TWENTY-FIVE
YARDS OF WAR

TWENTY-FIVE
YARDS OF WAR

THE EXTRAORDINARY COURAGE OF ORDINARY MEN
IN WORLD WAR II

RONALD J. DREZ

New York

Library of Congress Cataloging-in-Publication Data

Drez, Ronald J.
    Twenty-five yards of war : the extraordinary courage of ordinary men in World War II / Ronald J. Drez.—1st ed.
        p.   cm.
    Includes bibliographical references.
    Contents: The Halsey Doolittle raid, April 18, 1942 : Sgt. Robert C. Bourgeois—The Battle of Midway, June 4, 1942 : Ensigns George Gay and Albert Earnest—Tonolei Harbor and Kahili, October 16–17, 1943 : Lt. Jack Bolt, U.S.M.C.—Betio, Tarawa Atoll, November 21, 1943 : Pvt. James Russell, U.S.M.C.—The invasion of Normandy, June 6, 1944 : Pvt. Kenneth Russell, 1st Sgt. Leonard Lomell—The Battle of the Philippine Sea, June 20–21, 1944 : Lt. (j.g.) Arthur Abramson, U.S.N.—The Battle of the Bulge, Lanzerath, Belgium, December 16, 1944 : 1st Lt. Lyle Bouck—Namkwan Harbor, China, January 23, 1945 : Dr. Eugene B. Fluckey U.S.N.—Death Valley, Iwo Jima, February 25, 1945 : PFC Jay Rebstock, U.S.M.C.—The sinking of the U.S.S. Indianapolis, July 30, 1945 : Seaman 2/c Harold Eck.
    ISBN 0-7868-6783-3
    1. World War, 1939–1945—Biography.   2. United States—Armed Forces—Biography.   3. United States—Armed Forces—History—World War, 1939–1945.
4. World War, 1939–1945—Campaigns.   I. Title.
D736.D74   2001
904.53'092'2—dc21
[B]

2001039077

FIRST EDITION

Designed by Ruth Lee

10   9   8   7   6   5   4   3   2

For Judy

ACKNOWLEDGMENTS

I am especially grateful to the veterans featured in this book for granting me their interviews and sharing their stories. Their heroism and devotion to duty is an American heritage. Their leadership, patriotism, and selflessness should be taught in every school, and any search for role models should end here.

I am indebted to Dr. Stephen E. Ambrose, who has been my friend and mentor for twenty years. His example and inspiration challenged me to attempt this book, and he encouraged and delighted in every word. In the years that I served as his assistant director at the Eisenhower Center and we tracked down the veterans and walked the battlefields, he taught me every step of the way.

Perhaps most important was the enthusiasm of Dr. Douglas Brinkley, the able successor to Stephen Ambrose as director of the Eisenhower Center, who read the manuscript and introduced it to Hyperion.

His belief and encouragement were most appreciated and deserve my heartfelt thanks.

My editor, Leigh Haber, has been a professional joy and a champion of the manuscript. Her selection of the title was brilliant and her additions and erasures have enhanced the final work.

Leigh's assistant, Cassie Mayer, has handled details and communications flawlessly. She has made an enormous contribution, along with the Hyperion staff, to an excellent production.

My wife, Judy, has been a partner in this work as well as in every aspect of my life. Over the years, she has joined me in meeting the veterans and hearing their stories. She has delighted in their company and provided grace and a wonderful presence during interviews, at social events, and even when walking their battlefields. A more gracious, loving person does not exist.

My four children, Ronald, Jr., Kevin, Diane, and Craig, have reveled in meeting the veterans and being willing assistants at interviews, meetings, and recording sessions. They have been witnesses to history. I can give them no finer gift.

A final thank-you to all who read these stories. It is through you that our history and heritage will be forever preserved.

CONTENTS

FOREWORD

In September 1982, Ron Drez arrived twenty minutes late to my seminar, where we would meet for the first time. The seminar was on the Eisenhower Administration and life in general in the 1950s. As he was leaving at the end of the class, he stopped to apologize to me for his tardiness. He explained he was a businessman and had to complete his work for the day. I said, "You are a businessman and you're going for a Master's degree in History?" He said yes. I said he could be late any time.

There was a spark in that meeting. Instantly, we knew that a deep friendship had begun. We were so different yet so alike. Ron was forty-two years old. I was forty-six. He was a former marine company commander in Vietnam. I had been opposed to the war. He was Tulane, I was University of Wisconsin.

What we shared was more important. We were fascinated by history. We wanted to know what happened, and try to figure out why.

We had a respect for the men of World War II that impelled us to talk to them, read memoirs or books, talk to members of the unit, and gather and preserve their experiences.

That is what we do. That also started at our next meeting. Ron said he wanted to write about the life of Jack Nicklaus as his Master's thesis topic. I waved that away and steered him toward his experiences during the Vietnam War, then handed him some documents I'd just received about Khe Sanh and told him that there was his thesis—what happened at Khe Sanh.

He did the work. He turned out a solid result. I was so pleased and impressed that I hired him as Assistant Director of the Eisenhower Center. It was part-time, in pay at least, but almost full time with Ron. He went to reunions all over the country of World War II units, whatever service. He explained who he was, why he was there, and when the word got out that a rifle company commander from Vietnam wanted to interview them about their war, the men descended on Ron. He was interviewing veterans of D-Day in Normandy. All on tape. We would have student workers to transcribe the tapes and the interview would go to the Eisenhower Center Archives. I drew from that archive much of the material I used in my own book on D-Day, while Ron edited a script with the perfect title, *Voices of D-Day*. It was published by Louisiana State University Press, to flattering reviews and continuing sales. It is often cited and frequently quoted.

In the seven years after the D-Day anniversary, Ron has broadened his reach. He began interviewing Vietnam War veterans, especially those from Khe Sanh. And then he got going with World War II veterans on their war— what it was like, how it felt for them. All of those interviews are in the Archives. What he gives us here is the best of them.

For Drez and myself, our friendship has grown. In 1989 Ron and his wife, Judy, came to Normandy and my wife Moira and I guided them around for a week. Also in 1989 Ron and I taught a course on the Vietnam War. He had fought in it. I had worked to shut it down. He lectured the first hour, I did the second. His subject was the war, how it was fought, why it was lost. Mine was the politics of the war, how it fit into the policies of the Cold War, and how it almost tore

America apart at home. The auditorium was full, with students sitting in the aisles or standing at the back. Not one of them ever moved, at least in my memory. It was mesmerizing, for them and for us. I learned, Ron learned. It was one of my best teaching experiences, ever. At the end, to sustained standing applause, the Marine and the Professor embraced.

In the years since that occasion, Ron has started leading tours of battlefields in Europe and America, covering World War II and the Civil War. The participants in the tours cannot find the words to express how much they like him: He knows so much, is so enthusiastic, speaks with quiet authority but offers loud opinions, never tires, is eager to share what he knows with you, wants to learn. These qualities are also evident in his writing. In this field, I'm the teacher, he is the pupil. I've taught him something about pace, timing, organization, sticking to chronology, being always aware of his readers. He has added to what he has learned from the Professor and what he learned in Vietnam as a Marine in combat.

It is a fine gift Ron has. He can comment on or describe the individual's experience and achievement in World War II from the perspective of who he is and what he has done—and he can do so eloquently, through his prose. He has a sense of the dramatic and an ability to make his readers feel that they are there. *Twenty-five Yards of War* is a great book.

—Stephen E. Ambrose

PREFACE

The idea for this book was a natural follow-up to the successful Normandy Project conducted by the Eisenhower Center at the University of New Orleans under the guidance of Dr. Stephen Ambrose, Distinguished Professor of History. In that project, which started in 1983 and lasted for ten years, it was my happy task to "get the stories" of the men who had landed at Normandy on June 6, 1944. We knew the stories of the generals and admirals and the high-ranking officers, but Ambrose wanted the stories of the men who had fought their own "twenty-five yards of war." As his assistant director I traveled the length and breadth of this country to gather testimonies of men who had fought at Normandy. Over the years we collected more than fourteen hundred memoirs and interviews. Since I was a combat veteran myself, the men were at ease with me and that facilitated the collection. The culmination of that ten-year research was the publication of Ambrose's book *D-Day June 6, 1944: The Climactic Battle of World War II,* and my own book *Voices of D-Day: The Story of the Allied Invasion Told by Those Who Were There*. Both books were released just before the dramatic Fiftieth Anniversary celebrations in England and France in June 1994.

D-Day was the talk of the year and any veteran who could get to Normandy was there to witness the once-in-a-lifetime celebration. Interest was again resurrected in 1998 with the release of the movie *Saving Private Ryan* by Steven Spielberg. Dr. Stephen Ambrose served as a consultant on the film, and both of our books were credited as references in the writing of the novel of the same name by Max Allan Collins.

This new interest in World War II led the Delta Queen Steamboat Company, headquartered in New Orleans, to contract with me to lead a speaker's program for World War II–theme cruises up and down the great rivers of the United States. From the summer of 1995 until the summer of 1997, the company presented ten such cruises.

Because of my long research during the Normandy Project, I had many contacts and along the way I met many more veterans who shared their experiences with me and the passengers of the *Mississippi Queen*. The speakers were not only veterans of Normandy, but represented all services and battles in this very big war and were a wonderful cross section of the generation who had served in the war with quiet valor. They presented to their enthralled audiences the stories of their own experiences in the European and Pacific theaters.

I was suddenly aware that this was a unique opportunity. I wanted very much to record these men's experiences for future generations. I was also aware that many veterans who had not fought at Normandy felt more than a little slighted that so much was made over June 6, 1944. Here was an opportunity to showcase other battles.

The question of how to bring these stories to the reader was a difficult one. I did not want to present an entire history of the war or even a detailed account of the various actions in which these men fought, fearing their own experiences would get lost in a forest of words. Still, the reader would need sufficient background to place the situation, time, and geography firmly.

I decided to provide only a brief historical background and basic information of objectives and tactics of the particular action (a luxury not afforded the participants) to allow the reader to come along for the ride and be a silent witness. The reader would learn of the mission as the veteran lived it, watching the planning and execution from the unit level. There would be no bird's-eye view as a commanding general might have, far away with a large map posted on the wall plotting positions.

The reader would know the veteran by name and would climb into the cockpit or landing craft or submarine with him. The events would be presented in separate chapters in the order in which they happened. So the idea matured, and research and interview revealed wonderful stories.

The men in these stories have become my friends. Each one took the time to relate to me his memories, and it is to them, and to all warriors, that I dedicate this book. Here are twelve men in action in this gigantic war. Their common bond? Valor against the odds.

One is the recipient of the Medal of Honor and all have personal decorations. Another waited almost forty years for his valor to be recognized. But medals are not the measure of valor—courage and sacrifice are. All are ordinary men who faced adversity with courage in extraordinary times.

WARRIORS

Who are warriors? Perhaps it is better to ask *what* are warriors? And what is it about them that can, on the one hand, lead a grateful nation to figuratively genuflect in their presence or, on the other hand, cause a disappointed nation to treat them as second-class citizens or scapegoats of a failed political policy? What is it about them that inspires poets to immortalize them, and kings and presidents to speak in reverence of them, while, on many occasions, the people who benefit most from their life-threatening sacrifices treat them with indifference if not open hostility? The answer lies in the very fact that warriors are servants.

They are servants in a very special sense of the word, for the service they perform is like no other. They are called upon to bear unswerving allegiance to the nation in carrying out its political agenda; to risk life and limb with little explanation; to protect their fellow citizens with no promise of acceptance or gratitude; and to surrender part of their own rights and freedoms so the people they protect can better enjoy their own. And this service is predestined to be forgotten despite all resolves not to forget. And for what reward?

Gen. William Tecumseh Sherman said it best when he spoke about the manner of man who could perform the feats of a warrior when the best reward he could hope for "was to be shot dead on the battle-field, and have his name mis-spelled in the newspaper!" A warrior risks his life—and often loses it—for little pay, primitive living conditions, boredom, days of sheer torment and terror, separation from home and family, an early grave, or, perhaps worse, an old age surrounded with memories and stories few people are interested in hearing. "The first quality of a soldier is constancy in enduring hardship," said Napoleon Bonaparte. "Courage is only second!"

Yet, since the beginning, this certain breed of man has stepped forward and crossed the line from protected to protector; from citizen to servant; from civilian to military. And each new generation of this breed feels a certain camaraderie with all those who have gone before. Each new generation of soldiers, sailors, airmen, marines, legionnaires, or rangers, rediscovers the common bond that forever links it to its predecessors; and having rediscovered it, these new warriors scribble and etch this discovery on walls, helmets, and armor.

The words aren't always the same, but the meaning is. Some of the words are: "You haven't lived till you've almost died," and "Freedom has a special meaning the protected will never know." "Snafu" has its own special meaning to a soldier, as do the phrases "uncommon valor," and "conspicuous gallantry." Frustration has identified itself in other words, such as, "We are the unwilling, led by the unqualified, to do the unnecessary, for the ungrateful."

And what of that experience unique to combat veterans who, with constricted throats and hollow stares, have received the terse, sobering, three-word order, "Hold until relieved." It is rarely followed by an explanation, nor is there need for one. At such times, performance is less of a dedication to nation than a statement of personal fortitude and integrity and of duty to fellow comrades-in-arms.

Soldiers we are attacking. Advance as long as you can.

When you can no longer advance, hold your position.

When you can no longer hold it, die.

—GEN. JOFFRE, First Battle of the Marne, WWI

So strong is the bond of common experience among comrades-in-arms that it is not unthinkable to imagine a hereafter in which there would be common recognition. A certain nod between a Roman soldier from the Tenth Legion at Masada and a marine from the jungles of Guadalcanal; or a trooper from Rommel's Afrika Korps and a veteran from Longstreet's First Corps—all walking in the kingdom of the God that they knew was on their side.

And when the battles approach, instead of shrinking from their realities as might be expected, warriors hone their talents, develop a certain trust among their fellow comrades, make their peace with God, and then itch to go—to get it on—hoping that someone in charge will end the interminable waiting. And it is not the promise of certain victory that makes them anxious. To the contrary, it is often in the face of overwhelming odds that they strain at the leash—for to not join battle perpetuates the torture of waiting.

Nor are these remarkable servants stripped of courage in hopeless situations. In fact it appears that the more hopeless the situation, the higher the level of awareness of professional discipline. To the uninformed and ignorant, what often appears as a death wish or craving for destruction is, in fact, a resolve about the situation. That resolve, along with faith in one's comrades and a final prayer to God, precedes the step-up to a plane of human experience few achieve. It is at this level of trust and abandon that we find the defenders of the Alamo, Dien Bien Phu, Rorke's Drift, Bastogne, Wake Island, Corregidor, Camerone, and a list of other impossible, hopeless places too long to recount.

It is at this level of resolve that a young lieutenant, when informed that his meager force of one hundred faced a force of six thousand attacking Zulus, could blithely comment, as did Lt. Gonville Bromhead in the Battle of Rorke's Drift, the Zulu Wars, "Is that all? We can manage that lot very well for a few seconds."

And yet, except for a few of their leaders, the warriors remain nameless, faceless, and as time goes by, forgotten. Their eyewitness accounts of the battles in which they fought, their own particular "twenty-five yards of war," are eventually lost—sealed forever in the silence of the grave.

Twenty-five Yards of War is about warriors in ten climactic battles in the biggest war ever fought. These are accounts of extraordinary courage by ordinary men who, while facing overwhelming odds, abandoned themselves to the call of duty and met the enemy when survival was unlikely. This book represents an effort to remember and honor those stories and to capture the essence of their heroic experiences.

It is fitting then that to honor warriors facing overwhelming odds, a former comrade-in-arms should deliver an invocation. The words are similar to those used by countless other warriors before countless other battles, but no one has ever captured the spirit better.

O Lord, we are about to join battle with vastly superior numbers of enemy, and, Heavenly Father, we would like you to be on our side and help us; but if you can't do it, for Christ's sake don't go over to them; but lie low, and keep dark, and you'll see the damnest fight you ever saw in all your born days. Amen.

—COL. JACK HAYS, Texas Rangers, Mexican War

TWENTY-FIVE
YARDS OF WAR

ONE
THE HALSEY-DOOLITTLE RAID

APRIL 18, 1942

SGT. ROBERT C. BOURGEOIS

R obert Bourgeois was born on September 28, 1917, in the small
south Louisiana town of LeCompte, near Alexandria. He attended
a little school, typical of rural America in the 1920s. A school bus picked
up students from the far reaches of the district and delivered them to
the tiniest of schools. There were no strangers. When the Depression
came, small-town America was hit hard and when he was ten, Robert's
family was forced to migrate, hoping for employment in New Orleans.

Young Bob finished grammar school and then went to high school
and to Delgado Trade School and finished in mechanical drafting and
electric and acetylene welding, talents that would prove essential. When
he was twenty-two he sought to make his future in the world, but in
1939, with the country still suffering the aftermath of the Great Depression, he was uncertain where to begin. Friends in the Navy encouraged him to seek employment with the government, which at the

very least offered a retirement program. The promise of retirement and
security were powerful incentives to a generation of Americans who
had seen the soup lines and people selling apples on the street corner
to survive. No one had been spared the ordeal of seeing some family
member out of work. Bourgeois's friends told him that no matter how
bad things got, if he retired from the service, each month he would
have something coming in, and there were some great privileges for
when he got old or sick. This all sounded good to young Bourgeois.
Service people always seemed to be okay when everyone else was just
scraping to get by. They weren't rich, but neither were they wondering
about their next paycheck or their next meal.

In October 1939, Bourgeois decided to go down to the Air Corps
recruiter, raise his right hand, and sign up. They gave him a physical,
and the next thing he knew he was at Barksdale Field in Shreveport
for basic training. Bourgeois was given an aptitude test, during which
he told the interviewers that he was a qualified welder, which in turn
got him assigned to the welding shop and later to the mechanical drafting department. He developed skills right in the machine shop making
parts for aircraft. He also played baseball on the Barksdale team and
earned a permanently crooked finger for his athletic efforts.

After Barksdale, Bourgeois was sent to Denver to attend the Bombsight Maintenance and Automatic Pilot training school. It was a top-
secret assignment. In 1941, after finishing pilot training, he was assigned
to Pendleton, Oregon—getting married along the way—and began
training on the B-25 bomber. Bourgeois had been in training to fly the
aircraft when, on December 7, the Japanese attacked Pearl Harbor. In
the aftermath of the surprise attack, personnel were frantically thrown
together to make crews and Bourgeois was "anointed" a bombardier,
though he'd never dropped a bomb in his life. Nevertheless, he was a
logical choice for the position because he knew the equipment and had
been training bombardiers how to use the top-secret bombsight.

The United States had entered the war. In those first few days of
the war when rumor, fear, and uncertainty haunted America, the new
crews were assigned patrol missions off the West Coast. Bourgeois and
his crew took off and flew up the Columbia River gorge to Portland.
He remembered the breathtaking view of the mountainous terrain and

how hard it was, in this peaceful setting, to believe that the country was at war.

That illusion was quickly shattered when a sister B-25, flying a patrol around the mouth of the Columbia River, sank the first Japanese submarine of the war. Bourgeois and his crew were assigned farther north to patrol around Seattle. They patrolled Puget Sound as America geared up for war and the people of Seattle first experienced the new phenomenon of the "blackout." The patrolling B-25 crews watched as Seattle went dark after sunset.

Bourgeois had been on patrol duty for about a week when word came that the squadron would be transferred, not back to Denver but to the opposite end of the United States. They would leave the Columbia River and go to another Columbia, this one was in South Carolina, which had a new air base. Turned out the "base" was only a runway with no hangars, and they all lived in tents.

Less than a month after Pearl Harbor, in an office far removed from Bob Bourgeois and his B-25 squadron's tent city in South Carolina, Gen. Henry H. "Hap" Arnold, chief of the Army Air Forces, was greeted by the president of the United States in his study in the White House. He sat with the assembled group, which included Gen. George C. Marshall, chief of staff of the Army, and Adm. Ernest J. King, chief of staff of the Navy. Also present was a special advisor to the president and the secretaries of War and of the Navy.

President Franklin Roosevelt talked of Prime Minister Winston Churchill's arrival the next day and Gen. Marshall briefed those gathered on the global situation. Roosevelt then discussed the situations in Africa and in Europe, but it was when he turned the conversation to the Far East and to Japan that he was most forceful. He leaned forward and focused on the five men in the room. He repeated over and over his desire to strike back at Japan at the earliest possible moment. He told of the need for some sort of offensive attack to bolster American morale, which was suffering more and more each day. By the time the meeting ended, Gen. Arnold understood the urgency of the president's order.[1] On January 28, Roosevelt again pressed his military chiefs concerning progress on a plan to strike Japan.[2] He was now even more anxious as the Japanese continued to rack up one impressive victory after another.

Pearl Harbor had not been simply an isolated attack in a disjointed strategy: Japan followed with a series of devastating hammerstrokes. On that same "day of infamy," Japanese Imperial Forces began land and sea campaigns against Hong Kong and bombed Guam, Midway, and Wake Island. Less than twenty-four hours after Pearl Harbor, the Japanese caught Gen. Douglas MacArthur with his pants down and his planes parked in neat, close rows on the airfield at Clark Air Force Base in the Philippines. The planes were destroyed where they were parked.

Three days later, the news was no better. The British battleships *Repulse* and *Prince of Wales* were sunk in the Gulf of Siam and Japanese forces landed on Luzon.

The bad news arrived in sickening waves upon a stunned American population. During the next week there was one tiny glimmer of hope as valiant marine defenders repulsed an overwhelming Japanese force seeking to capture Wake Island. Thirsting for good news, Americans followed the gallant defense of Wake as day after day the outnumbered defenders thwarted the Japanese. The promise of a relief force raised hope.

But Wake Island was only a small oasis in a desert of gloom. On December 15, the British withdrew from Malaya and Burma, and on the nineteenth, the Japanese landed on Hong Kong and forced surrender on Christmas Day. But by Christmas, Wake Island had also succumbed. On December 23, Americans' tiny glimmer of hope had been snuffed out.[3] The proposed relief of the island had been called off. By the end of 1941, meaningful resistance to the Japanese attack in the Philippines was at an end and MacArthur departed, leaving fifteen thousand Americans behind. Those Americans and sixty-five thousand Filipinos assembled at Bataan to fight on with the hopes that some relief force could save them.

As 1942 began, the Japanese forces continued their undaunted march of conquest, invading Burma, pressing on in Bataan, and capturing Singapore. In a few months' time, the entire Pacific Ocean area

west of a line drawn from Alaska to Hawaii and southwesterly to
Australia was under Japanese control.

Back home, Gen. Arnold studied a daring plan to strike Japan in ful-
fillment of President Roosevelt's anxious order. It consisted of the possibility of launching aircraft from the deck of a carrier for a strike
against Tokyo. The Japanese knew that the range of carrier-borne aircraft was about 300 miles, so they would position their defensive rings
at that radius and a carrier force would be detected and most likely
destroyed. To risk one of only four carriers in the U.S. fleet in a suicidal
attack would be foolhardy. With most of the fleet at the bottom of
Pearl Harbor, those carriers were all that stood between the United
States and the Japanese Imperial Fleet.

   But this plan was not devised to be suicidal. It did not call for
typical carrier aircraft to launch. The plan called for medium Army
bombers, which had a much greater range, to launch from a distance
outside the Japanese protective rings and outside the range of Japan's
land-based aircraft. This would decrease the exposure to the carrier.
There was no thought of recovering the bombers since they could not
return and land on the carrier. They were too big, had a nose wheel,
and were not equipped for carrier landings, and even if they somehow
could land, they could not fit on the elevators to be lowered to the
hangar deck to clear for the next plane. Once launched, the bombers
would have to seek safe harbor on land. Landing in the Soviet Union
was out of the question since it had signed a nonaggression pact with
Japan. That left China the only friendly land nearby—but China was
infested with Japanese troops. There was no other choice, however, so
the bombers would have to land in China and be given to forces there.[4]

At the beginning of March 1942, Sgt. Bourgeois was working on some
equipment in his tent at the airfield in Columbia. In his tent was the
vault containing the top-secret bombsight. He was bent over his bench
working on a servo unit for the automatic pilot when he was inter-
rupted. He looked up to see his squadron commander stride in accompanied by "a little short guy" with a leather jacket. The squadron

commander told Sgt. Bourgeois that he wanted him to meet Jimmy Doolittle, indicating the "short guy." Bourgeois shook hands with the lieutenant colonel and the commander announced that Col. Doolittle was looking for some boys to go on a little trip with him and that they'd be gone for a few weeks and then come back home. He said it as casually as if the colonel were planning a fishing trip and when they caught their limit, they'd be back to continue the war.

As Bourgeois listened, the commander said that Doolittle needed someone to take care of the automatic pilots and the bombsights. Bourgeois nodded, and then Col. Doolittle spoke. He said that this trip was strictly a volunteer thing, but that added caveat did not deter the young Louisianian. Bourgeois shrugged and said, "Okay, I'll go." Doolittle accepted him and as they walked out he told the sergeant that they'd be leaving in a couple of days and would be going to Eglin Field in Florida.

Bourgeois was then assigned as the bombardier to aircraft 40-2247, which was always called 2247, and it was then that he met the rest of his crew: pilot Lt. Edgar McElroy, copilot Lt. Richard Knobloch, navigator Lt. Clayton Campbell, and engineer-gunner Sgt. Adam Williams. The newly formed crew left for Florida two days later, becoming part of the B-25 Special Project.

On March 3, Col. Doolittle addressed his new group of approximately 140 volunteers, assembled before him at Eglin Field. Bourgeois listened as the colonel informed them that this project would be dangerous and demanded absolute secrecy. He told them, "Don't talk to anybody. If someone wants to know what you are doing, tell them you don't know what you're doing." Bob Bourgeois thought that would be easy because he surely didn't know what the hell he was doing. Doolittle invited anyone who had any doubts about the mission to leave now and said no one would think the less of him. No one left.

The crews were placed in a virtual quarantine. No one was permitted near them except the few civilians who were working close by. They trained at auxiliary fields around Eglin, away from the main traffic. Their main practice area was little more than a macadam strip.

After Doolittle's talk, the crews saw little of him. He was gone most of the time conferring with Gen. Arnold and spending time in

Minneapolis where they were trying to solve leaking fuel tank problems. Newly designed self-sealing tanks weren't working, and Doolittle was exploring possibilities to increase fuel capacity. The bombers for Doolittle's mission would be modified to add a 265-gallon tank that would fit into the bomb bay, leaving just enough room for four 500-pound bombs underneath. There would also be a collapsible rubber tank placed in the crawl space separating the front and rear compartments. Other special modifications were made as the bomber crews continued to train at Eglin.[5]

There was one other great modification. It was not made in Minneapolis but right at Eglin Field. The Norden bombsight, a new, state-of-the art bombsight, was considered too valuable to risk being captured, and so a rudimentary sight was invented and constructed for the cost of twenty cents. It consisted of a sighting bar and a protractor. Knowing the altitude and air speed, the bombardier could set the angle of the sighting bar so when the target lined up, the bombs could be released.

One day a naval officer, Lt. (j.g.) Hank Miller, showed up among the volunteer crews. He had recently graduated from the Naval Academy in Annapolis and was assigned as a flight instructor at Pensacola. Miller began talking to the crews about a procedure called "jump takeoff." This procedure called for the pilot to rev the engine to maximum rpms while holding the bomber back on the brakes. When the engine was screaming at maximum power and the aircraft straining to be freed, the brakes were released and the bomber lurched forward in a modified, jackrabbit takeoff. To the Army pilots this was not the way to fly an airplane. At flight school Bob Bourgeois had been told, "You can't do such a thing. You need to fly this aircraft off the ground with about a mile of runway."

But it could be done and, after some practice, on a runway marked to show distances, some of the B-25s were getting airborne in 500 to 600 feet. Of course, these aircraft were light. There was no gasoline or bomb-load weight. But Miller had made some calculations and he concluded that if an empty bomber could get off in that short distance, then a loaded aircraft, with full flaps, might be able to get airborne also if there was a 25 to 30 knot wind blowing across the wings. Many of the bomber crews were skeptical of Miller's assessments. They could not envision this big bomber with a gross weight of 27,000 pounds, getting off in 500 feet with a ground speed of 50 miles per hour. What Miller and the crew didn't know was that the target weight of the loaded aircraft would not be 27,000 pounds, but a whopping 31,000 pounds, 2,000 pounds over the maximum designed load.[6]

The B-25 was a big airplane. It had a wingspan of almost 68 feet and was over 53 feet long. In addition to practicing short takeoffs, the crews practiced bombing runs over the Gulf of Mexico. On any given day, the crew of 2247, with Sgt. Bourgeois in the nose of the bomber, made bombing runs on little oil slicks on the water on which Bourgeois would drop little blue sandbags.

"I got real proficient in dropping those damn things," he said. "I was hitting those slicks from fifteen hundred feet in the air. I didn't need the sight. I could line up the target on my shoelaces and hit it."

In addition to bombing practice, each crew received about twenty-five hours of navigation, gunnery, and formation flying. Additional training was cut short because of the need to further modify the aircraft for increased fuel capacity. The lower gun turret was removed and a 60-gallon gas tank was installed in its place; ten 5-gallon gas cans were added to the carry-on cargo to be stowed in the rear compartment. This extra gasoline would be manually poured into the new turret tank to top it off as the gasoline was consumed in flight. The final configuration of the B-25 brought the gasoline capacity up to 1,141 gallons. This was almost 500 additional gallons over the standard configuration.[7]

The mechanics responsible for the inner workings of the B-25 had worked like Swiss watchmakers and had tuned the engines and carburetors to perfection, idling back for the least fuel consumption possible. Factory representatives worked side by side with the mechanics in order to tune the engines to run on the stingiest supply of gasoline: The 1,100 gallons of gasoline would have to take the aircraft more than 2,000 miles.

On March 23, the crews filled their bombers with fuel and received a short talk from Col. Doolittle, who still did not reveal their mission. He told them to man their aircraft and fly west to McClellan Field near Sacramento, California. On this route from Eglin the crew would be flying the same distance as if they had taken off from 500 miles east of Japan, then flown over Tokyo and on to the mainland of China.

As the aircraft flew westward, Sgt. Bourgeois was having a good time flying 25 to 30 feet off the ground across the state of Texas. As the big bombers buzzed the farms, Bourgeois laughed and said, "I could see white chickens flying over the fences. I think every chicken must have left the barnyard." The need to fly low over the countryside was just part of the training and the crews did not know why they had to do it. They were told to fly low, so they flew low. No questions asked. In fact, as the planes approached San Francisco, one of the aircraft flew under the Golden Gate Bridge.

The flight had also been a test of the distance monitored against fuel consumption, and the specially tuned carburetors seemed to be working perfectly. The crew landed at McClellan for final inspections and to have the propellers replaced with special pitches to ensure maximum fuel efficiency. It was here that the strangest modification was made: Capt. David Jones saw two black broomsticks placed in the tail to look like 50-caliber shotguns. The real guns weighed too much, so the broomsticks were used in the hopes of scaring off Japanese interceptors from flying behind the plane and making a rear attack.

On April Fool's Day, the B-25s were ordered to fly to the Naval Air Station at Alameda. When Sgt. Bourgeois and his crew arrived in Alameda, they got their first view of a large aircraft carrier sitting at the dock. As soon as they landed they were greeted by the Navy's little mechanical donkeys that hooked on to each bomber's nose gear and began pulling the aircraft to the dock. The crew then saw the name of the ship for the first time: on the side, in big letters, was *Hornet*.

"This must be the son-of-a-bugger that we're going to get on," Bourgeois said, and he was proved right as a big crane reached out and effortlessly picked his bomber up and set it on deck. There were some quizzical looks from some of *Hornet*'s crew concerning the loading of the big land-based bombers, but soon sixteen were loaded and two were left on the dock. All eighteen crews, however, boarded the ship. The two extra crews were just that, extra. They were there as standbys in case some crew members got sick or were incapacitated, but they would not fly the mission otherwise. The loading took place in the early afternoon, and afterward *Hornet* moved out of the berth and anchored in the middle of the bay in full view of the whole world.

"We sat out in the middle of the bay all afternoon with all these cars going by," said Bourgeois. "They must have wondered, where the hell are these guys going? And we still didn't know anything.

"We sailed the next day and went past Alcatraz and under the Golden Gate Bridge. I'll never forget that; it was beautiful.

"We were a day out in the Pacific when the captain came over the PA and addressed us all. He said that he knew that all of us were wondering where we were going and what we were going to do, and that was when he announced, 'We're going to Tokyo.'"

What had seemed far-fetched was now a reality. Bob Bourgeois remembered it.

"It was like a football game when the score is three to three and there are only a couple of seconds left, and some guy kicks a fieldgoal, and then everything is bedlam. That was the way we and the Navy boys were. There had been all kind of fighting and squabbling between the different branches of the services before. Now we had none of that. There was nothing but cooperation. They were cheering us on."

To Sgt. Bourgeois and the rest of the B-25 crews all the training suddenly made sense: the short takeoff, the low flight over the countryside, the finely tuned carburetors, the special extra gas tank modifications, the carry-on gasoline, the absolute secrecy. It all made sense now. They were going to bomb Tokyo.

The ship headed for Japan accompanied by two cruisers, an oiler, and four destroyers. Five days later, on April 7, Adm. William "Bull" Halsey, on board the carrier *Enterprise* with two more cruisers and four additional destroyers, left Hawaii and rendezvoused. Halsey and his force would provide a screening force for *Hornet* as she and her task force steamed toward Japan and the launch area 400 to 500 miles off shore.[8]

Here were sixteen ships from a crippled U.S. Fleet, including two precious carriers, defying the odds and exposing themselves to possible disaster. What a plum it would be for the Imperial Japanese Fleet to bag this task force. To bag Halsey and his men and send *Hornet* and

Enterprise to the bottom would be the brightest trophy of their collection.

Adding to the danger, *Hornet*'s fighter planes were blocked from access to the flight deck by the sixteen B-25s sitting there like nesting birds. Should the task force be discovered and attacked by enemy planes, one could only imagine the terrible sight of the ship's crew and the bomber crews pushing the bombers over the side in a frantic effort to get the fighters on deck and into the air to protect the carrier and the rest of the force. The B-25s were an obstacle to *Hornet*'s self-preservation.

After the announcement on board the ship's PA that Tokyo was their destination, Col. Doolittle assembled the crews in the mess hall and gave them details. He told them that their targets would be in Tokyo, Yokohama, Nagoya, Osaka, and Kobe. He told them that the Navy would get them to within 500 miles of the Japanese mainland. His would be the first plane off in the early evening, two hours prior to the rest of the force, and would carry incendiary bombs. He would arrive over Tokyo at night and would light the city up for the main strike. After the strike, the force would fly to China and would land on some small fields, refuel, and take off to fly to Chungking.

On the second day out of San Francisco, Bob Bourgeois and the entire crew of 2247, now known as Crew 13, because their aircraft was lashed down and in position to take off in the thirteenth slot, was called to be briefed on their mission. They were briefed by *Hornet*'s intelligence officer, Lcdr. Stephen Jurika, who had the unique distinction of having graduated from the University of Tokyo. He told them that he had frequented the Russian Embassy for some vodka sessions and that the personnel there had given him quite a few pictures of Tokyo. As he laid these out before Crew 13, Bourgeois whistled under his breath. He had never seen so many war plants in all his life. There were smokestacks blowing smoke in great industrial billows everywhere. Jurika then revealed their target.

"We were told that we had been assigned this naval base," Bourgeois said. "We were told that it was very important that we get it and that the base was right on Tokyo Bay and was about twenty-five miles south of Yokohama. We were told that knocking it out would help the war effort a great deal."

Bourgeois thought that Lcdr. Jurika was extremely thorough. As he briefed the crew he showed the men positions where various ships were berthed or docked. All through the voyage, as the ships plowed closer to their destination, Jurika constantly updated the locations of ships and targets.

After the briefing Crew 13, along with the rest of the crews, worked their way out to the flight deck. Each crewman carefully paced that awfully short distance from the first B-25 to the end of *Hornet*'s deck and then stared down into the rolling sea. No matter how they paced it off, it was only 467 feet from the start to the end of the deck. They shook their heads knowing that, in all their practices, they had never gotten off in 467 feet.

The aircraft looked huge sitting on the deck with its left wing hanging over the edge of the carrier and its right wing jammed against the ship's island, the superstructure located midships on the starboard side of the flight deck. There was no room for error. The Navy had painted two white lines all the way down the deck to the bow. The idea was that those lines were meant to guide the aircraft. If the pilot kept his left wheel on the left line and his nose wheel on the right line, he'd be fine.

On April 9, as the task forces headed west, there was more bad news. American forces on Bataan had surrendered. Most Americans had never heard the name Bataan. Later, as details of events there unfolded, they would associate it with a horrible death march and, like Pearl Harbor, its name would be remembered in infamy.

Ten days out of San Francisco *Hornet*'s task force plowed through stormy seas with high winds and reduced visibility. Bourgeois watched the tanker *Cimarron* conduct the delicate maneuver of inching close to *Hornet* and extending fuel hoses to fill the carrier's tanks. The two vessels plowed on side by side creating a thrashing sea between their two hulls while the tanker pumped its fuel into the big ship. When it was finished, *Cimarron* retracted its hoses and departed to the east, leaving the task force to go on.

As the launch date, April 18, approached, the crews constantly checked and rechecked the planes. They'd been over everything a thousand times. Each crew lined up on deck and had their pictures taken to record this daring moment in history that, for better or worse, would be something to remember.

By April 17, shipboard life had become routine, though Bourgeois never could get used to beans for breakfast. Every day seemed the same. It was the day before their big day and if he had thought there would be something special, like a last meal, he was wrong.

"I'd never eaten beans for breakfast in my life," he complained. "The Navy had pork and beans for breakfast, and I said, What the hell kind of chow hall is this?"

Even though the additional Army crew had crowded the Navy personnel, the Navy tried to make their guests as comfortable as possible forfeiting their own bunks down below.

"They also had ice-cream parlors. It was like a city," Bourgeois recalled. Capt. David M. Jones, the pilot of Crew 5, recalled that there were many amenities but the strangest was a billiards table—billiards being an odd choice on a rolling and pitching ship. "However, it made a first-class craps table."[9]

On April 17, the bombs were loaded on 2247. In recent days, Lcdr. Jurika had defined their target in more detail. They were to hit the dock area at Yokosuka, the largest naval base in Japan, and their target was, more specifically, an aircraft carrier that was in dry dock. The mission called for them to be armed with three high-explosive 500-pound bombs and one 500-pound incendiary cluster. The target was really a double target—the carrier and the dry dock.

"The incendiary cluster was specially made," Bourgeois said. "It contained 128 hexagon-shaped pellets about fifteen inches long with an explosive charge in the middle. The explosive charge dispersed these pellets and they were capable of burning through a three-quarter-inch piece of steel.

"Some targets, especially those over Tokyo, were very susceptible to fire. Lots of paper and wood." The bombers assigned those targets would carry more incendiary bombs. After the planes were armed there was nothing left to do but wait.

"It was the night before," Bourgeois said, "and we had planned for Doolittle to leave the next day in the early evening, and we were going to follow, flying low to keep the radar from picking us up."

Sgt. Bourgeois went to bed with that thought in mind, hoping to get a good night's sleep for what would obviously be a busy day. As he retired, the seas kicked up and the wind increased to 30 knots.

At 0330 he was shocked to consciousness by the ear-splitting sound from the ship's Klaxon calling everyone to battle stations. Throughout the dark quarters, crews sprang to life and grabbed their clothes, equipment, and B-4 bags. They scrambled for the aircraft on deck, which were being lashed by gale-force winds as the sea sent torrents of spray over the bow. It was a false alarm, though, and forty-five minutes later the "all clear" sounded.

Crew 13 checked the guns, manually pulled the props through 360 degrees to ensure correct ignition and firing sequence of the engine, stowed their gear, and made last-minute checks. By 0730 all was ready and the crews had eaten and were standing by in scattered areas of the ship, still expecting the takeoff to occur at dusk. Fifteen minutes later an announcement from the loudspeaker shattered their plans.

"All hands man your battle stations!" The Navy personnel went into action manning guns and taking up other positions. Bob Bourgeois was on deck, and from his position by the aircraft, he watched cruiser *Nashville* lunging forward in the heavy seas. At 0805 she suddenly opened fire. To the young sergeant it seemed that she was red on one side. The word spread like wildfire. Japanese boats had been sighted, and the task force had been discovered. The bombers had to get off even though they were still 200 miles from the launch point. The ship was threatened and the Navy needed the deck to defend her.

Now the ship's horn bellowed out, "Army crews, man your planes and prepare for immediate takeoff!" From various positions around the ship, the bomber crews scrambled into their aircraft and, in the howling wind, wheel chocks were removed from under the first plane, and it was pushed and shoved until the left wheel and the nose wheel were on the white lines leading down the pitching deck and off the end.

Doolittle was in this plane, and he was taking off in the morning instead of at dusk. The B-25 vibrated as its engines started. The right wing tip seemed as if it would surely scrape the ship's island and the left wing hung over the side like a great albatross too big for its perch.

All eyes on board ship and in the other fifteen B-25s sitting behind him were glued on Doolittle. They watched as the engines revved-up to full power and the aircraft strained against the brakes.

A flagman on the end of the carrier also drew everyone's attention. He was first silhouetted against the skyline, and then against the horizon, and finally against the boiling ocean as *Hornet* rose and sank from one wave to the next. He rotated his checkered flag in great circles signaling the pilot to increase power. The engines screamed higher and higher. When he was finally satisfied that the aircraft was at full power he watched as the carrier plunged into the trough of a wave so her deck was tilted downward. It was at that moment that he whipped his flag forward, signaling the pilot to release the brakes. The big bomber lurched forward and seemed in slow motion as it gathered speed. *Hornet*'s deck was now on the upstroke as she climbed the next wave.

In the aircraft, the pilot knew the takeoff procedure cold. It had been practiced on land many times, but this time it was for real—on a pitching deck with the distance to the water growing shorter by the second. Release brakes; wait three seconds; pull the yoke back into the chest and wait. When and if the nose came whooshing up, push the yoke forward and try to trim the aircraft. In this case, if the nose didn't come up, the bomber's destination was the sea.[10]

Down the deck ran Doolittle's plane. Up rose *Hornet*'s deck, reaching for the sky as she crested the next wave. Doolittle's bomber vaulted into the air, lifted by a combination of the springboarding deck and the 30-knot wind. At 0815, he was airborne, with room to spare.

Confidence among the remaining fifteen crews soared. Crews 2 through 6 took off in the next eighteen minutes. Bourgeois watched as each plane seemed to take off vertically, "hanging on the engines," and then leveled out. The wind was now so strong that the seventh aircraft took some of the pitch out of its flaps since the plane was being buffeted badly. The pilot feared the wind would push his bomber overboard. With their flaps at a decreased angle, Crew 7 headed down the deck.

From his place back in the line, Sgt. Bourgeois watched the run.

At the end of the deck, instead of jumping into the air like those that had gone before him, the seventh bomber dipped below the carrier's deck and the retracting wheels touched the top of a wave before receding into the wheel well. The aircraft then gained altitude and was off to join the rest of the airborne force.

A solitary figure raced across the deck among the waiting aircraft and stopped at 2247. It was Lcdr. Jurika, who even at this late time brought Sgt. Bourgeois's crew the latest intelligence about where ships were located in Tokyo Bay.

Suddenly it was Crew 13's turn. They would be the thirteenth aircraft to run down the pitching deck. Bourgeois was not superstitious; he had no doubts. He'd seen the rest of them go. He was part of history. The two backup crews had offered all that was in their pockets to replace anyone for this mission, but there had been no takers among the eighty raiders.

Aircraft 2247 raced down the deck, forty-five minutes after Doolittle's plane. Bourgeois watched as they became airborne with more than 100 feet of deck to spare. Their greatest worry—to get off in less than 500 feet—was unfounded. It had been easy.

"We'd hoped for a strong wind to help us," Bourgeois said. "We didn't expect a hurricane!"

They circled 360 degrees and flew back over the ship and down the exact line that the carrier was traveling. Out on deck a Navy man held a blackboard skyward so they could read it. It said 300 degrees. Since the aircraft only had B-type compasses, which could be very unreliable, this last flyover confirmed their direction. They joined Crews 11 and 12 and headed for Tokyo.

It was a strange flight. The three aircraft flew 25 feet off the ocean to avoid radar detection. The white-capped waves whipped past the plane giving a sense of increased speed and reminding Bourgeois of the white chickens frantically flying over the fences in Texas.

Everyone was aware that the raid would now take place in broad daylight instead of at night, as had been planned. The plan was 180 degrees out of sync. The flight out of Tokyo, if successful, would place the crews over China at night with the unenviable task of making a night landing at the remote airstrip at Chuchow, which had no runway lights. But all that was in the future—for now the focus was getting to Tokyo.

For several hours the three-plane formation flew west. The crew members could sometimes wave to each other. Some snacked, some talked, and in 2247, the crew listened to Tokyo Rose over the radio. She taunted her American listeners with her lilting voice. Her theme was how beautiful it was to live in the land of the cherry blossoms where all the Japanese were free from the dangers of bombing and how wonderful it was to feel such safety.

As they flew on, Tokyo Rose brought her usual variety of music and propaganda. Suddenly, about an hour before Crew 13 was scheduled to make landfall in Japan, they knew that Jimmy Doolittle had arrived. Tokyo Rose told them.

Her voice, which had been so peaceful and content, was now frantic as she announced, "We're being bombed!" After a few panic-stricken minutes, she went off the air.

It was noon as the flight reached the Japanese coast and the three planes broke off from each other. Crews 11 and 12 headed for Yokohama while Crew 13 plotted a course toward Yokosuka and the dry dock. But, as they crossed the coast, nothing looked familiar and, after some map study, they concluded that they were too far north. Feeling their way along, they flew over a Japanese airfield at 25 feet. The field had 150 aircraft on it, half of them cranked up on the end of the runway. Realizing their error, they did a quick about-face and headed back to the coast, drawing fire from the antiaircraft guns along the Japanese coast.

Bourgeois thought the impacting rounds looked like hailstones falling on the water as the pilot barely avoided the fire. Flying low along the Japanese coast, he could see the people working in the rice paddies. It was midday with not a cloud in the sky. It was absolutely beautiful weather. What a change from the stormy weather during takeoff from *Hornet*. It was spring in the land of the rising sun.

Now the crew was on track. They quickly identified Yokohama and turned south. As they approached Yokosuka, Bourgeois, from his bombardier's position, could identify all the boats—just where Lcdr. Jurika had told him they would be.

The bomber climbed to 1,500 feet and Sgt. Bourgeois opened the bomb bay doors out over Tokyo Bay. He was used to looking at 15- to 20-foot targets when he had practiced bombing in the Gulf of Mexico and he would hit those targets "smack-dab" in the center. Now he was looking at a target so big, "a blind man couldn't miss it," he said: an aircraft carrier in dry dock.

The B-25 flew its target line. As it came closer and closer to the big ship, Sgt. Bourgeois had his thumb on the release. He dropped the three 500-pounders, then dropped the incendiary bomb. He couldn't see the results from his position in the nose as the bomber zoomed over, but the copilot turned and watched as the bombs impacted. A huge ship-loading crane flew skyward and fell, shattering into pieces. The dry dock, with aircraft carrier, shook and toppled onto its side and the incendiary bomb cluster scattered its 128 shards on the oil-storage tanks and the machine shop area, creating a roaring inferno.

Bourgeois closed the bomb doors and Lt. McElroy, the pilot, swung the plane to the left to head southwest toward China just as if he were heading back to Eglin Field following a successful drop of Bourgeois's little blue bags on the slicks in the Gulf of Mexico. This extraordinary bombing mission was conducted with such routine efficiency that the copilot, Lt. Knobloch, munched on a sandwich throughout.[11]

They flew along the Japanese coast for an hour, constantly checking for enemy aircraft, seeing none. But then they ran into a Japanese naval task force. Bourgeois estimated twenty-five ships, in two columns. The pilot avoided antiaircraft fire by flying straight down the middle of the formation, reasoning that neither column would fire lest they hit the other. He was right. Not one shot was fired at the bomber as it skimmed the water.

After flying through the task force, 2247 headed for China. Now that the attack was over, the crew faced the discouraging facts. Prior to the mission, they had been briefed by weather experts that the prevailing winds that they would encounter on the way to China would be in their faces: wind on the nose would decrease their ground speed and that meant increased fuel consumption. They had already flown more than 200 extra miles because of the early takeoff. The pilot had leaned the engines so that every so often they coughed and sputtered, thirsty for fuel. Only then was the richer mixture grudgingly given, followed shortly by a renewed attempt to lean them back in an effort to keep fuel consumption at a bare minimum.

Aircraft 2247 flew along for hours, its engines stretching every drop of fuel, but to the west, the weather was deteriorating. The beautiful spring skies over Tokyo turned black and ugly and rain fell in torrents. The crew could see nothing, but in those dark storm clouds was a miracle: The prevailing wind that had buffeted the nose turned into a 30-knot tailwind boosting the bomber along. Again the engines were leaned until they coughed.

The plan had been to land at Chuchow in daylight, refuel with smuggled fuel from Chinese partisans, and take off again for Chung-king, where they would eventually meet up and deliver the planes to Gen. Claire Chennault and his famous Flying Tigers. To aid the bombers, two Chinese signalmen equipped with a hand generator were to fly to Chuchow and tap out a Morse code signal, "5-7" over and over, that would guide the raiders toward the airstrip, which they would find visually and land on. That was fine in the daytime. This was night in a storm. The best they could hope for was to receive the signal and fly close to the sight. No one ventured a guess how to find the strip at night.

As they flew, the only instrument to aid navigation was their hand-held B-type compass. They could not take a reading on the stars, because there were no stars. The storm had blotted out the sky.

They flew at 6,000 feet, hoping they were on a course over the South China Sea and not over land where high mountain peaks thrust into the sky. They had no idea where they were. No one talked about what they all knew. They just flew on in the dark of the storm in zero-visibility weather. As the hours passed, they could only listen for the Morse signal from the ground. They were never to hear it: The aircraft carrying the Chinese signalmen became a casualty of the same storm buffeting 2247. It crashed, killing its crew.

Despite the fact that they were in a difficult position, there was no panic. They had been flying in the zero weather for about five hours; it had been eleven hours since takeoff. The scant conversation that did take place concerning their predicament was laced with gallows humor.

Knobloch munched more sandwiches, remarking, "May as well die happy."

From his bombardier's position in the nose of the aircraft, Bourgeois chimed in over the intercom, "I hope Columbus was right that if you go far west, you get to the ... east." From the tail section, in his gun turret position, Williams liked that thought and said, "Maybe we'll come down in England." On and on they flew.[12]

Thirteen hours after they roared off *Hornet*'s deck the moment they hoped would not come came.

"The first time we really knew we were in trouble," Bourgeois said, "was when we actually ran out of gas. The red light came on the left engine and we kept running along until it quit. Mac [Lt. McElroy] feathered it while we still had power."

The fuel gauge for the right engine showed a little fuel, so 2247 flew on, on one engine. McElroy finally broke the silence.

"Well boys," he said, "we've got two chances. We can stay in here and we can all die, or we can try and get out and see what happens."

No one said anything, and 2247 continued along until the right engine started sputtering. McElroy ordered the hatch cover to be pulled. Bourgeois had a chest-type chute on and was in the tunnel up front in the bombardier's position, so he crawled back. Sgt. Williams crawled over the top from the aft section, not wanting to be the only one to go out of the aft hatch. The five men stared down, at the black hole in the floor.

Sgt. Williams started up a conversation to prolong the inevitable jump. He realized the momentousness of the day's events and did not want to see the mission end this way. But the sputtering engine and threats from the crew forced him to disappear down the black hole. Bourgeois followed him out.

The bombardier fell into the black void, which was wet and cold. He tried to remember his bail-out instructions from training as he plunged into the blackness. They were easy: count to ten to prevent the shroud lines from being entangled in the aircraft and to let your body slow down, pull the rip cord, and brace for the opening shock. By that time your body would have slowed somewhat and the aircraft would be well ahead.

In his hurry to open the chute, Bourgeois made an abbreviated count, "Five, ten," and pulled, and since his body was still traveling at the speed of the aircraft, the opening shock almost jerked him into a knot. He floated down in the silence of the night and stared down, looking for the telltale phosphorescence of the water in the South China Sea. He knew that this day would surely end with him as supper for a shark or a barracuda. He could see nothing.

It didn't seem fair: a heroic flight from the deck of *Hornet* ending with a crunch in the mouth of a shark. Then, suddenly, he made a very soft landing.

"I landed in crap," Bourgeois remembered. "I had been told that all these Orientals used human waste as fertilizer in their fields and I found out that was right. Boy, did I stink."

After gathering his wits, he grabbed his chute and tried to walk out of the rice paddy from the thigh-deep muck. He popped the quick disconnect on the chute so the wind wouldn't billow the silk and pull him down and drown him.

As he got to the embankment, he was able to survey his situation and found that he was in a low paddy with other paddies all around rising like steps up the side of a mountain. All along, the crew had thought they were flying over the water, and he now wondered just how close they had come to smashing into one of those upthrusting peaks. He thanked the good Lord for watching over them.

It was close to 10:30 at night and he was cold and disoriented and all he could think to do was to sit down, so he sat in the rain for an hour.

Finally Bourgeois decided to move and tucked his chute under his arm and walked a little distance and rested again. After a rest he walked a little more and in a flash of lightning, he saw a thatched hut. He didn't see any people, but a dog started barking.

The dog wouldn't stop and Bourgeois figured that this would wake everybody up and he might really be in trouble, so he again sat down in the rain. This time he stayed put for six hours, until daybreak. The only thing he could think about during that miserable night was his good, warm bed back in southern Louisiana.

As day broke, he picked a direction and started walking and

walked into a poppy field, all in bloom, where a man was picking poppies. Bourgeois's mind raced to remember his training and the only thing that came to mind was the tip he had been given on the way to distinguish Chinese from Japanese: "We were told that the Chinese would smile at you if you smiled at them. The Japanese would not."

He reached down into his trouser leg and retrieved his .45 and loaded and cocked it. "Here I go," he said, "I hope this sucker smiles."

He walked in laughing it up and the farmer laughed back. He made signs like he was hungry and, after much arm-waving, the farmer made a motion to follow him. He took Bourgeois to a little village. There were a few huts with mud floors and boards for beds; hogs lived in the rooms with the people.

Bourgeois was taken to the elders, who were boiling rice in a can. He watched as they added what looked like whole pogy fish to the mixture—eyes and all. The sergeant was the first white man they had seen and they offered him some of their food, which Bourgeois politely refused.

"I was hungry," Bourgeois said, "but I wasn't that hungry."

He then tried to draw pictures in the mud. He drew an American flag, but got nowhere until one of the elders suddenly got it and then smiled broadly, knowing the strange man standing before him wasn't a bad guy.

Bourgeois gave the villagers his silk parachute and his first-aid kit, which brought more smiles until a runner came and announced that Bourgeois would have to be hidden. Someone was coming up the trail. Inside a hut, he sat on the bed, which was a board on two sawhorses, and listened to what sounded like a huge argument outside. Suddenly the door opened and Lt. Clayton Campbell, the navigator, was pushed inside. He'd found the same village.

The joy of meeting Campbell was cut short when the villagers told them they had to leave because a Japanese patrol was close by looking for them. There was no question what they meant as the Chinese spoke excitedly while making "bang-bang" sounds while pointing to the two Americans. The Chinese escorted them along a primitive trail between rice paddies and ran across a Chinese man who had on a Japanese uniform coat that he had taken off a dead Japanese soldier. It still had medals on it.

This was a strange traveling party. A Chinese farmer guide, two lost Americans, and another Chinese in a Japanese uniform. They walked for miles, following their guide and with no idea where they were or where they were going. They only knew that the Japanese were around and search patrols must be looking for them.

The next day, their guide led them to a village and, to their happy surprise, they were reunited with McElroy and Knobloch. Later that day Sgt. Williams was brought to them. Crew 13 was reunited. The Chinese celebrated the reunion by offering their guests hot towels to refresh themselves, but before they could get too comfortable, their hosts told them that they had to move again and they trekked off to another village. Along the way, Lt. Knobloch snapped the most improbable picture of his mates, all with silly umbrellas, and their guide and the man with the Japanese uniform.

For the first time, Crew 13 knew where they were. They were 100 miles west of Chuchow. They were dumbfounded. Not only had they made up the 200 miles lost because of the premature launch, but they had actually *over*flown the proposed landing site by 100 miles. The providential tailwind had made up the distance.

The Americans continued their odyssey. The Chinese brought them "horses" that were about the size of large dogs. Bourgeois could have put the animal across his shoulders, and the feet of the big Americans dragged the ground when they mounted the animals. Knobloch chose to walk to the next village, where they stayed the night.

The following day, sedan chairs, carried by two men, were brought. The flyers were placed in the chairs and the curtains drawn to hide them. Off they went again, toted by small men, who changed shifts often. Along the way unsuspecting farmers were forced into service to act as bearers to carry the big Americans. They arrived at a big city of more than three hundred thousand people, and they found out this was Poyang. They'd traveled 40 miles by foot, horse, and sedan chair.

As they rested in a hut, Bourgeois had terrible stomach cramps and figured he needed a latrine. His best arm and hand signals made no sense to his guide. He tried stooping down and grunting, and then made all kinds of panicked motions—and finally the guide understood and took him outside. The sergeant was horrified to see a huge crowd of Chinese people surrounding an open-air privy of the sort he remembered from his boyhood days in Louisiana. Disdaining modesty in favor of his irresistible urge, Bourgeois sat in the center of his witnesses. As soon as he was finished, a man ran up and claimed the "honey bucket" and its contents for his garden.

The Americans were then greeted with a tumultuous welcome as they paraded in the streets. There were fireworks and flowers and waving and banners for miles and miles. A makeshift band, which had stayed up all night to play, rendered their version of the "Star-Spangled Banner." "They missed a lot of damn notes," Bourgeois said, "but you knew what it was, and there wasn't a dry eye among the five of us."

As night came, the group was off again, staying one step ahead of the Japanese. This time they were taken to a mission, which opened its iron gates and allowed them in. There was a priest who told them that they couldn't stay long because of the Japanese. The mission cared for 200 orphaned girls, who, the next morning, offered flowers and sang for them.

Again the sedan chairs brought them to Lake Poyang and across to another mission and finally to the railroad station at the town of Ying Tan, only 100 miles from their original destination, Chuchow. The train trip took all night and the next day, traveling at about four miles an hour. Fittingly, as it came into view of the Chuchow station, the train jumped the track and Crew 13 completed their journey on foot. A bus took them to Doolittle and eight other crews who had made it there before them. It was April 26—eight days since they had taken off from *Hornet* and bombed Tokyo.

EPILOGUE

The assembled raiders were eventually taken to Hengyang and then to Chungking, where Generalissimo and Madame Chiang Kai-shek fêted the crews. Doolittle was whisked off to Washington, where he was made brigadier general and awarded the Medal of Honor.

The raid raised the morale of the people of the United States and convinced them that the Japanese were not invincible. In Japan the surprise was complete. For the Japanese, the fact that American aircraft had been able to threaten the capital city and the emperor himself was a serious blow to their honor. After the war, it became known that the attack provoked Adm. Isoroku Yamamoto, the commander-in-chief of the Combined Japanese Fleets, to order the push on to Midway in the hopes of flushing out the American carriers. Yamamoto craved a show-down with the "weak" Americans.[13] Whether that urgency was the result of sound strategical thinking or the desire to extract vengeance for a humiliating attack will never be known. Yamamoto was killed on the first anniversary of the Tokyo raid when his aircraft was inter-cepted by Army fighters and shot down over Bougainville.

Such was the shock of the Doolittle raid to the Japanese leaders that it spawned one of the more bizarre weapons of the entire war— the balloon bomb. In an effort to retaliate against the homeland of the United States, Japan embarked on a weapons project whose goal was to carry destruction to the North American continent. Massive balloons, 30 feet in diameter and filled with hydrogen gas, were constructed of layered paper or rubberized cloth and attached to antipersonnel and incendiary bombs. These huge balloons were launched into the westerly jet stream with the hope that they would be carried 6,000 miles to the West Coast of the United States.

Schoolgirls worked pasting and gluing panels the size of a stretcher that were then pieced together. It took six hundred of these panels to make one balloon, and they began launching them in November 1944. By April 1945, more than nine thousand had been launched, with little success. Some balloons reached the continent and started some forest fires, but most were easily shot down by coastal defending aircraft. The most damaging incident was the discovery of a balloon bomb on the ground in Oregon by a woman and five children, who were killed when it exploded.[14]

But the raid was not without costs. One crew, because of a badly modified carburetor, consumed too much fuel and had to land in Rus-sia, where they were interned. Of the rest, all but two of the crews evaded the Japanese search patrols. Crew 6 crash-landed, killing two of its members; the other three were captured. Crew 16 bailed out and was captured. Of the eight captives from the two crews, three were executed and one died as a result of harsh treatment. The other four spent forty months in captivity in the hands of the Japanese. Speaking about the members of his crew, Lt. George Barr, the navigator of Crew 16, summed up the inhumanity of their treatment: "There were forty months of hell waiting for Hite, DeShazer, and me," he said. "Spatz and Farrow were spared that. They were executed."[15]

The greatest price was paid by the Chinese people, who received the full force of the vengeance of the Imperial Japanese Army. In their bloodlust to track down the raiders and regain their honor, the Japanese killed more than 250,000 Chinese. Many of the items that the grateful Americans had given their saviors, such as parachutes and cigarette lighters, became smoking guns that condemned their new owners. Entire villages were wiped out. The orphan mission that hosted Crew 13 was flattened by the Japanese Air Force the day after the Americans departed.

Many of the raiders, like Sgt. Bourgeois, stayed on and fought in the Burma-China-India theater. For his action in the raid, Sgt. Bourgeois was awarded the Distinguished Flying Cross.

TWO
THE BATTLE OF MIDWAY

June 4, 1942

Ens. George Gay and Ens. Albert Earnest

When Jimmy Doolittle's B-25 revved its engines in preparation to take off from *Hornet,* the deck was filled with spectators. Among them was Ens. George Gay and his fellow pilots from Torpedo Squadron 8, all of whom were anxious for the bombers to be on their way once the carrier had been sighted by a Japanese patrol boat.

Gay had gotten to know Doolittle's Raiders aboard *Hornet,* and all the Navy pilots had befriended and respected them for the mission they were about to launch. Despite this respect, Gay and the men of Torpedo 8 were more than a little envious that the Army was getting the first chance to strike back at Japan. They wished it could have been them.

As they stood on the windblown deck on that historic day, a sailor standing near the young ensign walked across the flight deck and removed a small metal box from his pocket from which he extracted a rosary. He kissed the crucifix and made the sign of the cross on one of Doolittle's plane's tires and then kissed the crucifix again before returning it to its tiny box. The young sailor then resumed his place as a spectator as the carrier turned into the wind. Doolittle rolled down the deck and into the Pacific skies and the other fifteen bombers followed.

The *Hornet* crew watched until the last bomber was out of sight. The carrier reversed course and headed east at high speed. The cruiser *Nashville* steamed over the horizon and engaged two Japanese boats, sinking them both. Ens. Gay was proud to be an American and felt sufficiently moved to write a poem about the raiders that night.[1]

George H. Gay, Jr., was born in Waco, Texas, on March 8, 1918. His family moved to Dallas, where George went to school. He grew up with BB guns and .22 rifles and always used and respected weapons. He was like most young boys, an adventuresome Huck Finn type, devising strategies to get secret notes to quarantined boarding school girls and fighting with bullies. On one occasion, after a fight, young George was ambushed by the bully, who hit him with a board as he rounded a corner. Some days later, an irate George—with fresh stitches in his face and armed with a baseball bat—crashed down onto the bully from the roof of a garage, aiming for his skull but settling for breaking a shoulder. After that George and his antagonist warily coexisted.

George's first experience with flying was at the Dallas State Fair, where the most popular attraction was the Ford Tri-Motor that took people up for rides. The youngster first asked his dad, and then his mom, and was told no by both. The boy was dejected. His grandmother saw George's disappointment and strode forward and took George by the arm and said, "Come on, son, I came here in a covered wagon, and I'm not afraid of that thing."[2]

In 1936 Gay enrolled in Texas A&M and spent two years there, but the war clouds in Europe, the family finances during the Depression, and his desire to fly if there was to be a war, cut his college years short. He decided that war was inevitable and reasoned that the way to avoid the draft was to get into the service he wanted.[3]

In July 1939, Gay tried to sign up for the Army Air Corps but flunked the physical with a supposed heart abnormality. He spent the next eighteen months working odd jobs as the war heated up in Europe. If he could not fight as an American airman, he thought he would go to Canada and join the RCAF or to England and the RAF. But before he could put either plan into action, a friend informed him that the Navy was looking for pilots and, though he didn't know that the Navy even had aircraft, he took the test and passed. On September 6, 1941, Ens. George Gay was commissioned.[4]

As he stood on the deck of *Hornet* it was hard to believe that his commissioning had been less than eight months before. The carrier was steaming toward Pearl Harbor after launching the first strike by the United States against the Japanese homeland. Seven days later, on April 25, she was back home berthed near the sunken battleships.

Admiral Yamamoto was shocked when he heard the news of the Doolittle raid. It was several days before he could deduce that the bombers must have been carrier-launched, however unlikely that conclusion sounded. No other explanation fit. President Roosevelt's assertion that the planes had taken off from "Shangri-la," an imaginary utopia from the novel *Lost Horizon,* was no help.[5]

It took several weeks for Yamamoto to learn the true origin of the raid. When the Japanese headquarters finally learned that it had been carrier-launched and led by Col. Doolittle, they scoffed in an effort to downplay its importance. Spokesmen for the high command said that the raid was less than "do-little"; it was in fact a "do-nothing" attack.

But the Japanese reaction to the raid belied those words and showed the extent of the blow to Japanese pride. Within two weeks of the Doolittle raid, Imperial General Headquarters Navy Order No. 18 was issued in the name of the emperor himself. It directed Yamamoto to carry out the occupation of Midway Island, and Yamomoto himself approved the details for "Operation MI," the capture of Midway and islands in the Aleutian chain. He would avenge the bombing of Tokyo.[6]

Takeshi Maeda, an Imperial Japanese Navy pilot on Japan's massive carrier *Kaga,* which had participated in the Pearl Harbor attack, was in Tokyo when Yamamoto's order was received to push forward with Operation MI. *Kaga* had returned to Tokyo after the attack on Pearl Harbor for repairs, and Lt. Maeda was a hero, having torpedoed the battleship *West Virginia.*

On April 18, Maeda had been ordered to stand by for a possible attack by U.S. carriers, but his commander told him the attack would most likely not come before April 19. To his horror, around lunchtime, he watched three low-flying two-engine planes fly over Tokyo. There were no Zeros, the superior Japanese planes, around to intercept, so they could do nothing. They were helpless—and furious. Maeda's commander briefed him that Yamamoto was pushing up the Midway operation in an effort to regain the confidence of the people, and especially of the Japanese Navy.[7]

The last days of May were days of extreme boredom for Torpedo 8. George Gay tried to carve a model of the new Torpedo Bomber F (TBF), which was due to arrive any day and to replace the older Torpedo Bomber Ds (TBDs) that they were now flying. The TBF was called the ghost ship because no one had ever seen it but everyone had heard about it. In fact, half of Torpedo Squadron 8 was still in Norfolk waiting for the arrival of the ghost ship so they could fly it out to join the rest of the squadron. The wait had been longer than expected. *Hornet* had left Norfolk on March 7, sailed through the Panama Canal, delivered Doolittle's Raiders, sailed back, made another patrol toward the Coral Sea, returned to Pearl Harbor, and was now preparing for a huge battle, and still Torpedo 8 Detachment waited in Norfolk for the mystery plane.

Now, two and a half months later, George Gay tried to pass time by carving a model of the new aircraft based on what others had told him about it. Other men of the squadron slept or read or walked around. There were constant games of acey-deucey and cards, along with the endless stories bragging of hometowns, romantic conquests, and what would happen in their first combat. It was the talk of warriors on the eve of battle.

After each day's briefings, to help pass the time, each man took a turn talking on a subject about which he had special knowledge; it became a popular way to kill a half hour. Gay talked about drilling an oil well. Another man talked about making plywood. Naturally, this forever after earned him the nickname "Plywood," which was actually good because calling him Plywood caused fewer fights than calling him by his real name, which happened to be Teats. Since Ens. Teats was the biggest man in the squadron, there were terrible stories about the fate of those who, for whatever reason, mispronounced his name.[8]

On May 26, the boredom ended. Rumors had been floating around for days that there would be a major engagement soon. The carrier *Yorktown* arrived a day later and Ens. Gay listened to friends returning from the Battle of Coral Sea tell of torpedo bombing exploits. He also found out that the U.S. carrier *Lexington* had been sunk by the Japanese. The pressure was building. The pilots of Torpedo 8 let off steam at the club at Barber's Point above Pearl Harbor. Here the warriors, girding for battle, passed around large gallon jars filled with ice, a little cola, and a quart of whiskey. Before the battle, the "Barber's Point Special" was a wonderful distraction.

On May 28, the men of Torpedo 8 were sleeping soundly after a night at Barber's Point when shots rang out just outside their rooms. They jumped out of their racks and heard the command to "hit the deck." Then the shouting voice said that this was no drill.

The startled pilots shook the cobwebs from their brains and realized that their squadron commander, Lcdr. John Waldron, was firing the shots from his .45 pistol and calling them to battle. George Gay thought that Waldron was a man who was driven to complete a task even if he was given little time to prepare. The twenty-one-year veteran pounded discipline and teamwork into his green squadron, and the only word he knew was *attack*. To the squadron commander, there was no other job more important than carrying a torpedo to a target and returning your aircraft safely.

Now this charismatic leader had literally blasted his men from slumber and had them running to the revetments and cranking engines. In minutes they were off, and shortly after noon were aboard *Hornet* as she steamed for Midway.

Two days later they were briefed on the situation. A large force of Japanese ships was expected to attack Midway in the next few days. The odds against the U.S. force scrambling to meet the massive attack would be about two and a half to one. The commander also briefed them about a diversionary attack by another Japanese force in the Aleutians, but *Hornet*'s mission would be at Midway.

Ens. Gay grimaced as the briefing went on. The attack was expected to come on June 4. The Americans would wait to see where the enemy would attack before committing their own forces. If the attack did not come on the fourth, then the plan was for *Hornet* to pull back and prepare to intercept an anticipated second strike on Pearl Harbor. If that attack on Pearl did not come by the fifteenth, then it would be presumed that the Japanese force was heading for the West Coast and *Hornet* would steam to make a stand there.[9]

On the day after Ens. Gay and Torpedo Squadron 8 took off from Hawaii to land on *Hornet,* Torpedo 8 Detachment, after its long delay in Norfolk, finally arrived with the new TBFs. But the carrier was gone: They were just in time to be too late.

Ens. Albert K. Earnest was with Torpedo 8 Detachment. He had been born in Richmond, Virginia, and spent his boyhood there. Like others of his generation, he had not escaped the hardships of the Depression. His father had been in the construction industry, making and selling bricks, but during the Depression, there wasn't any construction going on. The plant closed down and the family found other means of support, which was good enough to get young Albert into Virginia Military Institute. He graduated in 1938 with a B.S. in civil engineering and a commission as a second lieutenant in the Army Reserve. However, due to the reduced armed forces of 1938, only two graduates were taken by the Marine Corps and none by the Army. Earnest had taken the Air Corps exam while at school but had marginally failed the eye exam.

There was another program that offered a chance, albeit slight, of getting into the regular Army, and that was the Thompson Act program: Sign on for a year, after which there was an eight out of a thousand chance to be accepted for regular duty. Earnest did not like those odds, so he went to work for the next two years as a civilian in Richmond.

In 1940, the Navy came through town looking for aviator recruits. Earnest tried again and this time passed the eye exam. He had his commission in the Field Artillery Reserve, but a commission in the Army was not what he wanted and, despite his Army background and training, when the Navy offered flight training, he gave up his commission and joined the Navy.

Earnest received his Navy Wings in November 1941 and joined Torpedo 8 just as *Hornet* finished its shakedown cruise and departed for the Pacific. Like most of the new ensign aviators he was as "green as grass." He knew that a torpedo was supposed to be dropped from the aircraft while traveling at a speed of 85 to a 100 knots, and he knew that the torpedo should be dropped from a height of 100 feet, but that was the sum of his knowledge as a torpedo pilot. For that matter, most of the experienced pilots hadn't dropped a torpedo either.

When the carrier got orders to the Pacific in March, Cdr. Waldron decided to split the squadron in half and leave half in Norfolk to wait for delivery of the new TBFs and take the other half, those "experienced" with the TBDs, to sea on *Hornet*. The group remaining in Norfolk consisted of about twenty-five men: the executive officer, a few other experienced pilots, a couple of warrant officers, and the balance, who, like Earnest, were green ensigns.

By May, the group had accumulated twenty-one of the new planes, which came in dribs and drabs. Finally they got their long-awaited orders to the Pacific and flew across country and then to Honolulu. They arrived on May 29, but *Hornet* and *Enterprise* had sailed the day before, and *Yorktown* was in dry dock. The new ensigns had missed the ship and retired for the day, wondering what the next day would bring. When they awoke, they discovered that *Yorktown* was also gone.

Now a new plan developed. There was room for six of the new TBFs to park on the runway at Midway, so six would be sent to become part of the air force there. The word went out that the first six aircraft that could be ready would go. Ens. Earnest thought this all sounded interesting and exciting and he, like everyone else, volunteered to go. The other fifteen aircraft would be left behind, possibly to be placed on *Saratoga* whenever it arrived.

Ens. Earnest was delighted to learn that he would be one of the six pilots to fly to Midway, and, on June 1, took off from Honolulu for the 1,200-mile flight. It would take eight hours. Earnest was glad that two navigators from a VP squadron volunteered to go with them to navigate on the long trip to Midway.

When they arrived, they were given positions at the airstrip and a place to sleep. Each morning for the next three days, Ens. Earnest and the rest of the Torpedo 8 Detachment went to the runway and cranked the engines, warmed the aircraft up, and checked and rechecked everything.[10]

Midway Atoll was 6 miles in diameter and consisted of two islands, Sand Island and Eastern Island. It had a 5,300-foot airstrip and, with battle imminent, was armed to the teeth. One veteran compared the place to the Little Big Horn and Custer waiting for the Sioux to come. All the guns were manned and the marines were dug in. Everything from bombs to drinking water was bunkered for protection from air attack. There were also plenty of weapons not normally found, weapons created for a last-ditch stand: There were pipe bombs driven into the sand offshore to greet an invading force and stacks of Molotov cocktails; empty whiskey bottles contained a new kind of firewater.[11]

On the third night that Ens. Albert Earnest was on the island, he took a walk on the runway after dark. His thoughts were of the coming fight and of home and the unknown, and as he walked he saw something rolled up on the ground. It was a two-dollar bill. He knew that tomorrow would be his lucky day.

On June 3, Torpedo Squadron 8 consisted of the fifteen TBDs on *Hornet* and the six TBFs on Midway. The rest were back at Hawaii. The aircraft on board were part of Task Force 16, which consisted of *Hornet* and *Enterprise,* six cruisers and twelve destroyers. Task Force 17 was the carrier *Yorktown* with two cruisers and six destroyers. There were also four supply ships. There were 255 planes on three carriers and 110 more on Midway.

This fleet, with its three precious carriers, eight cruisers, and sixteen destroyers was everything the United States could scrape together. It was tiny in comparison to the naval juggernaut approaching from the west. Yamamoto's Combined Imperial Fleet consisted of the Mobile Force of four carriers, two battleships, three cruisers, and eleven destroyers, along with five supply ships and 275 carrier-based aircraft. Following closely behind was the main body of seven battleships, one light carrier, two seaplane carriers with midget submarines, three light cruisers, and twenty destroyers. Heading on a course for the Aleutians was the Second Mobile Group with two more carriers and its own support and screening ships. In all, Yamamoto had almost two hundred ships and seven hundred aircraft.[12]

His plan was massive, involving far-flung operations in the northern and central Pacific. His carrier task force, heading for the Aleutians, would strike on June 3 and the forces would land and occupy the islands of Adak, Attu, and Kiska. The Japanese hoped the Americans would respond to that attack and head for the Northern Pacific, leaving the Central Pacific and Midway open. On June 4, the Mobile Force with its four fleet carriers would attack Midway, bombing and destroying the base and aircraft in preparation for the invasion force. The invasion would be launched on June 5 with five thousand men. Midway would then become a Japanese fortress. If the American Fleet moved to contest the invasion or to try and retake the island, the carrier force would attack, followed by a devastating surface attack by the main body of heavy battleships and cruisers, which would be the final stroke to give Japan absolute control of the seas and finish the job begun at Pearl Harbor.[13]

The Midway operation would be also the beginning of an overall plan formulated by Yamamoto's Combined Fleet Headquarters. On May 4, the plan was war-gamed on the flagship, *Yamoto,* a massive battleship with eighteen-inch guns. The Midway invasion was to be a starting point for the second-phase plan, followed by a July operation aimed at the capture of New Caledonia and the Fiji Islands to cut the supply line from the United States.

From there, the air strikes would be launched against Sydney and other points on the southeast coast of Australia. Finally, sometime in August, the entire weight of the Combined Imperial Fleet would be hurled against Johnston Island and Hawaii. The plan war-gamed to a successful conclusion, with the help of some less-than-objective umpires.[14]

But the starting point for this ambitious plan was Midway. On the evening of June 3, the Japanese Mobile Force, with its four fleet carriers, plunged on in dense fog toward a position northwest of Midway.

On the evening of June 3, the pilots of Torpedo 8 sat in Ready Room 4 on the carrier *Hornet.* Cdr. Waldron passed out a mimeographed message to his men. George Gay slowly read his. It said that the commander felt that they were ready even though they had very little time to train. Despite the newness of the squadron, he felt that they were the best in the world and he hoped to fight the battle in a favorable tactical condition.

"But," the message read, "if worse comes to worst, I want each of us to do his utmost to destroy our enemies. If there is only one plane left to make a final run-in, I want that man to go in and get a hit." He finished with, "May God be with us. Good luck, happy landings, and give 'em hell!"[15]

When the squadron finally stood down from the ready room, most wrote letters. They were the letters of men going into battle. Most of the letters assured the loved ones that all was okay and expressed confidence they would return. There were also some "but ifs." Some talked of the next life and others gave permission to their young wives not to become old maids. Some letters were written to be sent only "if I don't return."

George Gay did not write a letter.

On board *Enterprise,* Lcdr. Richard Best, the squadron commander of Bomber Squadron 6, had been briefed on the latest intelligence for the upcoming battle. He had been called to a meeting in the cabin of Adm. Raymond Spruance, who was commanding Task Force 16. When he arrived the other three squadron commanders and the group commander were there. Spruance's staff was also present and the meeting got under way.

Cdr. Best was surprised at the detail of the briefing. The staff laid out the complete plan of the Japanese attack. They covered the June 3 diversion plan to the Aleutians, naming the ships. He found it strange that the briefing labeled that attack a "diversion." How could they know that?

The staff then laid out the complete battle plan—the approach from the southwest of Midway with the battleships and transports ready to take the island. The briefer drew a line from the northwest, which would be the path of approach for the carriers, and then he named them: *Akagi, Kaga, Soryu, Hiryu*. These were the big four from the attack on Pearl Harbor.

Best thought to himself that it was impossible to have information this detailed. You can't learn these kinds of details of an enemy's plan just through spies, you might get some indications of possible objectives, but this was very detailed. They even named battleship divisions, who was accompanying, and when they would be there. This was more than an educated response to conventional intelligence sources. The staff officer concluded his brief.

"I couldn't believe it," Best said. "I thought it was a script. When the whole battle plan was laid out, here we are, waiting behind the garden gate to assassinate these poor innocents, stumbling in, unaware that we know about them, that we've been reading their mail!"

Adm. Spruance asked if there were any questions. For a moment, no one raised his hand. Then Cdr. Best had one.

"Suppose they don't hit Midway and go into Pearl," he asked, thinking about his wife and four-year-old daughter living there.

The silence was deafening. It was not just a few seconds' pause, but one that went on for forty-five seconds and it became uncomfortable. It seemed as if the admiral was wrestling with telling Best why he should feel confident that the Japanese Fleet would not go to Pearl, but in the end he simply said, "Well, we just hope they won't."[16]

At 0130 on June 4, general quarters sounded on *Hornet*.

George Gay and the rest of the pilots of Torpedo 8 gathered in Ready Room 4 and sat to await dawn, which would come shortly after 0430. The projection screen was down, and on it was the latest tactical update, stating that four PBY aircraft had made torpedo attacks on enemy ships southwest of Midway.

The pilots settled back in their leather-covered chairs and reclined. The launch was most likely to be at dawn, but for now everything was quiet, including the Teletype machine. Some of the men soon dozed off—Daybreak came and they were still in their chairs. Waldron went off to find out what he could.

The pressure building in Ready Room 4 was tremendous. Some

thumbed through books, then tossed them aside. Others tried to discuss the tactics they should employ, but no one could agree. Fingers tapped on the arms of the big leather chairs. The pilots got up, stretched, and then sat again to continue the damnable waiting: 0500 came and went as did 0600, and still they sat. Finally, Waldron returned and said that the Japanese Fleet had not been located. He then secured the squadron from the ready room and they all stretched and yawned on their way out the door.

Waldron thought the sun was a factor and he felt that if the Japanese intended to strike Midway, they would have to hit soon. The squadron went to breakfast for the usual, including baked beans. The tension of being in the ready room was eased by breakfast, and the pilots were laughing and ribbing each other as the crisis seemed to have passed.[17]

At Midway, Ens. Earnest watched patrol aircraft take off at 0415 followed by the B-17s, which took off to prevent their being caught on the ground should the Japanese attack. The pilots of Torpedo 8 Detachment warmed the engines of the new TBFs, just as they had each morning since their arrival.

At 0545, one of the patrol aircraft pilots transmitted that many planes were headed for Midway, bearing 320 at a distance of 150 miles. Five minutes later the distance had closed to 93 miles and the island's radar picked them up. Two minutes later the patrol plane reported two carriers bearing 320 at 180 miles.[18]

Earnest and the other pilots were standing by their aircraft when a staff officer suddenly ran to them and reported the enemy sighting. The six crews manned their TBFs and taxied to the runway while the fighters took off. Torpedo 8 Detachment took off right after them. Ens. Earnest made his first takeoff with his 1,000-pound WWI torpedo in the bomb bay.

Once airborne, the young ensign looked to join up with the Marine dive-bombers. The Marines were flying the older SPD2s, an aircraft that the Navy had given up on. He understood that they were to rendezvous. The Marines had not had the aircraft long enough to perfect the art of dive-bombing, so they intended to glide-bomb, which made the plane more vulnerable to fighter attack. There would be no dive-bombers from Midway Island today.

The marine aircraft were nowhere to be seen, so Torpedo 8 Detachment turned to 320 degrees and headed toward the Japanese Fleet. They were flying only a few minutes when Earnest saw a Japanese fighter make a pass on the formation but not shoot. The fighter disappeared, and the six TBFs flew on. In the rear of Earnest's aircraft were his two crewmen: a turret gunner, Jay Manning, and under the plane's belly in the tunnel gunner position radioman Harry Ferrier.[19]

One-half hour after Ens. Earnest and the TBFs departed Midway airfield, the Japanese attack arrived. The island seemed to turn into a mass of flames with fuel tanks exploding, emitting huge columns of black smoke that could be seen for hundreds of miles around. Some buildings had been hit, including barracks, the mess halls, and the hospital, but the runway remained virtually intact and the damage, for all the fire and smoke, was light. Twenty minutes later, the Japanese aircraft were on their way back to the carriers.[20]

On *Hornet*, George Gay and his friends finished their breakfast and walked out of the wardroom. They had only taken a few steps when the bell started to clang and the shrill boatswain's pipe sounded over the PA.

"General quarters, flight quarters!" the voice boomed. "All pilots to the ready rooms." This time the Teletype in Ready Room 4 was not quiet. On the screen was the notice that Midway was being attacked by enemy aircraft. The pilots frantically wrote down the flight information.

The booming voice on the PA now ordered scout bomber crews to man their planes. It gave the wind direction and *Hornet*'s position, and then canceled the order for the scout bomber crews to man their planes.

George Gay wrote furiously as the voice continued. "Two carriers and battleships bearing 320 from Midway, 180 miles, course 135, speed 25 knots."

The adrenaline was really pumping as the voice paused for a moment. Then, "Enemy naval units sighted within striking distance. Expected strike time 0900. Looks like this is it!"

The order of launch would be fighters off first, then scouts, and finally the bombers and torpedoes. Hands were shaken, "Good luck," "Same to you!" The entire ship was a beehive.

Ens. Gay saw that there were only six of Torpedo 8's planes up on the deck, which was all there was room for. They would be the last to launch and they would be alone. There would be no fighter protection for the low, slow-flying TBDs despite Waldron's pleas. The fighter pilots had never encountered a Zero, and the advice from the Coral Sea veterans was to get altitude on the Zero or it would end bad. Besides, it was the bombers at Coral Sea that had really caught hell from the Jap fighters, so they would get the fighter cover. Ens. Gay was not comfortable with that. He knew that while the bombers may have caught hell, it had been the torpedo planes that had scored the hits at Coral Sea—and you could bet that the Japanese were very aware of that.

Without fighter cover, Waldron ordered his men to fly close to the water so the Zeros could not get under them. The squadron also knew it would have a tough time arriving at the battle area with the fighters and bombers since, after the six aircraft on deck were launched, the remaining nine would have to be brought up from the hangar deck while the launched planes circled.

The scout planes took off at 0700 followed by ten of *Hornet*'s fighters. George Gay watched as thirty-five bombers were waved into the air. Torpedo 8 began to start its engines when the loudspeaker announced a twelve-minute delay. Ens. Gay reflected that he was not carrier qualified. His first carrier takeoff had been just weeks ago when he flew a four-hour mission and returned and landed the aircraft. Cdr. Waldron had slapped him on the back and informed him that "two more" and he would be carrier qualified. This would be his second carrier takeoff and the first one with a torpedo. Most of the squadron had never even seen a TBD take off from the deck with a torpedo. Gay was dubious about the increased weight. Another pilot, dubious about the chances of the slow-flying TBD to get the squadron through the upcoming fight, dubbed Torpedo 8 the Coffin Squadron. They were all skeptical about the WWI torpedo that they carried, knowing that it had a history of problems, one of which was that on impact, it was often a dud.

There was no order regarding who would take off first. Whoever the deck crew spotted would go first and, as luck would have it, Ens. Gay's plane was rolled forward, first up. Oh, great, he thought, and then told the second pilot that if he went in the drink he'd have to ask for more ship speed to get more wind over the deck.

Gay was in the cockpit and his engine was running. He watched the signalman on deck wave him forward to the takeoff position. When he was far enough forward, he unfolded his wings and locked them. To his right front, the signalman's hand rotated rapidly, ordering him to rev the engine to full speed, and he pushed the throttle forward. Then the checkered flag whipped down, and at 0815 George Gay was rolling down the deck in his TBD with his first torpedo secured beneath him. His second carrier launch was perfect, and as he banked to his left to circle back over the carrier, he felt that he'd passed another test. One more launch and he'd be a qualified carrier pilot.

The next five aircraft were off quickly, but it seemed to Ens. Gay that it was an eternity before the rest of the aircraft were brought up to the flight deck and launched. As they rendezvoused, Waldron grouped them in two sections. The first had eight aircraft and the second had seven. Gay flew as the last plane so he could concentrate on navigation for the squadron.

He was very nervous. Normally he was aware of everything around him, but this time he did not trust his memory to keep him up-to-date on the performance of his aircraft. He did something he had never done before: He wrote everything down. He noted the rate of fuel consumption for each tank. He wanted to ensure that each tank was used proportionally so no one tank became empty; an empty tank is prone to explode if hit by fire. He plotted their course over and over.

They flew on for almost an hour with only the ocean and sky to look at. Gay wondered what the fighters and bombers were doing. Had they found the fleet? Had they attacked? There was no way that old, slow Torpedo 8 would be there for a coordinated attack. They would arrive late and react to the situation.

Around 0910, Waldron broke radio silence. "There's a fighter on our tail!" he exclaimed. Fourteen heads turned to see a Japanese scout plane flying over them at 1,000 feet. George Gay knew that if there had been any chance of them arriving on the battle scene unnoticed, that chance was gone.[21]

Ens. Albert Earnest had been flying for an hour in his new TBF from Midway. He was at 4,500 feet when his eye caught what looked like a transport. As he positioned himself in his cockpit for a closer look, the whole Japanese Fleet appeared before him. The six TBFs of Torpedo 8 Detachment and four other torpedo-carrying B-26s were the first aircraft to find the Japanese Fleet. Earnest could see two carriers and set his sights for them. The sight of the massive armada made him stare in disbelief and he opened the bomb bay. He did it automatically because he knew that if the hydraulics were damaged by a fighter, he wouldn't be able to open the bay and that meant he could not get rid of the torpedo. A second later his gunner shouted that they were under attack. The first fighter bore in on him and fired its 7mm guns, knocking out Earnest's hydraulic system. He thanked God that he'd opened the bomb bay.

But the loss of the hydraulic system created an unexpected problem. The loss of pressure dropped the tail wheel from its retracted position, which masked the tunnel gunner and prevented him from firing. The turret gunner continued the fight against the swarming Zeros for a few seconds until he suddenly slumped over, riddled by Japanese fire.

The six aircraft of Torpedo 8 Detachment were in two three-plane sections and, as they flew on, Earnest estimated at least twenty-five fighters were swarming on them.

"They were getting in each other's way trying to shoot at us," he remembered.

A moment later his tunnel gunner was also hit, and Earnest took the plane down to 200 feet and pushed the throttle full open in an attempt to avoid the Zeros, but the enemy was all over him firing 7mm and then 20mm cannon fire. He looked to his right to see the 20mm hitting on the wings; then one round came through the Plexiglas and hit him in the cheek. The blood poured down his face and the inside of the TBF looked like a butcher shop. The two gunners were down in the back and Earnest's face was covered with blood.

The young ensign flew on. "I was too young and dumb to do anything else," he said.

But the Japanese were relentless. Again and again they poured in and on the next pass they cut his elevator wires. He could not keep his nose in the air, and the plane dipped gently forward and started down. Earnest knew now that he was going to hit the water. There was no way he could make an attack on one of the carriers, so he looked around and saw a destroyer off to the port and kicked the plane to the left with his rudders and ailerons. Out went the torpedo. He never saw it hit the water and never knew where it went. The TBF was on a gentle glide to hit the water just as if it were going to land.

Earnest then went through the mechanics of landing. He rolled his elevator control tabs, just as he always did, and was shocked to see the nose come up and the aircraft jump into the air. He'd forgotten about the tabs when his wires had been cut. Now he was flying again.

But the two Japanese fighters that had been attacking him like lions on a zebra were not happy at his good fortune and were determined to make his plane go down. They chased him for what seemed like three hours but was actually more like three minutes. Earnest did everything he knew to evade them. He flew the plane like he'd never flown before, but it seemed hopeless. At every turn, the fighters were on him.

After a final series of frantic escaping maneuvers, Ens. Earnest was suddenly aware that there was silence. No more bullets ripping through the plane and no more zooming fighters rushing past him. He was alone. He checked in every direction. No fighters—just him and his beat-up airplane, which had come within inches of the ocean, only to rise again. He estimated that it had been four minutes since he had first spotted the fleet.

Earnest tried to get his bearings and found that the chase had taken him to the northwest, and now the Japanese Fleet was between him and where he thought Midway was. His compass was shot out, so he used the sun to navigate. He was definitely not going across the Japanese

Fleet again. Once had been enough. So he flew south, and when he thought he'd gone far enough, he flew east to a spot where he thought he was opposite of Midway. From there, he'd try to sneak in.

Suddenly there was a voice in his ear. His tunnel gunner was not dead, and he now climbed into the rear seat. He'd been knocked out by a Japanese 7mm that grazed his skull.

On they flew, seeing nothing. Earnest decided to fly above the clouds, which were broken at 4,000 feet. From that altitude he saw smoke and came down to see what was causing it. It was then that he spotted a small island that he knew was a short distance west of Midway. A few minutes later he saw the smoke was from Midway and flew in on the smoke from the burning fuel tanks on Sand Island.

As he approached the island, Earnest put his wheels down. Only one would lower, but after his recent excitement, he considered that a minor problem. As he approached the runway with his one wheel down, the ground control people waved him off. He came around a second time and got another wave-off.

The ground crew was frantically transmitting to Earnest to not land, but to take his plane up to altitude and bail out. They had seen the crippled aircraft and did not want it blocking the runway. But Ens. Earnest's radio had been shot out and he heard nothing.

"I had one wounded man, and I was wounded, and I had a dead man," Earnest said. "I took two wave-offs, and the third time, I said the hell with it, and came on in."

On one wheel, he landed the riddled aircraft and came to a great sliding halt. He got out and jumped to the ground and waited for the rest of his squadron to return. They never did.[22]

Ens. Gay checked his navigation note from his aircraft in the rear of the Torpedo 8 formation. He calculated that they'd been flying long enough that they should have found the enemy fleet. Waldron must have thought so also because suddenly Gay saw the first section break formation and form a scouting line. The eight planes spread out and formed a line, even with Waldron's plane, to be able to see more of the ocean below. But, due to their inexperience, the formation drifted wider and wider and soon the end planes were out of sight.

Waldron called them back, realizing that was a bad idea, and no sooner had they reformed than they saw smoke columns on the horizon. It was 0925. The whole panorama was below. Surface ships were belching smoke, and George Gay could see aircraft landing on the carriers. Because of the smoke he instantly assumed that they were late for the battle, but they weren't late. They were, in fact, the first carrier aircraft to have found the Japanese Fleet.

Waldron signaled for Torpedo 8 to spread out and bracket the biggest carrier for an attack. No sooner had they spread than the Zeros were on them, and Waldron ordered them to reform for mutual support. He broke radio silence and ordered the attack.

George Gay watched Zeros come in from all sides and from every angle. They were like a swarm of bees and they targeted the lead planes first. But the formation flew on, heading for *Kaga,* which now swerved and twisted in evasive maneuvers.

On the hangar deck of the huge carrier, Lt. Maeda was busy trying to change armament back to torpedoes. He had been waiting, his plane armed with a torpedo, when the order came to switch to bombs. Now it was back to torpedoes. *Kaga* was evading at full speed and it was no easy task to switch the weapons of thirty-six planes. There was also mass confusion and chaos because waves of aircraft were returning from the strike at Midway demanding to land. From the hangar deck, which was open, he could see the approaching formation of Torpedo 8.

The planes of Torpedo 8 began falling into the sea. As they fell, Gay watched some do a half roll flying upside-down for a moment and then crashing on their backs. Some were on fire, and he saw that one of them was Waldron. As he headed for the water, Gay flew by him. He saw the commander had stood up to get away from the flames and had one foot outside the cockpit. The aircraft hit the water and everything disappeared. Gay was witnessing a nightmare.

From behind him, he heard his gunner, Bob Huntington, yell that he'd been hit. The young ensign looked back and could hardly see the gunner, who was slumped down low. Gay screamed, "Are you hurt bad? Can you move?" But there was no sound.

Gay watched his squadron fall from the sky. It was like being on the last car of a roller coaster and watching all the cars in front take the loops and dips knowing full well that your turn was coming.

Gay took his TBD to the water. He flew right off the waves and had the throttle wide open, which only got him moving at 180 knots. He abandoned the straight flying glide and started dodging and pulled up and took a few shots at the Zeros. Machine-gun rounds thudded into the armor plate protecting his back and seat, and the Plexiglas shattered on his canopy.

The remainder of the squadron flew on. The Zeros' attack and the twisting of *Kaga* had placed the American aircraft to the west of their target. They turned and vectored to fly a course starboard and slightly ahead of the big carrier. The range to the torpedo drop point closed rapidly as *Kaga* began to turn toward her attackers, now numbering three aircraft. One of the planes was directly in front of Ens. Gay and the other to the left front.

Suddenly the plane in front went down while the one to the left was losing control. The stricken aircraft seemed to go down in slow motion, arching gracefully until it shattered on the water. Ens. Gay flew on alone.

Kaga was still in her hard starboard turn and that left Gay now approaching her forward port quarter. He was pleased with himself for having maneuvered for an excellent shot. He aimed a hundred yards in front of her bow and gripped the throttle to slow down to 80 knots to launch his torpedo. If everything went right, the torpedo should splash and travel its course just as *Kaga* finished her turn and strike her midships. He punched the release button, but nothing happened. The electrical release failed. As badly as his plane was shot up, it was no wonder. He reached for the mechanical release with a wounded left hand and yanked and pulled as if he were trying to rip it from the panel. He wasn't sure, but he thought he felt the torpedo release from the TBD.

He slammed the throttle forward and flew straight at the big carrier trying to make a tiny target for the enemy gunners. If he tried to pull the nose up to make a turn, he would expose the belly of his plane and make a big target. He closed in on *Kaga* and thought the ship looked enormous and wondered why *Hornet* didn't look as big when he was trying to land.

He focused on a gun emplacement right in front of him and flew right at it. The gunner jumped from his position as Gay zoomed over him. On the bridge he saw an officer with binoculars and his samurai sword. He was frantically pointing at the buzzing TBD making Ens. Gay chuckle at his antics.

Once over the deck, he kicked the plane into a right turn to fly out over the stern so the gunners on the starboard side would not get a free shot at his tail as he flew away. He flew right down the deck and saw a swarm of planes, men, bombs, and gas lines. Clearing the stern, he again hugged the water, flying wildly through several ships and out past the line of destroyers. The surface ships all banged away at him as he flew by. This wasn't all bad since his low, fast pass-by required the gunners to make radical changes to try to get him in their sights. Their chances of hitting him were small and, for the first time since he had arrived on the battle scene, the Zeros were not on his tail. They had opted not to run the gauntlet line between ships and risk being shot down by their own antiaircraft fire.

But they were waiting for him on the other side, and the lopsided fight began anew. They greeted him with 20mm cannon fire. One of the rounds ripped into the cockpit, shattering his left rudder pedal and piercing the firewall, setting the engine on fire. The flames licked at his feet as the aircraft faltered and, with some difficulty, Gay managed to get the nose up and cut the engine to slow the doomed TBD so he could glide for a watery landing. Doomed or not, he continued to be hammered by the Zeros. One wing hit the water slightly before the other, and the aircraft cartwheeled in a gigantic splash. The force of impact slammed Gay's open canopy shut, and when the violent spinning stopped he found that he was trapped inside. The hood would not budge despite frantic beating and pushing. The water rose to his waist and he sat on the instrument panel pounding the Plexiglas that threatened to entomb him and send him, and his TBD, in a final, 6,000-fathom dive to eternity. As the water rose to his armpits, with a mighty heave he finally opened the hood and scrambled out. He paddled to the rear seat and saw that his gunner was indeed dead and the water in his flooding compartment was red, but he still tried to free the body from its harness. The TBD nosed down, tugging his gunner loose from Gay's grasp, and began its descent. As if to extend a parting handshake, the tail brushed his calf as it went down.

The Zeros made a final strafing pass and flew away. Gay treaded water very much alone for a few seconds before his survival raft made a miraculous appearance, popping to the surface along with a seat cushion that he used to try to cover his head as if it were a camouflage net. He wore it like a bonnet. Torpedo 8 had begun its attack at 0925. It was now 0930.[23]

On *Kaga,* Lt. Maeda had seen the torpedo aircraft attack. He watched as the planes were picked off one by one, and he stood in awe of the ever-thinning line as they bore in.

"They had the Kamikaze spirit," he said. "The Devastators came in one after another; the Zeros were busy knocking them down one after another, but still they came. They really had their stuff—the bravery."[24]

Kaga continued to twist and turn because at 0951, just minutes after Torpedo 8 had been disposed of, Torpedo 6 from *Enterprise* arrived. *Akagi* and *Soryu* made similarly erratic evasive maneuvers. Torpedo 6, without fighter cover, fared little better than Torpedo 8, losing ten of fourteen planes. Then, at 10:00, it was Torpedo 3's turn to hammer itself on the anvil of the Japanese fighters. Only two of twelve TBDs escaped.

On board *Akagi,* Capt. Mitsuo Fuchida, the senior air wing commander who had led the attack on Pearl Harbor, watched the attack of the torpedo bombers. He could not fly in the Midway attack because he was recovering from an appendectomy.

All morning he had watched the aircraft from Midway try to attack the Imperial Japanese Navy Fleet. Now electricity filled the air of the ship as screening ships reported enemy carrier planes approaching. Soon he could see fifteen tiny black specks just above the horizon off the starboard bow. From a distance he could see one after another of the specks burst into flame and plunge into the water, trailing black smoke.

Soon a Zero group leader reported that all fifteen planes had been shot down.

A few minutes later, lookouts reported two more groups of torpedo bombers off both the port and starboard bows. Fuchida watched the two groups flying in two single columns heading straight for *Akagi*. He thought it impossible to dodge all their torpedoes. As the bombers approached their release points, the Zeros hammered them into the sea. Still the survivors plowed on and Fuchida cringed as he waited for the torpedo splashes, but none ever came. On the flight deck there was cheering as each of the planes was shot down. Of more than forty attacking planes, Fuchida had seen only seven release their torpedoes, and none of them had hit. There was great relief.[25]

As the last of the aircraft of Torpedo 3 from *Yorktown* splashed down, the Japanese Fleet had been under air attack for three hours. Fifty-two various aircraft from Midway, including the six planes from Torpedo 8 Detachment, had flown strikes against it. Then forty-one planes of the torpedo squadrons from the American carriers had tried their luck. All had been swatted away like pesky flies. Not one of the ninety-three aircraft had scored a hit, and, to make matters worse, the fighters and bombers from *Hornet* never even found the battle area. They returned home without having fired a shot. The fighters from *Yorktown* seemed a mere annoyance to the Japanese as they became engaged in a furious dogfight, while the fighters from *Enterprise* became high-altitude observers until low fuel forced them to return to base.

After three hours, the Japanese Fleet was not only intact, it was unscathed. One hundred fifty-two carrier aircraft and another fifty-two from Midway had flown to the battle area and now were either shot down or struggling home. Only fifty aircraft were left to stop the Japanese armada.[26]

George Gay had been in the water less than an hour watching the Japanese Fleet moving around him. He was watching *Kaga* land aircraft when he suddenly saw American aircraft diving down. Small objects separated from the planes as they pulled out of their seventy-degree dives. The first three bombs aimed at *Kaga* were near misses, but the next four smashed into the swerving carrier. Enormous explosions rocked the massive ship and further detonated the exposed bombs and torpedoes that littered the deck. Fuel lines criss-crossing the deck to refuel the planes returning from Midway ruptured and ignited in massive sheets of flame. The ship was ripped apart. A second group of dive bombers found *Akagi*. Two bombs smashed into the flight deck and the same secondary detonations and fiery explosions doomed her to the same fate as *Kaga*.[27]

Captain Fuchida, on *Akagi*, had watched as the big ship turned into the wind to launch aircraft. All planes were in position, with their engines warming up. In another five minutes, the deck would have been empty and the aircraft headed to attack the American force that had launched its torpedo planes against them. At 1024, the order came to start launching aircraft.

The air officer whipped his white flag down, and the first Zero raced down the deck and into the sky. It would be the only aircraft to take off. Suddenly a lookout screamed, "Helldivers." Fuchida looked up to see three black aircraft diving down on him. The bombs they released looked like they were headed directly for him, and he hit the deck.

The first thing he heard was the roar of the bombers pulling up hard after their near-vertical dive. The second was the explosion of the first bomb and then the flash and explosion of the second bomb. When no more bombs fell, he got up and looked skyward, but the planes were gone. He looked at the flight deck and could not believe what he saw. The deck was twisted beyond recognition and aircraft were scattered, some with their tails in the air, but all on fire as fuel ignited in yellow and black balls. Shortly, the ship began shuddering from the explosions of its munitions.[28]

Although Gay didn't know it at the time, the bombers from *Enterprise* had at the last minute found the fleet and swooped down unopposed while the Zeros were busy handling the earlier torpedo attacks and a small group of American fighters.

Simultaneously, a third carrier, *Soryu*, erupted in flames from the bombs from *Yorktown*'s aircraft. A flight of seventeen aircraft had peeled off from 14,500 feet and plunged down in a seventy-degree dive. Four of the aircraft had no bombs due to faulty switches that inadvertently jettisoned them during the flight to the Japanese Fleet. But the rest did, and four 1,000-pounders found their mark, and *Soryu* was finished.[29] In less than ten minutes, three of the four Japanese carriers were destroyed.

Gay couldn't believe it. Japanese ships cruised all around him. One passed less than 50 feet from him. He felt he was sitting in the bull's eye. "Give them hell, boy," he said to no one, but secretly hoped that the American bombers would ignore the cruiser passing next to him. He had just been shot down by this invincible enemy and now he was watching his enemy being destroyed in spectacular explosions. In an effort to shake the thundering American strike force, the whole Japanese Navy steamed over him and disappeared over the horizon—but it wasn't long before they were back. The three burning carriers were downwind of him but other ships criss-crossed all around him. The explosions that rocked the carriers were hurting his stomach. As the ships passed and repassed him, he hid under his seat cushion hoping to look like just another piece of bobbing wreckage.

The life raft was a problem. It was a big bundle that bobbed around and at times Gay tried to ride it to keep it out of sight. Later in the day he saw some other Japanese ships steaming close to the carriers, picking survivors out of the water. He waited for another American strike and was disappointed that it never came. Slowly the Japanese Navy drifted away and, as dusk settled on the battle area, Gay's hopes for survival soared. He felt sure he would be picked up from the debris of battle.

He watched as two of the destroyed carriers were towed over the horizon. Only one remained in his area. He was thinking about opening his raft when tremendous explosions almost made him leap from the water. A Japanese cruiser began firing to try to sink the remaining carrier to avoid capture.

When it was almost last light, Gay inflated the raft and it looked beautiful. He scrambled in and was relieved not to have to tread water, but he also discovered that the compressed air from the bottles soon leaked out of three out of four of the flotation compartments. Try as he might he could not pump fast enough to keep those ruptured compartments full. The one good compartment seemed enough to keep the raft afloat, so he abandoned himself to the trust that he would be okay. He became very cold and his teeth chattered throughout the night. His other wounds added to his discomfort and he longed for the warmth of a new day.

At first light he felt some relief. The hours he had spent out of the water had revived him and he had the presence of mind to start thinking of his next moves. He examined his .45 and found it to be in working condition. He surveyed the area, which had some wreckage floating, but found nothing useful, and then set up a watch for himself, keeping a sharp lookout.

At 0620, twenty-one hours after crashing into the ocean, he heard what he described as, "the most beautiful sound I have ever heard."[30]

He saw a patrol bomber, a PBY seaplane, obviously scouting for the Japanese Fleet. It flew straight over him having sighted his yellow raft. He waved his arms, and the aircraft rocked its wings and continued on its mission. Ens. Gay knew that a report would be made and he could almost hear his location being sent out.

A report was one thing. A rescue was something else. These were still dangerous waters, and he knew nothing of the situation. Where was the enemy fleet? For that matter, where was the American fleet and was it still afloat or were both navies shattered by yesterday's events? He chose to think positively, especially since the recent flyover, and began to take inventory of just what existed in his little raft world. His several wounds didn't seem to be too bad. He found patches for the raft, a survival knife, flares, a signal mirror, dye markers, a survival book, and even some food: some K-ration and concentrated candy. There was also a Bible.

The warmth of the sun made everything feel better, but later on in the morning he felt sick and was worried about capsizing the raft. He patched the raft as best he could and then made two stacks of all his possessions. One stack was to keep no matter what, and the other was to throw overboard should the Japanese pick him up. In one of the stacks was $800 that he had taken with him when he flew from *Hornet,* not because he was afraid it would be stolen while he was gone, but because he was afraid that the carrier would be sunk and he couldn't bear the thought of his money at the bottom of the ocean.

In mid-afternoon, an albatross landed on the raft and stayed a while before flying off. But as the day wore on, he knew his chances for pickup were diminishing and he prepared himself for another night. At least he had had a chance to dry off.

Much later in the afternoon, he heard those wonderful sounds again. It was the PBY returning from its patrol. Again it flew over him and again Gay waved his arms, knowing that this second flyover was to determine his exact position and how much he had drifted from the morning sighting. Help would be on its way. Maybe tomorrow he would be picked up. He did not expect this plane to land in the water and make itself a sitting duck for an enemy aircraft out on its own patrol—but that's exactly what it did.

After flying over him the aircraft circled and touched down close to the sole survivor of Torpedo 8. The door opened and a sailor asked, "Seen any Jap planes lately?"[31]

With that Ens. Gay climbed aboard. The pilot was Lt. Cole. Cole had indeed radioed Gay's position that morning and continued his mission. On the way back Cole and his eleven-man crew decided to pass over and see if they could find that guy in the raft. When they did, they knew that a surface vessel could be a couple of days getting there and might not even find him. So, despite the extreme danger to which they exposed themselves, the crew voted unanimously to land and pick the "poor bastard" up.[32]

Lt. Cole turned his craft into the wind, lifted off the ocean, and flew to Midway.

EPILOGUE

George Gay was patched up from his minor wounds and was visited by Adm. Chester Nimitz, to whom he gave a firsthand report of the attack on the enemy carriers at Midway. He was the only living eyewitness.

After his report, Gay was singled out to be a spokesman for the war effort for the Navy, and as such, became a celebrity following the speaker's circuit and telling the people back home that the war effort needed them. That mission was bittersweet. While he loved getting out the message about the war, his fame and publicity were a source of heartache to the families of those who did not survive, and on occasion there were some hard feelings.

In April 1943, Gay served a second combat tour, flying out of Henderson Field at Guadalcanal. For his heroism on June 4, 1942, at Midway, he was awarded the Navy Cross.

On the Japanese side, for Lt. Takeshi Maeda, things did not go as well. When the aircraft from *Enterprise* dropped the bombs that smashed *Kaga,* he was on the hangar deck attempting to change ordnance. He was badly wounded and taken off the doomed carrier later that day. *Kaga* sank that night.

Maeda was taken back to Tokyo on a medevac ship that arrived in broad daylight. But he and other survivors, like Capt. Fuchida from *Akagi,* were held back from disembarkation until well after midnight and then taken to the hospital through a back gate so they could talk to no one. He needed six months treatment and during that time was isolated. Those from the battle who were not injured were placed in a hangar and kept out of sight for months.[33]

Gay's aircraft, the TBD Devastator, was devastating only to the crew that flew it. The aircraft flew its last combat missions at Midway. The horrific losses suffered there caused the aircraft to be removed from service.

Ens. Albert Earnest waited for his fellow pilots to return to Midway. The day after the battle, PBYs flew search and rescue missions over the battle area. On June 5, he was somewhat encouraged when one of the aircraft picked up George Gay and another aircraft picked up some survivors from Fighting 8.

"I didn't have much hope," he said, "but I had some hope for several days." For his actions on June 4, Earnest was presented with two Navy Crosses; one for flying the mission and the second for getting his wounded gunner and his new TBF back to Midway.

Earnest was sent back to Hawaii and given three days leave at the Royal Hawaiian. He later supported the Guadalcanal landings from the carrier *Saratoga.* After *Saratoga* was struck by a torpedo, he flew missions out of Henderson Field on Guadalcanal, where he earned a third Navy Cross.

The American attack on the Japanese Fleet began at 1022 and was over in eight minutes. Three Japanese carriers and a heavy cruiser were ablaze. The fourth carrier, *Hiryu,* launched a strike against *Yorktown* and severely damaged the American carrier, but the American bombers found *Hiryu* and sank her.

Yorktown would sink three days later when a Japanese submarine put a final torpedo in the badly damaged ship. The battle of Midway was over. Japanese losses were four carriers, a heavy cruiser, 234 aircraft, and 2,500 men. The Americans lost one carrier, one destroyer, 147 aircraft, and 307 men.

Ens. Gay had been a witness to the attack on the carriers, but he had not been the only American eyewitness. Frank O'Flaherty and Bruno Gaido from Scouting 6 had also been shot down and were recovered by the Japanese destroyer *Makigumo.* After being interrogated for a week the two men were blindfolded and bound hand and foot. The Japanese dragged them to the edge of the deck, tied them to containers full of water to weigh them down, and threw them overboard.[34] The final two American victims were the result of a Japanese atrocity.

The undaunted advance of the Japanese had been stopped at Midway, six months after the attack on Pearl Harbor. A week after the battle, the Japanese canceled the planned July invasion of New Caledonia, Fiji, and Samoa.[35]

THREE
TONOLEI HARBOR AND KAHILI

OCTOBER 16–17, 1943

LT. JACK BOLT, USMC

John F. "Jack" Bolt was born on May 19, 1921, in Laurens, South Carolina, and moved with his family to Sanford, Florida, when he was five years old. He attended school there, but was not a very good student, perhaps because, from the age of ten, he worked to earn spending money and buy his own clothes.

He managed to get into the University of Florida in 1939, but, instead of beginning his college career as a poor student, he entered as a transformed student. While he had cared little for studies throughout most of high school and just skimmed by, he had the good fortune, in his senior year, to have an inspiring teacher who revolutionized his scholastic habits.

His first year in college, Bolt carried a maximum load and was an honor student. He developed an inquisitiveness that compelled him to question, examine, and tinker with everything he touched. He was never satisfied with just accepting that something worked; he wanted to know how and why, and if there was a better way.

The wars in Europe and Asia were a long way off, but as time went on, those far-flung events came closer and threatened the United States. Typically, the student body was against U.S. involvement in the wars and, in fact, quite hostile to President Roosevelt's warnings of the dangers of war.

But Bolt remembered the event that seemed to change the thinking of many Americans. If it didn't change people's minds about American involvment, it at least created an openness to heeding Roosevelt's warnings. The previously pacifist student body suddenly became more hawkish after September 16, 1941, when the American destroyer *Reuben James* was attacked and sunk by a German U-boat with the loss of 150 officers and men.

By that time, Jack Bolt's college career was close to an end. He had joined the Navy in July 1941 because he knew he could no longer stay in school with a younger brother due to enroll in the fall. It was a matter of money: The family finances could not support both boys, and the Navy offered $500 a year for reserve pilots who signed on for a four-year hitch. That sounded good. The regular salary plus flight pay of $225 a month and the new $500 reserve incentive was more money than Bolt had ever seen, and he leaped at the opportunity. There would be plenty of time for school after his hitch, when he would return to campus and enter law school.

The Navy called him in November to begin his service. One month later, Pearl Harbor was bombed and then most everyone else was called. When he began flight training in Atlanta, he had never flown before, but he quickly became a natural, even attempting some daring maneuvers not authorized by his instructors. He tried some loops on his second solo flight when everyone else was doing the more sedate figure-eights. Of course, Bolt would stall and fall out of the loop since he didn't have the proper technique, but that didn't stop him from trying.

Following his basic aviation training, he went on to advanced training, first at Jacksonville and then to Opa Locka in Miami for gunnery training. Along the way he opted to be commissioned in the Marine

Corps upon completion of flight training. He pinned on his gold second lieutenant's bars in August 1942, just as the Marines landed at Guadalcanal in the South Pacific, marking America's first offensive strike.

The only other Marine aviator in his flight in advanced training was immediately sent off to the Pacific for combat duty. Bolt thought he would receive similar orders to combat in the Pacific, but he received the worst possible orders for a young marine straining for action: His orders assigned him to be an instructor and to impart his flying knowledge to new classes of fledgling aviators. He was going to face young eager students, not the aviators of the Imperial Japanese Navy. It was a great disappointment.[1]

What Jack Bolt didn't know was that a frantic Naval Department needed his instructional skills more than his combat skills. After being surprised at Pearl Harbor, the Navy faced the sobering statistical fact that they would have to turn out thirty thousand pilots a year if they were to win the war against Japan.

After Pearl Harbor, the Navy realized that it only had four thousand qualified combat pilots in the entire Navy, and it would need eight times that many for each year the war went on. Bolt and his fellow instructors would be the backbone of the Naval aviator training program.[2]

Even had the young marine aviator known these details, they would have offered him little comfort. He cared little about the big picture or the long haul. He was a warrior, and the only thing that he knew was that the war was going on without him.

From September 1942 until February 1943, Bolt instructed. His daredevil spirit continued to show itself as he mesmerized his students by doing outside loops in an aircraft not designed for that maneuver. Bolt escaped unscathed and became a legend to his students.

In the South Pacific, while Bolt instructed in the art of flying, the war entered a new phase. The euphoria following the smashing victory at Midway soon ebbed as the Japanese Navy regrouped and pushed anew to conquer vast reaches of the Pacific Ocean. Its proposed targets included the Solomon Islands, which would protect its southern flank and threaten Australia. The key to this conquest would be Guadalcanal and, anticipating its importance, the Japanese began building an airstrip there.

Rabaul was the final fortress northwest of the Solomon Islands, which ran along a northwest to southeast line. At the northwest end was Bougainville; at the southeast extreme, 700 miles away, was the island of San Cristobal. Between lay the many islands of the archipelago, popping up like sentinels on either side of a narrow waterway called the Slot. Three hundred miles to the southeast was the island of Espíritu Santo, an American jumping-off point for entry into the hopscotching Solomons.

The Marines landed at Guadalcanal on August 7, 1942, and wrested control of the island, and its airfield, from the surprised Japanese, who had not prepared a proper defense. But Lt. Bolt could only read about that operation while shackled to his instructional duties.

In the days that followed, the United States suffered a naval defeat at Savo Island, and then lost the services of the carrier *Saratoga,* the victim of a Japanese torpedo, for three months. But as bad as that was for the carrier-short Navy, it was only the beginning of a disastrous two months. In September, a Japanese submarine sank the carrier *Wasp,* and on October 24, a dark day for the Navy, *Enterprise* was damaged and *Hornet* sunk.

With the sinking of *Hornet* on that October day, the United States, for all the hand-clapping after Midway, could only field one damaged carrier in the ongoing Solomons sea battle. It was also an emotional loss as the veteran lady of the Halsey-Doolittle raid and Midway now lay at the bottom of the Pacific.

Meanwhile Marines held on to Guadalcanal by their fingernails, repulsing a series of fanatical Japanese ground attacks while the U.S. Navy slugged it out with the Imperial Japanese Navy for control of the seas. For months the battle raged, with so many ships sunk in the waters north of Guadalcanal that the area became known as "Ironbottom Sound." It was not until February 1943 that U.S. forces secured Guadalcanal.[3]

Bolt at last had orders to the war in the Pacific. He boarded the troop carrier *Rochambeau* in San Diego and started the fourteen-day,

10 knot-per-hour trip across the Pacific to New Caledonia, 1,000 miles east of Australia. It was a long, hot, and crowded ocean voyage across the equator, and Bolt was glad when it was over, but when he arrived, he was still no closer to combat than when he had been an instructor. He was immediately sent north to Espíritu Santo to a little base called Turtle Bay, a beautiful place with clear winding streams and a 3,000-foot runway called the Fighter Strip.

Bolt saw that the runway was made of coral, which packed beautifully and, other than being hard on tires, made a first-class strip. But the war, and the fighting, was still a long way off. His assignment was not to the battle area up the Solomon chain, but to remain at Espíritu Santo and be consigned to "the pool"—a dreaded place. It was actually a replacement pool for pilots, and all one could do was sit around and wait, and hope to be sent to a squadron in action. Of course, that only happened if a pilot was killed or disabled. Worst of all, the time spent in the pool didn't count as time required to fulfill an overseas tour.

The pool was also a disheartening place. For those like Jack Bolt, there seemed little chance for escape. It was like being a spare part on the shelf waiting for the engine to break down so that you could be used. And the pool was not just for new pilots: Pilots assigned to squadrons and pilots working on their combat tours also dreaded being sent back to the pool. If a pilot got sick and left behind, he was put back in the pool, where the combat time clock stopped.[4]

From Guadalcanal, the action had moved up the Solomons. The Marines had gotten a free jump to the Russell Islands because the Japanese had not defended it and, after setting up a runway, the next leap was to New Georgia and the Munda airfield.

New Georgia was not a free jump. The battle for the Munda airfield had developed into a long ground battle. The air action, however, had produced few air casualties and most of the downed pilots were picked up, so there was no call to the pool for replacement pilots. Jack Bolt and the others in the pool languished at Turtle Bay. It wasn't until June 26, after four months in the pool, that Lt. Bolt got to fly out of the pool—and that was to only log ten junk hours on a ferry run to Guadalcanal.[5]

At that time, also languishing on the island of Espíritu Santo, was

a disgruntled thirty-year-old major named Gregory Boyington. This
ten-year veteran, who had an aeronautical engineering degree from the
University of Washington, had a reputation as a hard-drinking trou-
blemaking streetfighter, a Marine Corps renegade.

The stories did not take long to circulate in the pool. He had gotten
into the war early, volunteering to fly in China with Gen. Claire Chennault and the Flying Tigers. He shot down six Japanese airplanes in
China, but then feuded with Chennault, made himself persona non
grata with the old, leathery-faced general, and returned to the Marine
Corps after Pearl Harbor.

Boyington had come to Espíritu Santo and had been assigned as
assistant operations officer of the Fighter Strip. He called it a "next to
nothing" job. "All I did was count the planes when they went out for
training flights, and count them again when they returned."[6]

The months dragged on for Boyington and the pool. Nothing happened. Finally in May, Boyington got a break and was assigned as
executive officer of VMF 222* and was off to Guadalcanal. His luck
seemed to continue when the commanding officer was promoted out
of the squadron and he found himself in command.

For four weeks, the action-seeking Boyington escorted bombers on
missions up the Slot and patrolled the skies over Guadalcanal, but he
never saw one enemy aircraft. He returned to Espíritu Santo and got
acquainted with the new fighter that was making its debut in the war,
the Corsair. Boyington thought it was the sweetest flying aircraft he'd
ever flown. Finally the Americans had a fighter that could compete
with the Japanese Zero, which had dominated as a fighter with speed
and maneuverability.

He was delighted and anxious to take the new Corsairs back into
combat on his second combat tour with VMF 222. But the hard fighting, hard-drinking major squandered his opportunity and blew his
chance at command when he broke his ankle in a drunken brawl.
Instead of taking the Corsair back into combat, a hospital ship took
him to New Zealand, and VMF 222 went into combat without Gregory
Boyington.

*Marine Fighter Squadron 222; the Navy designation was VF.

Life went on at the Fighter Strip without him, and the pilots in the pool continued their waiting. Despite the disappointment of not being in a squadron, Bolt enjoyed the life that Turtle Bay and the Fighter Strip offered. He was ingenious in pursuing activities to pass the time: He loved diving in the crystal-clear waters and, after many meals of mutton and powdered eggs and other distasteful service food, he relished the opportunity to supplement his daily diet with some fresh delicacies from the sea.

Bolt noticed that some sort of tuna came into the springs at night to feed, and that sent the lieutenant into action. Armed with explosives, Bolt soon had the stream mined, placing his charges at critical spots. When a school of fish would swim by he would blast it, sending the survivors back upstream only to blast them again when the startled fish tried another frantic run to escape. Then he simply picked up the fish floating on the surface and returned to the strip for a fish fry. Bolt's fishing escapades reached their zenith when, on one memorable evening, he mined and shot a school of mullet, racking up 240 fish.

As a hunter he was no less adept. Pigeons, wild chickens, and wild pigs were not safe with Bolt on the prowl. One day an antiaircraft fellow told him of a problem they were having at their camp with wild pigs constantly in their garbage pit. The commanding officer would not allow any shooting around the camp, so the pigs were unchallenged and grunted and snorted through the garbage to the dismay of all concerned. The attempted solution had been to fence off the garbage pit with reinforcing rods and heavy mesh wire to keep the porkers out and, while it kept them from the garbage, it did not get rid of the pigs.

As the man spoke, Lt. Bolt's eyes widened. This was no problem at all, he thought. This was an unseized opportunity. Instead of fencing the pigs out, why not open the gate and let them in? Then the gate could be closed and, to Bolt's way of thinking, you had a corral full of barbecue.

One night, he and an equally resourceful friend went to the pit and opened the gate, and then sat down, out of sight, and drank for a couple of hours. They could hear activity at the pit—grunting, snorting, and rooting—but they remained patient and waited. Finally, when enough time had passed, they ran to the pit and closed the gate.

Twelve pigs were in Bolt's trap, including a 400-pound boar who looked as mean as his tusks. Since there was no shooting allowed, and neither man wanted to tangle with the boar, they maneuvered to open the gate a little and encourage the boar out. The grunting animal was glad to oblige and stampeded out with five unintended cohorts. It was a small price to pay to be rid of the big tusker, and the remaining six pigs found their way to the barbecue spit.[7]

Young Bolt's fishing and hunting energy carried over to the jungle and its plants. When he found an Army manual on identifying edible plants, he organized jungle trips to identify them. There was little that escaped his inquisitive eye, and he was the most energetic pilot in the pool.

In the middle of August, Maj. Greg Boyington returned to the pool, still limping around on his mending broken ankle and using a cane. He became tremendously popular with the pool pilots and lifted their spirits. He also came to recruit.

Boyington had seized an opportunity, not easily recognized, to get himself another command in combat. Upon his return from the hospital, he had been assigned to one paper-shuffling job after another, when he noticed that the fighter squadrons up the Solomons were being rotated back to the States faster than planned and that the replacement squadrons were not arriving when scheduled. This left the fighting units short of fighter support.

Boyington convinced the group commander that he could form a squadron from the pilots in the pool, train them for a couple of weeks in the Corsair, assign them a squadron number from a unit that had rotated back, and give the fighting forces up north an additional squadron they had not counted on. The group commander agreed.

Boyington explained his plan to the pool pilots, who were ecstatic, and for the next three weeks they trained during the day and talked flying combat at night. Boyington, at thirty, was an old man to the rest of the pilots, who were between twenty and twenty-two, and quickly picked up the name Grandpappy.[8] The pilots never really called him that to his face, though. They called him Skipper, or sometimes just Gramps.[9]

They trained in the new F4U Corsairs built by Chance Vought and recently delivered for combat to the Solomons. The fact that the Marines were on the receiving end of what they considered the greatest aircraft ever built was the continuation of an old story: Marines forever complain that they only receive hand-me-downs when it comes to equipment and materiel, and the Corsair came to them as an aircraft rejected by the U.S. Navy. The Navy's aircraft carrier pilots found it too difficult to handle on takeoffs and landings and opted for the F6F Hellcat as their weapon of choice. To the Marines, the rejected Corsair was a chariot from heaven; a chariot that could exceed 400 mph.

"The Corsair was a sweet-flying baby if I ever flew one," Boyington had said of the long, sleek, inverted gull-wing fighter. "Here was a ship that could climb with a Zero, . . . and one that had considerably more speed."[10]

"It was a tremendous gun platform," Jack Bolt said. "But the main thing was its engine with twenty-five hundred horsepower. We could bang the throttle full forward, . . . and it just ran circles around the Zero."[11]

But the powerful Corsair required an expert pilot to handle it. It was delivered into combat in the Solomons in February 1943. VMF 124 was the first squadron to try it in combat.

By September, VMF 124 was ready to rotate home. It had knocked down an impressive sixty-eight enemy aircraft and had lost only eighteen Corsairs to the enemy. But the eighteen losses was a misleading number. There was also a disturbing statistic to be reported. In addition to the eighteen aircraft lost in enemy action, another twenty-one Corsairs were lost as nonbattle casualties. In the right hands, it could be a devastating weapon; in less capable hands, it was unforgiving.

On September 12, 1943, Greg Boyington and his new squadron escaped the pool and flew to Guadalcanal for their first combat tour. They were now VMF 214, having borrowed the numbers from a squadron just rotated back to the States. The pool pilots were, at last, legitimate pilots of a combat squadron, and they decided to name themselves.

Unanimously they ruled out anything that had a Walt Disney connection, and there were a lot of those floating around. Since Boyington had rescued them from the pool when nobody seemed to want them, they wanted to call themselves "Boyington's Bastards," but were advised off of that name by a public affairs officer. Other names were suggested, all to connote the idea that these pool pilots were outcasts. The name "Outcasts" was suggested, as was "Forgotten Freddies" and "Bold Bums," but none had the charisma of "Boyington's Bastards."[12]

Finally the squadron came up with the compromise name "Black Sheep." It defined them perfectly and was socially acceptable. It spoke of outcasts, orphans, rejects, the unwanted and abandoned.

A Black Sheep emblem was created using the black bar sinister, which in heraldry signifies illegitimacy. To the left of the bar was a swayed-back, sorrowful-looking black sheep; not at all intimidating. It had no steam snorting out of flared nostrils, no threatening curved horns, no flashing teeth or any belligerent look at all. It simply looked lost and forlorn.

To the right of the bar sinister was the number 214—the number borrowed from the squadron that was back in the States. The crest was formed by the Corsair. The illegitimate squadron was now thoroughly legitimate.[13]

Around noon, the Black Sheep landed at Henderson Field and the following morning flew to the Russell Islands, where they were immediately assigned scramble alert duty. Unlike Henderson Field, whose knocked down trees and cratered landscape showed the signs of fierce battle, the Russells were untouched by war: Tall coconut trees dominated the landscape, the air was clear, and the water a deep blue contrasting with the white sand.

As the squadron sat in the ready room, Boyington squatted down and talked tactics to his men. These tactics were different tactics; not the current fighter tactics. These were Greg Boyington's tactics.

Jack Bolt listened attentively as the skipper talked. He told them that the tactics that he wanted them to employ were not in the book. He'd thrown the book out, and he wanted them to focus on the advantages of their new airplane.

Fighter pilots had previously been taught to employ the Thach Weave, which had the airplanes constantly flying long, intersecting patterns, weaving through each other's trails like two water skiers, crossing slowly back and forth. An enemy aircraft that got on one plane's tail would soon find itself facing a deadly side shot from a weaving companion. The attacked plane would act just like an aircraft pulling a target sleeve. The sleeve would be the enemy plane on his tail, and the second plane would soon have a killing shot at the intersection.

Boyington wanted to use the strengths of the Corsair. He told his pilots not to try to loop with a Zero or to turn with him. Get above him with superior power and come down on him in a stern pass and blast away at close range. If you miss, don't stay to dogfight. Climb away from him and come down again. "Let him have it, and watch him burn," Boyington said while drawing diagrams on the ground.[14]

The essence of Boyington's tactic was attack. Attack and always accomplish the mission. Jack Bolt admired his skipper and thought he was a great and exciting tactician. In Greg Boyington's world, every man was a shooter, because when you were a shooter you could not offer help or protection to a wingman, and no wingman was going to remain out in left field with no one protecting him. He was going to dive into the fight also. They would be a squadron of gunfighters, not weavers and wingmen.[15]

As gunfighters, they couldn't have asked for a better gun. The armament on the Corsair was six .50-caliber machine guns mounted three on either side of the fuselage. The four inboard and intermediate guns each had 400 rounds of ammunition while the two outboard guns had 375 each. The total of 2,350 rounds made it a formidable weapon.[16]

The next day, the Black Sheep flew their first combat flight. They were itching for action. The mission was to escort Army-24s to bomb Kahili, which was one of five airfields on Bougainville. Boyington led and Bolt and the rest of the Black Sheep followed with their eyes peeled for the fast-flying Zero. Despite high expectations, the bombing mission was a dud with most of the bombs missing the strip and not one enemy plane spotted. The Black Sheep returned to base, each with their full load of 2,350 rounds.

Two days later, on September 16, twenty-four Corsairs of the Black Sheep roared off the dazzling white coral strip and over the deep blue water around the Russell Islands. The mission was a strike on Ballale, an island off Bougainville with lots of Japanese aircraft.

The Black Sheep flew high cover over the bomber force. Again, eager eyes searched the skies, but still nothing. Sixteen of the twenty-four pilots were still looking for their first action. They flew on, approaching the target area, and the bombers started their dives. As they did, the previously empty skies suddenly were filled with Japanese Zeros. It looked like forty to fifty planes, and the fight was joined with sweeping, diving, plunging aircraft zooming in all directions. The fight spread over a 200-mile radius as the new squadron attacked.

Bolt attacked with the rest. He plunged into the fight. The first Zero he saw just zipped by and presented no shot. "It was a great big Meatball with the sun over my shoulder," he said. "I was in a state of shock. It takes awhile to develop real expertise."[17]

In his first fight, Bolt was not as effective as he would have liked, but he dived and fired with the rest of the squadron in this huge aerial melee. Despite the intense firing, he hit nothing.

After thirty minutes, an eternity in any fight, it was over, and the Black Sheep headed back for home. When they landed, they reviewed the tally for the day. Eleven Zeros down, with another nine listed as probable. Boyington had gotten five of them and had become a Corsair ace in one day. One pilot never returned.

The next day, the pilots and Boyington excitedly discussed the day's fight in the ready shack. Boyington critiqued and the young Black Sheep listened. He told them that the chance to shoot down an enemy aircraft was a fleeting and infrequent opportunity. If one of those opportunities happened, the pilot must have planned it in his mind. He must have planned how to get into position and what to do once there. The target would be moving and there would only be split seconds to react before it would be gone.

Boyington looked around at his men, who hung on his every word. "There is a split second when everything is right," he said. "The target will remain anything but stationary. The range has to be just right, the deflection has to be accurate, and the first squeeze of the trigger has to be smooth and perfect." Pacing the floor he told them of the months of preparation necessary to face a moment when the enemy is in the crosshairs. "The judgment of a split second is what makes some pilot an ace, while others think back on what they could have done."[18]

It was a dramatic message, and it was forever etched in Lt. Jack Bolt's mind. At the conclusion of the meeting, Boyington announced that the squadron would hop up the Solomon chain once again. In the morning they would fly to a new base at Munda on the island of New Georgia.

If the Russell Islands looked like the picture postcard South Seas isle, then Munda looked like a bombed-out junkyard. A large part of the area had been flattened by the savage battle necessary to take the place. Only stumps remained from what had been tall, stately coconut trees, and wrecked aircraft, both Japanese and American, littered the place. Bulldozers tried to clean it up and repair the runway for future use by shoving many of the wrecks into piles. Some planes were on their ends with tails in the air, others were upside-down; some planes bore American stars, while others bore the red meatball. Many planes were in pieces, with a wing here and a fuselage there, and in the air was the stench of unburied bodies. Flies were in profusion.

The Black Sheep had little time to enjoy the scenery as they were immediately sent into the air on patrols. Those day patrols were supplemented at night by Japanese air raids, and life on Munda became a day-in, day-out drudgery of morning-to-night patrol and escort flying. The night was a fight to sleep in the steaming temperature between air raids. The flies made their way from dead bodies to the Spam and beans, and dysentery was common.

There was nothing redeeming about Munda. Tree toads, rats, and lizards were regular visitors in the tents and, in the damp and wet, everything mildewed. On nightime Japanese raids, pilots dived into their water-filled foxholes only to find them already occupied by frantic rats that had fallen in and could not climb back out. The pilot's body must have looked to the rats like an island on which they could climb to safety from the foxhole. The thrashing and splashing that ensued was nothing short of spectacular.[19]

• • •

Since August 1943, after securing Guadalcanal, the Marines had moved up the Solomon chain, first to the Russell Islands, and then to Rendova, and now to Munda. The next target would be Bougainville, which when captured would allow the fighters to reach the prize at the end of the chain: Rabaul. It was at Rabaul that the main Japanese strength was concentrated. But Bougainville was a huge obstacle to overcome, with its five heavily defended airfields and accompanying swarms of Zeros. The largest airfield was at Kahili, on the eastern tip of the island.

On September 23, during the second week of the six-week combat tour, the Black Sheep were called on to fly high cover on a joint Army, Navy, Marine, and New Zealand strike on Bougainville. For Jack Bolt this could be one of his chances to bag a Zero.

The prospect of getting an enemy plane while flying an escort mission was almost nil. Low and intermediate fighter cover for the bombers was hard work indeed, with little to recommend it. Bolt had worked very hard on these missions, weaving back and forth over the bombers to protect them, and when the Zeros would attack the formation, they would tear through at such a rate of speed that there was no chance of getting one. The only way to get a Zero was to break formation and chase it, and that was forbidden.

After their initial success on their mission over Ballale, where Boyington had shot down five Zeros, the squadron had not had a single kill. They had flown never-ending escort and even more hazardous strafing missions, and there had been no chance to attack the Japanese fighters. Boyington compared this duty to linemen in a football game: a lot of hard work for the backs to score the touchdowns.[20]

But today the squadron would fly high cover, which offered more opportunity. They were excited to a man, and Jack Bolt was anxious to get a kill and join in the club of Black Sheep pilots who had knocked down a meatball.

If he had been less than focused on his initial aerial combat opportunities, he vowed to eliminate those early mistakes and profit from his experiences. He had seen many enemy aircraft in those first encounters, and he likened the situation to a hunter who shoots at a whole flock of birds, expecting his unaimed shot to hit something, instead of focusing on a single target. The result of his unaimed shot is that the birds usually fly away, leaving the hunter empty-handed. To be successful, he would be like the lion focusing on his selected prey, impervious to the whole herd stampeding in front of him. No matter how many other animals get in the way, the lion is not distracted.[21]

Nine Black Sheep Corsairs took off from the strip at Munda to provide the high cover for the joint, strike-force bombers flying to Bougainville. The flight up the chain was uneventful, and the bombers released their loads and began the return flight to Munda. Suddenly, the Japanese fighters came up after them. Forty Zeros closed in on the Army bombers, attacking them from the rear. From their high cover position, the Black Sheep attacked.

They tore into the Zeros, but because of the advantage in numbers, the Zeros soon had three Corsairs damaged and flying back toward Munda. The remaining six fought a wild battle with the Japanese aviators. Lt. Bolt flew in and out of the swarming fighters. He maneuvered, trying to get off a shot while at the same time trying to keep enemy planes off his tail. He kept the throttle pushed full forward and flew into a cloud bank and became separated from his division.

Three other Corsairs twisted and turned with great difficulty against the Zeros, which could turn in tighter circles, and they desperately fought to keep the enemy from getting behind into the killing zone. The Zeros peppered the Corsairs, but despite numerous hits, the big planes stayed aloft. Finally one Black Sheep pilot got off a shot, sending a Zero down in flames. The Americans, low on fuel, broke off and headed home.

Bolt emerged from his run in the clouds alone, and immediately began a powerful climb into the sun to 20,000 feet, just as Boyington had instructed. At that altitude he dived down at a flight of six Zeros and focused through his sight on one plane. His eyes never left his target. As he stared through the reflector gunsight on top of his control panel, he saw the Zero clearly in the center. The illuminated crosshairs floated on the target as the Corsair roared down, at tremendous speed, ever closer. Bolt held the stick firmly in his hand, with his thumb on the red button on top, and nudged the plane slightly, constantly keeping the Zero in his sights. Other enemy aircraft zoomed around him—

some attempting to escape him, others attempting to shoot him—but the only thing Bolt saw was the Zero in his sight. Finally, at a point blank 200 yards, he opened fire.

The six guns in his wings roared and sent out a mixture of tracers, armor piercing and incendiary rounds. Only then did he pull off the attack line. The Zero flamed like a giant flare and spun down to the water. Another Zero flashed in front of him, and in a diving turn, the young Marine managed to get behind this enemy plane also. From his stern position, he knew the pilot could not see him. Like the Corsair, the Zero had a blind spot behind the aircraft where the pilot could not see another aircraft in the "kill" position. This would be a zero-deflection shot: no lead, no adjustment to the line of fire; the point of aim was the point of impact—just shoot.

Again the illuminated crosshairs lined up the Zero: horizontal crosshair on the wings, vertical crosshair on the tail. With that perfect picture in his sight, Bolt pressed the red trigger again. The six .50-calibers roared again, and the second Zero erupted into an orange ball of flame, becoming a plunging comet with a black, smoking tail marking its path to the water.[22]

Two shots, two Zeros. Jack Bolt was now a Zero killer.

Twenty-six days after the Black Sheep had begun their combat tour, their count of enemy kills was impressive—twenty-six enemy planes confirmed, an average of one a day.

Between missions on Munda, the usual method of blowing off steam and unwinding was drinking and singing. Bolt and his comrades would gather in the hut where most of the squadron slept and sing songs that everyone knew: "When You Wore a Tulip," "I Want a Girl, Just Like the Girl . . . ," and other favorites. They also had their own "Black Sheep Song," with original words to the tune of the "Wiffenpoof Song." Their collection also included bawdy songs like "One Ball Riley," and songs with original lyrics to old tunes, like "After Rabaul Is Over" set to the waltz "After the Ball Was Over." These tunes were later collectively titled "South Pacific Serenade" and were a great morale builder.

Another morale builder was the radio program of Tokyo Rose. In the distant reaches of the South Pacific, Rose's program was the only good music that the Marines could pick up, and they enjoyed the Stateside music that she presented. If there was propaganda to contend with, then that was the cost of good music.

On October 13, however, Tokyo Rose had bad news for the men of the Black Sheep Squadron. She broadcast that, on that day, the white men on Munda would all be killed. It would be their last day; the Emperor had decreed it. The "South Pacific Serenade" was in full voice that night.[23]

Flying escort cover was, to the Black Sheep, as effective as sweeping dust under a rug. You never got rid of the dust, and the next day it was back again. The same was true of the Zeros. The fighters fended them off, and the next day, on another bombing run, the same fighters were back again, no worse for wear.

It was not enough to fend them off, they had to be eliminated, shot down for good. As long as the enemy fighters flew from Kahili and the other airdromes on Bougainville, the island could not be invaded and without invasion and capture of the airfield, Rabaul could not be attacked. As long as an effective force remained at Rabaul, the Solomons campaign would never end . . . and if the campaign would never end, they could never go home.

Boyington devised a tactic that would inflict maximum attrition on Japanese air strength. Just as he had introduced the new fighter tactics for the Corsair in opposition to the Thach Weave, he now suggested the fighter sweep: Instead of sending bombers with fighters to Bougainville and reacting to the Japanese attack on the bomber formations, let the bombers hang back and send the fighters in first. When the Zeros came up, they would be faced with a pure fighter adversary, and they would have to contend with the ultimate dogfight. The Black Sheep were confident that they could win the day.

Even if some enemy fighters remained to attack the bombers, by the time the bombers arrived on the scene the Zeros would be so short of fuel, they would have to break off and land. The bombers should then be able to make their run unhindered, and the refueling Zeros, on the ground, might offer another lucrative target to other American aircraft.

There was skepticism from headquarters, but that skepticism was quickly put to rest when, on October 15, on a bomber cover mission, Boyington and three other Black Sheep raced ahead to Kahili and attacked sixteen Zeros, destroying six enemy planes, with three more probable. There was no damage to the attacking Corsairs. Boyington's new tactic was adopted.[24]

Lt. Ed Olander of the Black Sheep described the fighter sweep as "picking a fight." He described it as a bully going into a schoolyard and saying, "Let's fight." If the enemy planes were not up, Boyington would get on the air and taunt them to come up, which they usually did, increasing Boyington's shoot-downs.[25]

A big fighter sweep was planned for two days later, October 17, and the Black Sheep would lead the sweep. The pilots were excited and could not wait to join the enemy in combat, but before the sweep, they were assigned one more bombing escort, scheduled for the sixteenth.

Twelve Black Sheep took off on that morning for a mission to Bougainville. On the way there, the weather turned nasty. The bombers first tried to get above the weather, but there seemed to be no top, so they tried to go under the clouds, but there was no bottom. They were socked in.

Jack Bolt watched the bombers fly into a massive bank. Suddenly they were out of sight, and the fighters lost them. They flew on for a while, but the bombers never reappeared. Instead of turning 180 degrees and heading back, Boyington lowered the fighters down through a little hole in the cloud bank and discovered that the fighters were above and behind the airstrips of Kahili and its sister strip on the small island at Ballale. They were in the vicinity of Empress Augusta Bay, where the proposed invasion would take place. From his cockpit all Bolt could see was an unbroken expanse of jungle. They turned in the direction that would take them toward Kahili, and Boyington ordered them to pull up in a close formation for mutual support. The flight crept past the airdrome and flew over the water separating Kahili and Ballale.

Suddenly, in full view of the fighters, a bustle of shipping activity appeared, not uncommon for a day with thick overcast. Any troop and supply movement would be done on a day such as this when the threat of an air strike was minimal because of bad weather. The Japanese were making a major troop movement, and the Black Sheep had stumbled upon it. Clearly visible to the tightly packed fighters were at least five troop-laden barges, along with a lot of smaller craft, ships, and other vessels. They presented a very tempting target.

Jack Bolt braced himself in his seat and was eager to attack. He had his hand on the throttle ready to go, but Boyington surprisingly called the attack off because of the foul weather and the chance that his men would become scattered and separated in the bad weather. Still Bolt considered making the attack alone and had just about convinced himself to break the formation and roar in on the troop carriers when that temptation was thwarted. He discovered that the pig-tail, the curled connector from his sight bulb to the electrical source supply, was broken. The bulb was fine, but the faulty pig-tail made the sight useless. This had been a common problem and he cursed his luck that the sight was out of action when such a target was in view.

Boyington led the fighters on a winding course back toward Munda, and all Jack Bolt could do was look longingly at the target retreating from his view. First he took the planes over to Choiseul and then toward Vella Lavella, crossing the Slot. Bolt thought the navigation was poor and he still chafed at the lost opportunity. How could they pass such a golden target? All the planes the squadron had shot down—at this point, thirty-five—paled in comparison to the sheer number of targets of men and materiel offered to them at the little harbor on the southeastern corner of Bougainville. He could not believe that twelve fully armed Corsairs with close to thirty-thousand rounds of .50-caliber ammunition were flying past them. Those men and materiel would be facing the Marines when they invaded Bougainville, but the Black Sheep had passed them up.

Boyington ordered the aircraft that had enough fuel to continue to fly on to Munda while those who could not make it would stop at Vella Lavella. Almost immediately one of the planes that had not been properly topped off coughed and began its descent toward the water. It was

Bolt's wingman, Lt. Harper, and he brought his aircraft to a belly landing in the water about 5 miles short of Vella Lavella.

Bolt circled his wingman, watching him escape the cockpit and inflate his life raft and climb in. He continued to circle until he saw a boat get under way from the island and head toward the downed pilot. Only then did he bring his aircraft in for a landing at the strip. He taxied toward the refueling area and noticed that another six Black Sheep had also been forced to land while the rest of the flight had continued on to Munda.

Bolt scrambled out and ran to his comrades, telling them that they should never have passed by the ships and barges; they should refuel and fly back and attack. Most of the pilots shook their heads, and Bolt pleaded again. He told them it was a perfect opportunity that would never come again. The risk would be minimal. In this weather their chance of being jumped by Zeros was almost nonexistent, and even if they were jumped, they could easily escape by pulling up into the cloud cover. But his pleadings fell on deaf ears.

Only two of the Black Sheep showed any interest at all, and they were squeamish about confronting Boyington's temper when and if they returned to Munda. They suggested getting permission, but this time it was Bolt who shook his head, knowing that would never happen. He knew that the slowness of the command structure and the necessary approvals would kill the mission before it had a chance. No, there could be no permission request; they had to take a chance for a great opportunity. They could only attack now and explain later.

What did they think? Come on, fellas, the target is there. His companions shook their heads, but one of the pilots offered the pig-tail off of his sight to Bolt if he wanted to go back on his own. For the rest, the fear of Boyington was too much to prod them on the daring, unauthorized mission.

The ground crews filled the Corsairs with fuel, and they lined up on the strip to take off for the return flight to Munda. Jack Bolt sat in his refueled airplane, and replaced his burned out pig-tail with the new one. His sight glowed again and was operable.

The seven Corsairs took off and six headed for Munda, but Bolt made a ninety-degree turn and took a course back toward Bougainville.

He set his course up to Choiseul, expecting to fly there and then turn to the northwest for an approach toward Kahili and Ballale.

As he flew toward Choiseul, the bad weather, which he had expected, had now improved dramatically. He wished that it had remained bad, with low clouds, but now the ceiling was much improved. It would have no effect on his attack, but the increased ceiling now removed his safeguard if he were jumped by fighters. Without that cloud cover that he could easily hop into, he wondered if he had not done a foolish thing. He would be no match for a pack of attacking Zeros.

Choiseul came into view and he turned to the northwest. Kahili was less than thirty minutes away and the Corsair ate up the distance quickly. Lt. Bolt checked his sight to make sure the bulb was working and saw it was illuminated.

Now Kahili and Ballale were visible and, sure enough, the barge and shipping traffic was still there. From 15,000 feet, at full throttle, he roared down on the first target and opened fire. The roar of his guns had the Japanese scrambling and he chopped up the first barge full of troops. As he pulled out, the barge was already sinking. Then he hit a second and third. Each time he pulled out he looked back for a new target. He bore down on the fourth barge, strafed it, and made his pull out over land.

About 10 miles east of Kahili, Bolt discovered a barge staging area in a small harbor. This was Tonolei Harbor. He roared up that harbor and shot up more barges, did a wingover, and came back out, shooting a tugboat for good measure. He saw a big orange tracer float by him as he departed the area. The tug had managed to fire some 20mm ammo at him. He'd seen that orange tracer before and knew exactly what it was. No other guns fired at him, and he tore out of the area at full throttle. Looking back he could see several vessels on fire.

He had plenty of fuel, but his ammunition was gone. His 2,350 rounds had found their mark and he plotted a course to Munda. He covered the 200 miles to the strip quickly. Boyington was waiting for him; he'd obviously been briefed by the pilots from Vella Lavella on Bolt's whereabouts.[26]

Boyington listened and then chewed Bolt a new rear end, but the chewing out was later soothed by the back-slapping from the other Black Sheep in the hut that night as they celebrated their new hero. More than one of his comrades now regretted not having joined Bolt on the unauthorized mission.

Ironically, this was the type of action that Boyington, with his attack mentality, would have taken had the shoe been on the other foot. In fact, he had often ignored orders in the past when the right opportunity presented itself. He'd attacked against orders, even leaving escort missions to chase Zeros and send them down burning. But that was he, and he was the squadron commander, and he was Maj. Boyington, with sixteen kills, and this was young Lt. Bolt of far less fame.

Bolt's chewing out did not affect Boyington's decision to include him in the "new" aerial tactic to be unveiled the following day. Disobedience or no, Boyington knew a good fighter pilot when he saw one, so Jack Bolt and twelve other Black Sheep filled out the roster to accompany Maj. Boyington on the "fighter sweep."

Before dawn on Sunday, October 17, the twenty pilots gathered in the ready room at the Munda airstrip. The thirteen Black Sheep were joined by seven pilots of VMF 221. In the glow from the Coleman, Boyington paced the floor and delivered one of his best attack speeches. There was silence as he spoke, and each pilot knew that this mission was not a defensive reaction to attacks on bombers; this was offensive, and they were out there to pick a fight and lure enough Zeros up so that they could shoot them down and not be bothered with those particular aircraft or pilots again. The next sweep would take care of more of them, until there would be none left.

"We'll go up at about twenty thousand feet," Boyington began. "One division will fly ahead at six thousand to act as bait and get the Nips to come up and fight." The word *bait* was not lost on his audience.

He paced as he told them that this was going to be action. He again warned them for the umpteenth time to keep their altitude and not get into a turning maneuver with the Zeros.

"If you lose your division," he said, "join with someone else. Let's stay in there. The sooner we shoot down all their planes, the sooner they'll have to give up."[27]

His talk was over and now it was time to fly. The Corsairs roared off and got into their formations with four bait aircraft out front at 6,000 feet. The other seventeen climbed to 20,000 feet and leveled off, heading north past Vella Lavella.

The sky was clear blue as the force reached Kahili without any sign of the enemy. They circled lazily over the field until, finally, black puffs of antiaircraft fire came up.

Bolt looked down and could see the telltale dust from the airstrip indicating that the Zeros were taking off in groups. Boyington talked into his throat mike and warned the pilots not to get too eager and to pick out their targets. As he tallied the planes coming up, he could see it was not going to be an even match. Twenty-one Marine Corsairs against fifty-five Zeros.

Boyington dived into the center of them and Jack Bolt was close behind. For almost an hour the aerial dogfight swarmed over hundreds of square miles. In the center of the storm, planes went toe-to-toe. Parts fell out of the sky, wings and propellers, as did parachuting pilots and flaming aircraft. On the air came the frantic chatter of, "Watch out," "Got him," "Get him off my tail," and "Look out behind you." It was the longest fight anyone had been in.

As the fight continued at altitudes closer and closer to the water, aircraft, seeking speed, dived for the increased velocity, and then resumed the fight at a lower altitude. In the melee, Jack Bolt lined up a Zero in his glowing sight and fired his six guns in a long burst. The Zero exploded and took its orange and black path to the water.

When it was over, the adversaries were down to the water, low on fuel and ammunition. The Corsairs broke off and headed for Munda; the Zeros limped back to Kahili, much the worse for wear.

The flight back to the airfield was a stragglers parade, and anxious comrades counted the planes one after another as they returned. Once the fight began, no one ever knew for sure how their comrades fared. You went out and engaged the enemy and returned to base. If someone didn't come back, well, he didn't come back. You didn't know what happened, he just didn't show up; he was missing, and if you didn't find him on a rescue search, then he was missing and presumed dead, and after all possibility of survival had expired, then he was just dead. He'd vanished off the face of the earth—no trace, no body, no plane.

As the planes limped home and landed, the count approached twenty-one, and miraculously the twenty-first plane landed to the wild cheers of the squadron. The tally was twenty Zeros for sure, with not one Corsair lost. Two pilots were wounded and three planes landed with a cumulative 123 holes in them, but the Corsairs brought them all home.[28]

The jubilant Black Sheep were not to be quieted. They all talked at once, showing with their hands the various attitudes they had been in during the fight. It went on for hours.

Jack Bolt, who, just twenty-four hours before, had launched his one-man assault against Japanese shipping, now was a three-time Zero killer. His chewing out by Maj. Boyington was a thing of the past, and even if it were not, a special telegram arrived and buried it forever. Adm. "Bull" Halsey sent heartfelt "Congratulations on your one-man war in Tonolei Harbor." The fleet commander had nullified the ass-chewing.

The next day, a second fighter sweep cost the Japanese eighteen more Zeros, and, on the twenty-fourth, the first combat tour of the Black Sheep Squadron ended. Fifty-seven planes had been destroyed in the thirty-two days that the "borrowed" VMF 214 had been in combat.

EPILOGUE

The Black Sheep Squadron spent one week on R&R in Sydney, Australia, before they returned to begin training for their second combat tour, which began on November 27, 1943, and ended on January 8, 1944.

Fittingly, the ever-curious Lt. Bolt wasted no time applying his tinkering and testing, which had made him a legendary fisherman and pig hunter, to the ammunition used during the squadron's first combat tour. While most of the squadron, especially Maj. Boyington, had simply been satisfied to blast the Zeros from the sky, Bolt had noticed some curiosities in the performance of the ammunition for the .50-caliber guns.

He was convinced that the belting of the ammunition—which consisted of one incendiary round, followed by one tracer round, and then one armor-piercing round—was not as effective as it should be. While the squadron had confirmed fifty-seven kills, there were almost thirty other planes listed as probable. "Probable" meant that the plane had not been seen burning, exploding, or crashing, even though it may have been hit with enough rounds to ensure its destruction.

When he returned to Espíritu Santo, Bolt went down to the "boneyard," a junkyard of wrecked planes, old oil drums, engines, and other discarded pieces. He set up machine guns and fired with the standard belting of ammunition. Few fires were set as the rounds struck the targets, and Bolt knew that the Zero, with no armor plating and no self-sealing tanks, should be easy to burn. Almost all of the Black Sheep kills were confirmed by burning, and here, at the boneyard, he had difficulty setting fires.

He fired at drums filled with gasoline, and the armor-piercing rounds went through them without igniting, but the incendiaries always worked. He tried firing only incendiaries, with a tracer every fifth round, and that combination was a winner. He showed Boyington the results and his boss was convinced. From then on, the new belting configuration was the standard and its success prompted other squadrons to change over, creating, for a while, a shortage of incendiary ammunition.[29]

During the second combat tour, the squadron increased its kills to ninety-seven, but the probables only increased to thirty-five, offering substantial proof that the new ammo configuration was working. Lt. Bolt became the squadron's fourth ace when he shot down two Zeros on the day before Christmas and added his sixth Zero on the day after New Year. That day, however, was a dark day for the squadron since their legendary squadron leader, Boyington, was shot down coming back from a raid over Rabaul. Rescue patrols never found him.

The whole squadron spent days searching unsuccessfully, and it was finally Jack Bolt who inventoried his belongings and packed them up to be sent back to the States. Several days later the squadron's second tour was over and, despite a request to keep the Black Sheep together as a fighting force, they were disbanded on March 20, 1944.

On April 12, Gregory "Pappy" Boyington, with twenty-six kills (actually twenty-eight including the two not initially recorded from the day he was shot down), was selected to receive the nation's highest award, the Medal of Honor. Strangely, it was the first medal for the ace of aces, and it is hard to imagine why such a warrior had not been cited before. To be sure, his hard-drinking, maverick past, and his swashbuckling style and ego were anathema to the politics of citations. Final recognition of his military exploits became an embarrassing necessity, even for his jealous enemies, who were legion. Perhaps, in their jaded eyes, the Medal of Honor was harmless to a dead legend.

Boyington was not dead, however, but a prisoner of the Japanese, who had picked him up in a submarine and kept him for almost two years. When he turned up among the living after the war, he felt that his award of the Medal of Honor was hollow, given to him only when everyone thought he was dead. In his writings, he made it painfully clear that he didn't appreciate this "so-called honor" and relegated it to the "dust of our garage."[30]

On the same day he was posthumously given the Medal of Honor in Washington, the Marine Corps also belatedly awarded him the Navy Cross. But this too only added salt to the wound, and Boyington thought the award was a makeup. He had shot down twenty-eight aircraft during the war, twenty-two during the Solomons campaign, and not one action had ever been cited. By normal standards, he should have had a dozen medals of every variety. His daring fighter tactics, which proved so devastating to the Japanese, would have garnered another commander a high award, but no one had seen fit to write him up for anything. The belated Navy Cross infuriated him and he called it his lone "booby prize"—it actually only cited a shootdown of "one enemy plane."[31]

Boyington was bitter, and perhaps rightfully so. His snubbing, demonstrated by his lack of awards, had begun in the Solomons, after a mission where he and his Black Sheep had stuck with an Army flight of bombers when even their own escorts had been driven off by the Japanese. That Army commander wrote a citation for a Silver Star for Boyington, but someone up the line squelched it.

His full resentment poured forth when he wrote, "This was the closest I ever came to being considered for so much as a Purple Heart, until it was believed that I had been killed."[32]

But Greg Boyington was not the only person who was snubbed, and unfortunately, it was he who did the snubbing when it came to one of his eight aces, and that ace was Jack Bolt.

Whether it was because Bolt had gone alone on the Tonolei Harbor raid without permission and upstaged him or whether Boyington resented Halsey's warm congratulations to the young aviator or whether he was frustrated because of his own lack of recognition and awards, Boyington did not award Lt. Bolt the Navy Cross that he richly deserved for the daring attack against a possible overwhelming force.

The standard procedure was to award a pilot who shot down three enemy planes the Distinguished Flying Cross. Boyington gave Bolt this award, but added one sentence in the citation referencing the Tonolei action—and that one sentence guaranteed that Bolt would not receive the Navy Cross. No second award can be awarded for the same action, so by including the brief reference, Boyington assured that the Navy Cross could not be given for the Tonolei Harbor action. It certainly wasn't because the fiery commander didn't think the award was deserved; on the contrary, he wrote in his book that he gave Jack Bolt the Navy Cross for his daring attack.[33] He described the attack in glowing terms, but the fact is, he did not recommend the award. For whatever reason, known only to him, he also ensured that it would never be awarded.

Boyington's lapse did not detract from Lt. Bolt's remarkable achievement. He was a combat ace with the most famous squadron ever to fly in the U.S. Marine Corps, and arguably, in the history of aviation.

But Jack Bolt's military excellence did not end with the Black Sheep. After the war, he spent a twenty-year career in the Marine Corps and fought again in the Korean War. He picked up right where he left off in the Solomon Islands and became an ace again, this time in the F-86 Sabre jet, shooting down seven MIGs and becoming the only jet ace in Marine aviation history, and the only naval aviator to become an ace in two wars.

Once again, it was his testing and tinkering that led him to that plateau. He was still the lion focused on his prey in the skies over Korea when he and another jet zoomed down on a MIG from 40,000 feet. At 15,000 feet, the other aircraft had the MIG in his sights and was in the kill position, but didn't shoot and just flew along. Bolt watched, anxiously wondering why, but still the jet flew behind the doomed MIG and still did not shoot. Finally, realizing that the MIG might escape, Bolt tore past his nonfiring partner and blew the Chinese aircraft out of the sky. The thing that Bolt knew, that his partner did not, was the difference that Pappy Boyington had taught years ago. "The judgment of a split second is what makes some pilot an ace, while others think back on what they could have done."

In jumping aircraft, coming down from extreme altitudes, like 40,000 feet, Jack Bolt knew that it was common for the windscreen in a jet to fog over, blinding the pilot. To avoid that condition, he had discovered that if, while making that dive, the pilot would put the armor glass defrost on full, so that the cockpit became so hot that it was almost painful, the windscreen would not fog up. In the dive on the MIG, Bolt was almost baking, the heat was so intense, but he could see, while his wingman could not, and Bolt got the kill.

Late in his career, Lt.Col. Jack Bolt commanded VMF 214, the Black Sheep Squadron. This remarkable aviator retired in 1962.[34]

In 1976, a television show called *Baa, Baa Black Sheep* was produced based on Boyington's book and his input as a technical advisor to the show. It protrayed the Black Sheep as a bunch of misfit criminals who Boyington had rescued and was anything but the truth. In fact, no pilot of the Black Sheep Squadron had ever stood or faced a court-martial, and they were not a bunch of brawling bums; the only brawler was Boyington himself. It was slanderous to the men who had served him so well, and forever stereotyped them with an image they had not earned. When they confronted him, Boyington told the Black Sheep that he only did it because he needed the money.

The pleasant, unexpected consequence of Boyington's indiscretions in the production of that television show is that it brought the squadron the fame it richly deserved for its combat skills. The show was very popular for a while, and the price the squadron paid for being depicted falsely was partially offset by the reward of being the most famous squadron in aviation history.[35]

FOUR
BETIO, TARAWA ATOLL

NOVEMBER 21, 1943

PVT. JAMES RUSSELL, USMC

On August 16, 1942, only four months after the dramatic Halsey-Doolittle raid over Tokyo, which had so lifted the spirits of America after the disaster at Pearl Harbor, a second dramatic raid placed U.S. Marines on the tiny island of Makin in the enemy-held Gilbert Islands. Two U.S. submarines, *Nautilus* and *Argonaut,* landed Lt.Col. Evans Carlson and two companies of Marines on the Makin beaches. The landings were unopposed, and the Marines only encountered opposition when Japanese soldiers straggled onto the battlefield in small groups. *Nautilus* provided some supporting fire, and sank two vessels in the lagoon.

The Marines destroyed the garrison on the small island of Butaritari, and generally created havoc among the Japanese defenders. Their mission had been just that—to create a diversion from the ongoing Guadalcanal invasion taking place in the Solomon Islands, a thousand miles to the southwest.

Japanese aircraft responded to calls for help from the defenders of Makin, playing cat and mouse with the submarines, forcing them below the surface whenever they flew over. On the next two nights, the submarines recovered the raiding force and departed. Carlson's Raiders, like the Doolittle Raiders, had provided another boost to American morale, but, despite the euphoria, the raid had not achieved its objective. No Japanese forces were diverted from the battle for Guadalcanal, and the excitement of the daring raid was somewhat diffused when it was discovered that nine of the raiders had been left behind and were captured and beheaded by the Japanese.

An unintended consequence of the raid was, however, to focus the Japanese on the task of reinforcing their island strongholds all across the Pacific, as they now recognized the direction that a cross-Pacific attack would take.[1]

The Casablanca Conference in January 1943 had decided that the main offensive against Japan could be a drive across the Central Pacific, rather than Gen. MacArthur's South and Southwest Pacific drives. The Navy was ordered to prepare for a Central Pacific drive and, by June, the American Joint Chiefs were ordered to prepare for such operations. Once the plans for the defeat of Japan had been formulated, the Navy brain trust envisioned an ambitious initial attack. They planned to seize the Marshall Islands, 700 miles north of the equator, as the gateway to Japan.

But it didn't take long for these planners to realize that the first step had to be more modest than the gigantic leap from the Solomons to the Marshalls. The lack of men, materiel, ships, aircraft, and a host of other factors, including the threat of the strong naval and air forces on the island of Truk, near the Marshalls, made that attack impossible. The prize of the Marshall Islands would be gained only after a series of stepping-stone attacks on other atolls leading up to the Marshalls.

Examining their maps, the planners realized that the opening attack in the Central Pacific would follow a line roughly parallel to the attack in the Solomon Islands. The offensive in the Solomons had originated at Guadalcanal and hopped up the chain, approaching ever closer to Rabaul, whose conquest or neutralization had been the ultimate objective. Now, the Marshall Islands, in the Central Pacific, like Rabaul in the South Pacific, would be the new objective, but it was clear that other battles had to be fought, and won, first.[2]

Although the execution of an island-hopping drive across the vast reaches of the Pacific Ocean would be new in the history of warfare, the idea of such a drive was not. It had been a contingency plan for the U.S. Navy ever since the United States had acquired the Philippine Islands as a possession in 1898. The need to defend this possession had led the Navy to examine the direct route across the Pacific. There were hundreds of tiny islands blocking this direct route, and any potential enemy would be faced with the task of defending certain islands in an attempt to block an attacking force. For the enemy, this posed a damnable question. Which islands to defend? Would the islands they chose to defend compel an enemy force to deploy, or would that defensive position simply be outflanked or bypassed, leaving men and precious materiel to wither on the vine?

For any defender, this was a formidable problem. Any defensive choices, by necessity, fragmentized his total strength. There was no hope of massing at any chosen battleground or reacting with reserve troops from a nearby position after a landing. The island's ground defensive forces were on their own. The battle would be won or lost by them.

On the other hand, an attacking force could not overwhelm the defenders with superior numbers. The small land spaces on these islands limited the number of soldiers that could be placed ashore to attack, and those soldiers would have to land in the face of a prepared defensive position.

Landing a force also required the attacker to expose his naval forces, and keep those forces exposed until the land battle could be won. A counterattack from opposing naval and air forces would be against an exposed, vulnerable fleet, possibly forcing the attacking fleet to withdraw and leaving the landed forces with the task of dislodging the defending force, without superior numbers for the job.

As the Japanese defenders began their fortification of certain key islands against a possible American drive in the Central Pacific, they felt they could force the Americans to attack the islands they chose to defend. Unlike the danger of being bypassed, which might have existed in 1898, they could choose the battleground. All they had to do was build an airfield on one island that would be a threat to an attempted bypass, and that island could not be ignored.

This then became the Japanese strategy for the defense of the axis across the Central Pacific. They would construct airfields from which to launch strikes against the approaching enemy, or his supply lines, and fortify these islands so that any attacking force would be compelled to expend great time and effort in the attack. Meanwhile, Japanese aircraft and submarines would converge on the vulnerable ships and transports in an initial attack while the main fleet sortied from Truk to deliver the final blow.[3]

To mount either a defense of the Central Pacific or conduct an offensive drive across the island-studded ocean required a strong, mobile fleet. In the beginning, Japan had such a fleet, but its backbone had been defeated at Midway and its air arm had been squandered away in the costly battles in the Solomons Islands. Now it was the U.S. Navy that was emerging as the dominant fleet.

At the time of the attack on Pearl Harbor, the Navy had ordered twenty-two new fleet carriers, and now, in 1943, these ships were ready. They offered a tremendous new potential, eliminating the need for land-based aircraft for support, as had been necessary in the march up the Solomons. The fast carrier task forces could isolate any area in the vast expanses of the Pacific, and strike at the Japanese in their dug-in positions.[4] Their only challenge would be a confrontation with the Japanese Fleet, and this confrontation would be the event the navy desired most of all. The outcome of a fleet confrontation, to the Navy's admirals, was a foregone conclusion. It would be the end of the Japanese Navy, and a quicker end to the war.

By June 1943, the Joint Chiefs, realizing that an attack in the Marshall Islands was too much of a risk, ordered preparation for an attack into the Gilbert Islands, six hundred miles to the southeast, astride the equator.[5]

Sixteen atolls made up the Gilbert Islands, and Tarawa was the largest, twelve miles at its base and more than twenty miles up its eastern coast. Its western face was a submerged coral reef with a single opening, three miles from the southern end, by which ship traffic could enter the lagoon. The names of the islands in the atoll were exotic: Naa, Buariki, Taritai, Taborio, Bonriki, Eita, Bairiki, and Betio.

It was at tiny Betio, the remote island at the western base of the triangular atoll, that the Japanese had chosen to make the Americans fight. They had constructed an airfield and had fortified it to the extent that the proud commander, Adm. Keiji Shibasaki, had boasted to his men that the "Americans couldn't take Betio with a million men in a hundred years."[6]

For fifteen months, since Carlson's raid on neighboring Makin Island, Shibasaki had first built, and then perfected the defenses of Betio. It was an island shaped like a bird lying on its back, with its head pointing west, and its tail pointing east. From its position in the extreme southwestern tip of the triangular atoll, only three and a half miles separated it from the opening in the barrier reef. Shibasaki's efforts had transformed the small island into the most fortified position on the face of the earth.

The main defenses of Betio faced seaward, toward the south, but extremely strong defenses also faced the lagoon. There were more than five hundred bunkers and strongpoints, and more than fifty coastal defense guns, antiaircraft guns, and beach defense guns. Some of the guns were up to eight inches in caliber.

This massive array of armament was set into hardened casemates. Bunkers, firing pits, and automatic weapons positions, as well as heavy guns, were encased in concrete structures designed to withstand heavy bombardment, even direct hits. Twelve-inch reinforced concrete walls were topped with numerous layers of coral, sand, and coconut logs almost two feet in diameter. Some blockhouses had roofs that were over five feet thick. These were also topped with more logs and steel angle irons. Even the angle of the walls, sloping to the ground, was planned to avoid telltale shadows that would be easily recognizable in aerial photographs.[7]

Despite these formidable man-made defenses, they were only secondary to Betio's primary defensive line: the barrier reef and the shallow water that covered the coral. Like a moat in a medieval castle, the reef stood between the attacker and the defenders. It could not be flanked or bypassed. It had to be confronted.

Jim Russell labored over his workstation at Inland Steel Company on Bienville Street in New Orleans. He was nineteen years old and working a summer job to try to make a few dollars. And it was few dollars that he did make, working for sixteen cents an hour as a spot welder making barrels.

As a barrel came off the roller, young Jim would open it and stick it on the spot welder and push a button. The ensuing blinding flash and countless sparks that erupted from the barrel left spots in front of his eyes as if he'd stared into a camera's flashbulb. The shower of sparks covered him and he continuously brushed himself off. After fifteen minutes of this procedure, he was given a new pair of gloves and a new hat. He was treated to these because the old ones were riddled with holes from the steel shards flying from the spot welder.

It was the best he could do for a summer job, and one day, a fellow worker suggested that he and Jim should join the service since they could definitely make more money, and they wouldn't get burned. Young Jim agreed and went home and told his grandmother that he was giving up his career as a spot welder and joining the service. His grandmother advised him against such a rash action, pointing out that in the war some people got killed. Jim was undeterred by her "life-threatening" warning, and told her, "Well somebody has to get killed, but it's better than that stupid spot welding!"

Granny reluctantly signed the papers, and Jim and his spot-welding friend joined the Marine Corps and were sent to Marine Corps Recruit Depot at San Diego. For twelve weeks they endured the rigors of boot camp, and then spent three more weeks on the rifle range, followed by more advanced infantry training at Camp Pendleton.

By February 1943, Jim Russell had been transformed from a sixteen-cents-an-hour spot welder to a well-trained, fifty-dollar-a-month fighting Marine. He received orders that sent him to Tulagi, in the Solomons, to join the 2nd Marine Division. As he arrived, the battle for Guadalcanal was still being fought, and he was assigned to Company K, 3rd Battalion, 2nd Marine Regiment, called 2nd Marines.

Again he trained on Tulagi, with additional training in the New Hebrides. Finally, the division boarded ship for Wellington, New Zealand. The rumors were rampant. Some thought that the Japanese had invaded parts of Australia, and that the 2nd Marines Division would be based in New Zealand for an eventual assault into Australia. But when they arrived in Wellington, it was apparent that Camp Wellington was a training camp where they would continue to prepare for future operations.

Wellington, New Zealand, would be to the 2nd Marine Division what Melbourne, Australia, was to the 1st Marine Division: It was a place of training, liberty, and refurbishment. The shot-up divisions from Guadalcanal went there for R&R (rest and rehabilitation).

While some of the Marines thought that they would be isolated from the main population of New Zealanders, quite the opposite was true. Camp Wellington was on the outskirts of town and frequent liberty and a railed tram brought the Marines into close contact with the local gentry. The New Zealanders adopted the young Americans, and the Marines were expected to be on their best behavior in their host country; except for some boyish pranks, like uncoupling the tram and letting the cars roll back down the hill, for the most part, they were.[8]

The New Zealanders were very aware that these Marines, through their victory in the Solomon Islands, had stopped a possible invasion of their homeland by Japanese forces, and they laid out the welcome mat. Five hundred marriages were celebrated before the 2nd Division departed, forever welding American–New Zealander relations.[9]

The Marines quickly adapted to the customs and "strange language" of the English-speakers from "down under," and became an integral part of New Zealand. Jim Russell thought that the people were wonderful and the country a delight. The only thing he questioned about New Zealanders was their custom of drinking warm beer. He never got accustomed to that.

But there was work to be done in New Zealand, and that included amphibious training. It was amphibious training like Marines had never undergone before. The training simulated attacking against a fortified beach. The standard doctrine had always been to land at the least defended place and, once ashore, to seek out the enemy and attack with superior forces.

Now Jim Russell and members of the 2nd Division found themselves charging ashore on practice beaches and simulating attacking in the face of an entrenched enemy. It was amphibious warfare stood on its ear. To add to the confusion, the orders were to attack only the positions that could not be bypassed. Move, move, move was the order screamed from commanders and NCOs. Bypass, bypass; let the follow-up forces take care of the bypassed enemy.

They were also introduced to a new vehicle of war: a landing vehicle tracked (LVT) or "alligator." These unarmored craft could hold upward of eighteen men and could move at 12 miles per hour on land and 7 miles per hour in the water. They were perfect for crossing reefs or going ashore in shallow water, and they had the added advantage of being able to carry assaulting Marines across the beach rather than just dropping them at the water's edge, like the Higgins boats did, the LCVP (landing craft vehicle; personnel) built by the Higgins boatworks. Seventy-five of these vehicles were serviceable after the Guadalcanal campaign, and the local Ford Motor Company set about attaching steel plates for protection of the driver.[10]

On the numerous beaches around New Zealand, the Marines of the 2nd Division practiced this new art of amphibious landing. One battalion got to use the new alligators for a couple of days, and then would turn them over to another battalion for training.

Jim Russell was a "BARMAN," the man who was issued the one Browning automatic rifle per squad. Later the Marines would carry three per squad. As they practiced in the alligators, Russell's position was in the back of one of the four columns of men. The squad leader and the point man were up front, and that suited Russell fine. To disembark, the outer columns of Marines had to go over the side in a sort of roll; then the inside columns. Climbing out presented too high of a profile and a tempting target. Russell figured that those in the front would be the most likely target of the enemy, and he was content to go out over the back.

The seemingly endless training was not a chore. Generous liberty in Wellington made it seem as if the war were far removed, and the

Marines enjoyed the months of getting ready. But one day, in mid-October, Jim Russell watched the 1st Battalion strike camp, packing things and rolling up tents. Everyone wondered where they were going. Next, the 2nd Battalion struck camp, and by now the rumors were flying. Finally Russell, and the 3rd Battalion, got the word to strike camp, and they moved out and boarded the troop transport, USS *Biddle*.[11]

The word was that they would be doing a practice landing at Hawkes Bay near Wellington, and then return before mounting out for their unknown final destination. There would be one final party when they returned from this final exercise. Dates and wives were coming up for the weekend; the hotels were full of Marines' clothes, and the streets full of cars. But the party would never be held.[12]

The fact was, the Marines were not coming back. They were off to their objective with a brief stop in the New Hebrides for a practice landing. New Zealand had seen the last of the 2nd Division. Life on the transports settled down to the usual boredom, but was made more intense by the heat of the equatorial climate. Every morning the Marines exercised, and then belted ammo, sharpened knives, cleaned rifles, wrote letters, and passed the time with bull sessions.

Whenever the question arose as to their final destination, the universal answer was "Truk." While most Marines didn't know one place from another, they all seemed to know Truk. It was a nasty place with lots of Japs, and it would be a bitch to attack. It didn't matter where you were going, the speculation was always Truk.[13] It wasn't until November 14, after the practice landings in the New Hebrides, when the assault force was again at sea, that the final destination was revealed to the men on board.[14]

It was after morning exercise that Jim Russell's platoon sergeant told everyone to sit down on deck. This was unusual since the formation was usually dismissed after exercise. Everyone took a seat, and Lt. Hopkins suddenly appeared, holding charts and maps roughly rolled in his arms. He laid them out and explained what he knew.

The operation was code named Galvanic, and it would be the assault and capture of the Tarawa Atoll. Looking at the maps, and seeing the more than forty islands that made up the atoll, the men groaned, thinking they would have to attack each and every one of them. Lt. Hopkins eased their fears and pointed to the only island to be attacked, the one shaped like a bird in the left corner of the triangular atoll.

All eyes studied the strangely shaped island and examined the beaches coded Red 1, Red 2, Red 3, on the northern coast, and Green Beach on the western coast. The southern coast had also been divided into two beaches coded Black 1 and 2. They studied the long pier that separated Red 2 from Red 3 and extended out from the bird's feet, over the reef to the deep water, 700 yards from the shore. Some of the men pointed to the break in the barrier reef on the western side of the atoll where the invasion forces would presumably enter the lagoon.

"Why are we attacking from the lagoon?" came one question. "It will be suicide to go through that opening to get inside. The Japs will have it zeroed. We'd be better off just launching the attack from the sea where the reef is not as wide."

The lieutenant fielded all questions and showed the obstacles on the sea side, by the Black Beaches: hedgehogs (crisscrossed barriers of steel to rip the bottoms out of landing craft), barbed wire, steel stakes, and mines. He also pointed out that the slight concave profile of the island from that side would allow the Japanese to enfilade the entire landing force on its way to the shore. The lieutenant also showed them that the guns facing seaward were more numerous than those facing the lagoon.

The men asked other questions and were told that there was a relief model of the island that was available to them between 1400 and 1800 hours in the officers' mess. Russell and his friends went up and examined the detailed model, which showed the airstrip clearly and the coastlines bristling with guns. It was even detailed with coconut trees.

The next day, the model was brought to their company to examine as a unit, and the main question was how many Japs were on the island. The commander told them that they estimated about five thousand Japanese. The Marines groaned, and then heard that the estimate of enemy strength had been determined from an aerial photograph that had clearly shown the number of Japanese privies, and by applying an arbitrary figure of how many men would be serviced by one privy, it was possible to estimate the enemy strength.

While the technique of estimating the number of enemy troops by counting the "shitters" elicited laughs from the men, even that rough estimate meant that the Marines would be landing six thousand men against five thousand defenders. This was not even close to the minimum ratio of three to one necessary to defeat a dug-in, defending force.

Each man was issued a checklist, which he was ordered to complete prior to D-Day. Russell read his over. There were eighteen questions beginning with, Who is the officer or NCO in charge of him on D-Day? The questions were simple: Where do I report? What special equipment do I take? What's my boat team number? Where is my debarkation station? The checklist made sure that each man knew what was going on, and what was expected of him on D-Day.

Jim Russell filled out his sheet, penciling in the answers.

What wave am I in? First.

What beach do I land on? Red 1.

When he got to question sixteen, he wrote the answer without hesitation. Question sixteen asked, "If separated from my unit, what do I do?" All Marines knew that answer. "Join the nearest friendly unit."[15]

At the next meeting, the men again pressed around their leaders. "What about the reef?" they asked, and the question was a troubling one.

Lt. Hopkins told them that it should be no problem for them since the LVTs would not be hindered by the reef, and they were in the first wave, and the LVTs would take the first three waves in. Waves four, five, and six would land in Higgins boats. The water over the reef was expected to be four feet, and that would float a Higgins boat, but should there be less water, the LVTs would come back and shuttle the next waves in. Should the tractors not be able to shuttle, then those in waves four, five, and six should be prepared to "wade in."

The announcement of a possible wade-in had all eyes snapped back to the mock-up and maps, where they could quickly see they would have to wade at least 700 yards. Jim Russell and the men in the first three waves were glad it wasn't them.[16]

The depth of water at any time over the reef was a ticklish question. Four feet was needed for a Higgins boat. To possibly learn more about the tides at Tarawa Atoll, the Navy called upon some Australians and

New Zealanders who had previously lived on the British-possessed island. The consensus was that there should be sufficient water, but
couched in that estimation was the suggestion that a full moon in late
December would ensure sufficient water at five feet.

But waiting until December was out of the question. A meticulous
military and political timetable had been set in motion when the Combined Chief had approved the Central Pacific drive. Future operations,
and their detailed planning, were contingent on maintaining that timetable.

Although most of the former inhabitants of Tarawa had expressed
a guarded optimism about the water's depth over the reef and had
produced tide tables to back this optimism, there was one man who
disagreed. Maj. F. L. G. Holland had kept tide records for the British
government, and he was not at all optimistic about the depth of water
over the reef. He brushed aside the other estimates and warned that
the tides could be low at this time of year.

There would only be a quarter moon, not the full moon that would
guarantee the higher tide, and this could present a problem. While the
major's presentation was passionate, everyone listening only seemed to
politely nod and dismiss his warning.

Those who were optimistic about the tide countered Holland's assessment. They again pointed to the charts that, they reminded, had
been generated by people who had actually lived on the islands. That
data, they said, clearly showed four and one-half feet of water over the
reef, and that would be enough to float the boats.

Holland's warning had been disregarded, but this brush-off did not
sit well with the feisty major, and as the naval officers carefully refolded
their charts, confident that they had diffused the volatile discussion
concerning the tides, Holland would not be silenced.

"You won't have three feet!" he barked.[17]

But the meeting went on, and as more experts weighed in on the
side of five feet of water, Maj. Holland again shook his head.

"You won't be able to cross that reef," he said, in a last attempt to
convince someone, but the subject was finally closed.

While the major's insistence that the water would be too shallow
seemed to fall on deaf ears, MGen. Julian Smith, the 2nd Division

Commander, was impressed. He knew that he could do nothing to create more water over the reef, but he could do something to warn his men. From then on he ordered that in all briefings, the troops were to be told of the possibility of a wade-in.

Other officers realized that even if there was barely enough water to float the Higgins boats, there would surely not be enough water for the deeper-draft landing craft mechanized (LCMs) carrying the tanks. Guides would be prepared to walk, as pathfinders, in front of the tanks to lead them ashore. Artillerymen were told to expect to learn what it was to be a pack mule.[18]

Pvt. Jim Russell, and the men of his Company K, assigned to the first wave, would land in tractors on Beach Red 1. His platoon would be embarked in two tractors, going in side-by-side. Their objective was to land in the vicinity of the bird's neck and work their way along the shore toward the bird's beak, where there were heavy fortifications. Sgt. Gresham would be his tractor commander, and Lt. Hopkins would command the second LVT.[19]

As D-Day approached, most of the men were filled with optimism. They had been thoroughly briefed, had seen the model of the small island, and had heard the bombardment plan and the planned air attack scheduled prior to their landing. The commander of the bombardment force, Adm. Howard Kingman, could not have been more optimistic. He sent a message to the men of the landing force.

"Gentleman," he said, "we will not neutralize Betio. We will not destroy it. We will obliterate it."[20]

Obliteration seemed to be the appropriate word to the Marines preparing to land. When told of the tonnage of shells and bombs that would impact on the island, which was less than one-half square mile, some wondered if the island would be there when the smoke cleared.

Three battleships, four heavy cruisers, and more than twenty destroyers would saturate Betio with 3,000 tons of ordnance in just over two hours. The only respite from this colossal naval bombardment would be the brief time that fire would be lifted for air strikes.[21]

But Col. Merritt Edson, who was the regimental chief of staff, presented a more pragmatic assessment, born from experience at Guadalcanal.

"Navy gunners make the mistake of thinking of shore targets as ships," he said. "When you hit it, it sinks, and is gone. On land, you need a direct hit on every gun."[22]

On the evening of November 19, 1943, the eve of D-Day for operation Galvanic, the Marines of the landing force tried to get as much sleep as nerves and the sweltering heat would allow. Bodies lay on the decks of the transports hoping for a cooling breeze. Reveille would be early, and H-Hour was set for 0830.

In the very early hours of D-Day, the transports carrying the Marines of the 2nd Division moved into an area about 5 miles off the western edge of Tarawa Atoll. Throughout the assembly area, the shrill whistle from boatswains' pipes could be heard as the winches lowered the Higgins boats into the water. They were soon circling in their rendezvous pattern off the stern of ships, waiting to move alongside to receive the Marines who would be coming down the cargo nets.[23]

The bombardment ships positioned themselves south of the transports and 4 miles off the western tip of Betio so they could deliver enfilade fire across the long axis of the island. In the light of the quarter moon, the low-lying silhouette of the target could be seen on the horizon.

On the deck of the transports, the Marines stared out into the night. Jim Russell had been to chow and had the traditional steak and eggs, and then gathered his gear and moved topside to wait for the order to embark into the landing craft. He could see the Higgins boats circling in the water.

Suddenly, to the south, the battleships opened fire. The entire bombardment force salvoed the island, and in the distance, flashes and explosions could be seen by the waiting Marines. Cheers went up as they watched the spectacle. Then the order came to go over the side and down the nets.

Four at a time, the Marines swung themselves over the rail of the transports and, with their feet on the horizontal strands of the net and their hands on the vertical strands to prevent being stepped on, they climbed down into the bobbing Higgins boats. As one boat was loaded from a particular station, it pulled away and began to circle off the stern, to be replaced by the next boat. The loading proceeded smoothly, until, suddenly, the order to cease embarkation was given. Half the force was embarked and circling, and the other half was aboard ship.

A southerly current had carried the transports into an area where they fell in the line of fire of some of the ships of the bombardment group. The transports began to move back to their assembly area, while the boats in the water were forced to follow like ducklings behind the mother duck. In the darkness some lost their way, and by the time all vessels were back in position, valuable time had been lost. H-Hour was reset for 0900.[24]

The Japanese had not been idle while the shore bombardment rained shells on them. They fired back with eight-inch guns, but only inflicted slight damage. Many of their shots were terrifying near misses in the transport area, again forcing the transports to move, with more confusion for the boats already in the water.

Now it was Russell's turn to go over the side. Down he went with half of his platoon, led by Sgt. Gresham. As the boat pulled away from the transport, it immediately went to an area to rendezvous with the LVTs. Seventy-five LVTs were placed in the water by the ten ships that had transported them to the assembly area. Incredibly, an additional fifty of the armored carriers rolled down the ramps of landing ship tanks (LST), having just arrived to join the attack force. In a remarkable display of logistical coordination, the remaining tractors necessary to carry the first three waves to the beach had arrived during the night from the West Coast of the United States.[25]

In a short time, the Higgins boats had moved into positions alongside the noisy tractors, and the Marines rolled from one vessel to the other. The tractors now began to circle in their own rendezvous while all eyes remained fixed on the sound and light show that was the bombardment of Betio. When the aircraft came in for their bombing runs, the Marines embarked in the LVTs and the Higgins boats were treated to a sight not seen before.

The dive bombers came in and sent clouds of smoke and flame shooting high into the air as they pounded the island from one end to the other. Wave after wave of aircraft hammered Betio until it vanished from view of the circling Marines.

When the last aircraft departed, the massive naval bombardment resumed as the assault waves moved to enter the lagoon. They moved in three single files toward the opening, which was three miles off the Betio beaches. Already inside the lagoon were two minesweepers, which had cleared the opening, and two destroyers, dueling with Japanese gunners.

One of the minesweepers sat on the line of departure, shining its light at the tractors, which were laboring to gain entrance to the lagoon. A strong westerly current slowed the LVTs to a crawl, and they fell more than twenty minutes behind schedule.[26]

The men in the tractors of Jim Russell's platoon knew nothing of the schedule, or the change in H-Hour. That meant little to them. What did concern them was the water lapping over the sides and pooling in the bottom of the craft and the shallow freeboard over the side. To Jim Russell, it seemed that the slightest pitch could send walls of water into the well and sink the LVT.

By 0800, the columns of tractors had gained the calmer waters of the lagoon, and as they passed the minesweeper at the line of departure, they turned out of their columns and formed an assault line. Russell watched as his tractor turned for Betio, and could see the long line of forty-two tractors in the first wave turn at the same time and churn for the beach.

At 0825, the fighters and bombers came in for their last passes on the beach, but the landing craft were still a long way from shore. That final pass was to have been made just minutes before the first craft touched shore. It would keep the enemy pinned down as the Marines got inland, but the last pass was finished while the LVTs were still twenty minutes from landing.

Except for the two destroyers in the lagoon, the preinvasion bombardment was over. The assault waves headed for the beach with no covering fires.

As the first wave made its run for the beach, Jim Russell looked from side to side and, from his low position on the water, he could see the long line of tractors making good progress and keeping a good line. Once in a while, a geyser of water erupted as Japanese gunners tried to get their range.

Directly ahead of them, they could see the outline of the reef reflecting menacingly just under water. To their left was the long pier, jutting out 500 yards from the shore. The tractors hit the reef on line.

Jim Russell felt the impact as his LVT made contact with the coral. The coxswain stopped the machine, but only temporarily, and then gunned the engine. The tracks grabbed the reef, and the machine crawled up onto it. For the first time, the tractor sat well above the water, and the men breathed a sigh of relief. The tracks crunched on the coral and waddled toward the shore.

As he looked back, Russell could see some of the tracks had gotten hung up, but most soon freed themselves, and they too were grinding for the shore. The noise of the crunching coral reef added to the already deafening noise of the engines, drowning out even the noise of explosions. Water geysers just seemed to appear with no sound attached to them.[27]

The assault line advanced across the coral reef, heading for the invasion beaches. Red 1 was 700 yards wide and corresponded to the area of the bird's beak and throat. Red 2 was only 600 yards wide and ran from Red 1 to the pier. Red 3 covered the area to the left of the pier 800 yards to a point opposite the airfield.[28]

Russell and other members of his boat team took cautious peeks over the sides, but were careful to make them short before pulling their heads back in below the level of the gunwales. To the left, a tractor exploded, sending up an orange ball of flame. A quick look again to the front confirmed that the shoreline was only a short distance away. The platoon sergeant passed the word for everyone to get ready.

As the engines slowed, Russell could hear a steady ping of bullets against the sides, and then the LVT crawled up the sloping beach. It lurched forward and began to crawl up the seawall of coconut logs before it stalled. Japanese fire whistled over their heads, and in the next instant, the tractor was hit by fire and stopped. Then a larger caliber shell slammed into the LVT, killing both the coxswain and his assistant.

"Get out," was the order, and Jim Russell rolled out over the stern. The rest of the men were out, running in a low crouch or crawling toward the wall. In their scramble out of the stricken vehicle, ammunition and other ordnance was dropped or left in the vessel. Ironically, despite the confusion among the landing craft, this LVT had made land exactly where it was supposed to land, in the salient to the left of the beak. It would prove to be the deadliest spot on the beach.

The new arrivers on Red 1 pressed themselves against the wall, but only until they had gathered themselves, then they moved to the west along the seawall toward the beak, which was their objective. Five men were wounded as the half platoon had debarked over the stern of the LVT, but when they moved out, they took their wounded with them.

They moved along, close to the coconut-log seawall, as the second wave came in. Jim Russell could see an enormous volume of fire whistling over their heads, directed against the approaching landing craft, but not much was being aimed against Gresham's force. They passed one pillbox, and then another, but the third one pinned them down.

They deployed and returned fire against the fortified position, and forced the Japanese away from the apertures. It was a Mexican standoff, with Gresham's men not able to advance against the strong position, and the Japanese defenders not able to direct fire against the approaching landing craft.

Using fire and maneuvering, they kept the enemy pinned down, and after thirty minutes were able to move past the pillbox and continue toward the beak. Along the way, this small force breached barbed wire and other obstacles.

The coconut wall was at least 4 feet high, and the tide was out, so they could move in a crouch without having to crawl. As they moved, they recovered weapons and other equipment from dead Marines in the water. However, the one weapon they wanted the most they did not find on the bodies they searched: They could not find a single hand grenade.

They did not encounter another strong position, and when they reached the point where the big guns were, they could see that they had been taken out by the shore bombardment. However, one large gun position, just inland from the wall, and able to cover both Green Beach and the cove by Beach Red 1, continued to hammer away at the approaching tractors and wading men.

Gresham formed his men in a defensive position. Twenty men, of the entire landing force, reached their initial objective, and they now dug in, or pressed themselves against the coconut-log seawall. From their position on the small point of land, they could look back and see a panorama of the assault: It was a panorama of death. The shoreline and reef were covered with smoke from burning tractors. Japanese direct hits smashed into the LVTs, which turned into massive fireballs as their fuel tanks exploded. Bodies were hurled into the water, and some men, their clothes on fire, leaped for the quenching waves.

In the salient where Russell's craft had landed, the destruction was the worst. Covered by fire from the front and both flanks, because of the curving shoreline, the tractors were shot to pieces.

Further out in the lagoon, a strange odyssey was taking place. Far out, at the end of the reef, small dots appeared in the water, like little bobbing corks. In small groups and clusters, these bobbing objects moved across the reef toward the shore. Russell and the men on the northwestern tip of the island were held spellbound as the fourth assault wave waded in.

Transported into the lagoon, across the line of departure, the fourth wave had run aground on the reef in their Higgins boats. The 5 feet of water optimistically predicted by the tide prognosticators was, in fact, just over 3 feet. Maj. Holland's Cassandra-like warning had been right, and the fourth wave, followed by the fifth and sixth waves, began the wade into the killing zone.

All around the little dark spots struggling through the water, Japanese bullets sent up water geysers; mortars landed in their midst. Seeking any type of cover from the deadly fire, the Marines crouched down so just their heads were above the waves. The fire from Japanese guns rose to a deafening roar. In ones and twos, and sometimes in groups, the Marines pitched forward as the fusillade shattered their ranks.

On shore, the rest of Russell's platoon, led by Lt. Hopkins, miraculously joined forces on the bird's beak. Unlike Sgt. Gresham's tractor, the lieutenant's had landed unscathed, and his half of the platoon got out safely. Hopkins deployed his men around the point, even on the Green Beach side, and began to fire at some of the bunkers to try and give the wading Marines some cover. From their position on the relative safety of the point, Hopkins's platoon became spectators to the grim wade-in.

Some of the heavily laden Marines in the lagoon were not victims of the Japanese fire. The sheer weight of their loads pulled them underwater when they stepped into holes made by previous bombings, and they drowned. The advancing men pushed their way through floating bodies, and those who made the beach collapsed among the packed numbers of other Marines pinned down on the narrow strip of beach in front of the seawall.

In a float plane, flying above the wading attack force, a naval officer had a bird's-eye view of spectacle. He looked down and was overwhelmed by the sight. "The water seemed never clear of tiny men, their rifles held over their heads, slowly wading beachward. I wanted to cry."[29]

As they looked out over this scene of death, the men of Jim Russell's platoon could see a separate group of wading Marines, far removed from the other groups that approached the shore. They seemed detached from the assault force and were coming in toward the extreme western boundary of Beach Red 1. They were approaching the beak itself rather than the bloody salient of the cove where Marines were dying by the scores. Although some of their numbers fell victim to the intense Japanese fire, they seemed to be making better progress.

This force was from the fourth wave. Unknown to Russell and the rest of the Marines on the point, this was Company L and part of H&S Company being led in by Company L's newly promoted commander, Maj. Mike Ryan.

Ryan had been scheduled to land in the center of Red 1, which now had become a terrible place of death. As his Higgins boat approached the reef, he saw one lone Marine jump over the wall, far to his right, by the bird's beak. Although this was far removed from his scheduled landing spot, he directed the boats carrying his company to slide to the right. When he could go no further inland as his boat nudged the reef, he was directly in line with the point.[30]

Ryan's men began their wade-in from 700 yards. It took almost an hour, as the Japanese gunners shot down a third of their ranks, but finally the exhausted men joined Company K on the northwestern tip of Betio. The arrival of this force placed two hundred men on the bird's beak, and the major took command of this mixed force. Then this small isolated force received a gift from heaven: Two Sherman tanks arrived.[31]

Ryan explained to his force what he wanted to do: use the tanks in a coordinated attack and drive down the west coast, clearing enemy positions as they went. It was now after two o'clock in the afternoon, and the men prepared for the drive down Green Beach.

Using the tanks, this mixed force jumped off in the attack and punched their way down the beach. Jim Russell used the tactics that had been pounded into his head all through his training. He moved out and bypassed what did not hold him up. The tanks blasted some targets, and the whole force suddenly found itself looking at the Pacific Ocean, only 300 yards from the southern shore.

Russell scraped out a fighting hole and took up a defensive position facing the coconut trees to his left. His back was to the lagoon. The tanks rumbled into defensive positions, but soon Maj. Ryan gave the order to pull back to their positions on the beak. He had been unable to communicate with superiors, and he felt he was too exposed in his new position. Many positions had been bypassed and that left a lot of Japanese to his rear. He had no flamethrowers or explosives, and without those he could not clear the bunkers.[32]

Back to the point went the Marines. This time Russell dug in, preparing for the eventual counterattack that he knew would come at night. The Japanese had consistently attacked at night during the Guadalcanal campaign, and there was no reason to think that this night would be any different.

Maj. Ryan moved from position to position, encouraging his men and telling them to dig in and sit tight. The following morning, they would attack to clear Green Beach.

As the sun set on D-Day, Jim Russell looked back toward the lagoon, and Red Beach. The sight was a disaster. Bodies floated in the lagoon, slowly moving back and forth at the will of the currents. The shoreline was a junkyard of destroyed tractors and equipment; Marines huddled against these wrecks for cover.

In front of him, the Japanese still held most of the island, and, although he didn't know it, the small pocket that he and the rest of Maj. Ryan's force occupied was the greatest success of D-Day. A Japanese counterattack would be guaranteed to inflict maximum casualties on the pinned-downed Marines, and mortar fire along the shoreline would produce multiple casualties for each round fired. Supporting arms offshore would be of no use if the Japanese counterattacked. Naval gunfire in these close quarters would kill both Marines and Japanese.

At the end of D-Day, the entire landing force, hunkered down or dug in on the sliver of Betio beach that represented a toehold, was literally shot to pieces. Nervous Marines prepared their weapons for the night attack, sure to come with whistles and soldiers screaming *Banzai*.

But the counterattack did not come, and for the men in Ryan's force, the night was really very easy. There were no bombardments, and surprisingly, the Japanese did not mortar the tightly packed ranks of Marines on the beach.

As day broke on D+1, Ryan's force was ready to attack down Green Beach. The two tanks—one light and one medium Sherman—having gained some tank/infantry experience the preceding day, were now joined by a naval gunfire spotter appropriately named Lt. Greene. By 1120, the combined force was ready to attack.[33] In front of them were a variety of heavily fortified Japanese positions, some of them able to cover both Green Beach and Red 1 at the same time, with apertures facing in both directions.

Minutes before the attack was ordered forward, Jim Russell and his buddy, PFC Joseph Herberski, checked their weapons one more time to make sure everything was ready. These two men had been together since boot camp. They had been to the Solomons and to New Zealand, and now they were in the fight of their lives. During the preceding month, they had spent their last days as teenagers, and yesterday they had become battle-hardened veterans.

The bodies of dead Marines still floated in the lagoon behind them as they faced forward to attack the dug-in Japanese force. Their fellow Marines, who formed this mixed bunch of "orphans," had all survived the gauntlet of the reef. Some had ridden in, but most had waded in, and much of their equipment had been lost along the way. Still others had straggled in, having sidestepped their own landing beaches where defenders had mown down their attacking comrades, and they had made their way to this small beachhead on the bird's beak. Joining them were an assortment of vehicle drivers, tractor drivers, and gunners, and members from all of the companies of the battalion.

Among the entire force, there was only one length of a bangalore torpedo, and a single bazooka, with only two rounds. No flamethrowers had made it across the reef. The 72-pound weapons had either been jettisoned or had dragged their gunners to the bottom.

The bazooka was a new weapon, and only PFC Herberski, among the Marines of Maj. Ryan's force, had any training with it; he had attended a weapons school. Russell had retrieved the launcher, along with one of the two rounds, and Herberski decided to carry it on the assault. Without hand grenades or explosives or flamethrowers, it was the only antibunker weapon they had.

At 1120 the attack moved out and was almost instantly pinned down by a large bunker shaped like an anthill. Machine-gun fire brought the new attack to a screeching halt; the main armament of the bunker was two 75mm guns.

Russell looked for cover and ducked down behind a large coconut log, almost 6 feet long and fully 18 inches in diameter. Herberski flopped down beside him, and they twisted to place the log between them and the fire from the pillbox. In positioning themselves, they discovered that the log moved rather easily, and they were able to roll it to their best advantage.

Peering from behind their cover, the two Marines could see the bunker easily. Its sides sloped to the ground, and it looked more like a sand dune than a fortified position. Some Marines began to fire at its openings, but were answered with a tremendous volume of fire from the bunker. There was no way to move as long as the bunker was active. Attacking seemed impossible, because an attack required an uphill run across open ground to get to the aperture. Naval gunfire was out of the question because of the proximity of the attacking Marines, and the two tanks were sure targets in the open for the 75mm guns.

As Maj. Ryan pondered his next move, he was surprised to see the massive coconut log rolling forward, pushed by Russell and Herberski.

As they pushed, they dragged their weapons, including the bazooka and the single rocket.

Bullets from the enemy position sent sand flying in front of the log, and those rounds that hit the rolling log simply ricocheted off or embedded a couple of inches in the hard surface. The two PFCs were sweating profusely and stopped every few feet to rest.

With the volume of fire that their journey was attracting, Herberski suggested that maybe, if they stopped pushing, the Japanese would forget about them. Russell dismissed that thought and grunted to his task. Fellow Marines, tucked behind their own cover, now alternately encouraged and then derided the two-man log crew as they imitated the mythical Sisyphus, rolling his stone up the impossible hill.

Now they were at the base of the slope leading toward the aperture. The exhausting push across the open ground was nothing compared to the uphill push that now began. Crouching, with their legs drawn up, they pushed forward with their feet. After moving the log a few feet, they braced it with their hands and their weapons so it would not roll backward. Again they coiled up behind the log, and pushed again, seemingly ignoring the rounds impacting nearby. The log was absolutely impervious to the enemy fire.

The gasping Marines rested momentarily, and then renewed their efforts. Up the slope rolled the log, forever wanting to roll back, but stopped by the two men behind it. Heads, arms, and shoulders served as chocks to prevent the roll back. In one of these grunting maneuvers, Herberski exposed himself slightly and was, instantly, shot through the neck.

Bracing the log, Russell bandaged him, and Herberski insisted that they go on. Blood soaked through the bandage, but he pushed with all his strength. The distance between the coconut log and the deadly bunker slowly closed. At 25 feet, they seemed close enough, but the two Marines did not stop. Finally they were barely 15 feet from the opening that spewed gunfire.

From their positions, the other Marines could see Herberski maneuver the launcher to load it. There were no catcalls now, and the other Marines laid down a base of fire to keep the enemy from the aperture. Despite encouragement, Herberski's movements were slow; loss of blood from his neck wound had weakened him.

Finally the bazooka was loaded, and Jim Russell readied himself for what he knew would be his only shot. He braced himself, and in an instant, he had bolted upright to a kneeling position, took quick aim, and squeezed the trigger. The backblast of the weapon temporarily obscured his view, but the rocket sailed straight through the aperture and an enormous explosion detonated within the pillbox. The force of the explosion blew the log free, and it rolled down the hill, rolling over Russell and the wounded Herberski, until it rested at the bottom of the slope.

Inside the bunker, the 75mm guns and the machine guns were now silent; six Japanese gunners were dead. The other Marines surged forward. The next bunker fell with the bangalore torpedo.

Russell brought Herberski back toward the rear and placed him with several wounded Marines, and rejoined the attack. Ryan moved forward and, in the next hour, completed a truly astonishing attack. Utilizing direct fire from Navy destroyers, pinpointed by Lt. Greene, all the positions on the west coast of Green Beach fell under his onslaught. Before 1230, he had gained the southern shore and signaled that he had a beachhead. For the first time, the embattled Marines on Betio controlled an area where they could land fresh troops.

Ryan's attack with his force of "orphans" had cracked the western defenses of Betio. Their trophies included seven large-caliber coastal guns, plus rapid-firing 37mm guns, and numerous heavy machine guns.[34]

By 1400, Green Beach was alive with activity. Ryan's force now faced to the east and had carved out a line several hundred meters in depth. They defended the newly won beach for a renewed amphibious landing. And a strange landing it would be.

The 1st Battalion, 6th Marines were transported to the offshore area of Green Beach. The whole battalion was embarked in rubber rafts, with six to ten men per raft. Higgins boats towed the rafts, six in a string, 12,000 yards in to the west coast, and advanced from the ocean side, until they bottomed out on the reef. From there, the Marines began to paddle the 600 yards over the coral, toward the beach. It was

a slow process, and the vulnerable rubber boats and landing craft offered targets to Japanese gunners, but by 1900, the battalion was ashore,
dug in behind Ryan's lines. Because the men of Ryan's command had
pushed the Japanese away from Green Beach, not one man was lost
due to enemy fire. The only loss was an LVT loaded with much needed
supplies that struck a mine and sank.[35]

The newly landed battalion took up positions behind Ryan's men.
Jim Russell watched them occupy many of the positions that had been
cleared by the morning attack. Their orders were to attack the following morning, and they dug in for the night.

Again that night, the Japanese did not counterattack. At 0800, 1st
Battalion, 6th Marines shoved off in the attack, passing through Jim
Russell and the men who had conquered Green Beach. They moved
forward, encountering the holed-up Japanese force and smashing their
bunkers, with few casualties of their own.[36]

Russell and the men of Ryan's force watched them depart, and then
watched a reenactment of the previous day's landings, when 3rd Battalion, 6th Marines came ashore. Before noon, these new Marines were
ashore, and by 1700, they followed in the path of the 1st Battalion,
which had moved forward six hours earlier.[37]

The back of the Japanese force was broken. That evening they
would launch a futile banzai charge from the eastern end of the island,
inflicting over a hundred casualties among the Marine forces, but suffering the annihilation of the last remnants of their fighting forces. The
following day, the island was declared secure, and carrier aircraft began
to land on the newly acquired landing strip.

EPILOGUE

The Battle of Tarawa, or more specifically, the Battle for Betio Island,
had taken a little over three days. The Marines had suffered three
thousand casualties, a statistic that appalled the American people when
the numbers were released. The Japanese force of five thousand men,
except for seventeen prisoners and some Korean laborers, were killed
or committed suicide.

On D+4, November 24, Jim Russell could see the transports anchoring in the lagoon. These vessels would take him and the other Marines away from this stinking, rotting place. At noon, there was a ceremonial flag raising, and the island was officially secured. The long pier, which had been a focal point of the attack just three days before, now became the pier that took them out over the reef, and to relief.

For young Jim Russell his war had just begun. He would later participate in attacks on Namur, Saipan, and Tinian, where he was wounded. For his heroic action against the bunker at Betio, he received the Navy Cross.[38] He also received a Bronze Star at Tinian for heroism.

PFC Joseph Herberski, Russell's friend and fellow attacker of the key bunker, did not survive his wounds. He died sometime during the evening from his neck wound. Russell never saw his body. He too received the Navy Cross, as did Maj. Michael Ryan. There were four Medals of Honor awarded at Tarawa.

Of the more than 1,100 men of the 2nd Marine Division who were killed, half could not be identified. The pulverizing Japanese fire, the drowning waters of the lagoon, and the stifling, equatorial heat robbed the dead of identification. Only one-quarter of the bodies were ever returned to the United States.

In a battle that saw the Marines suffer one thousand casualties a day, the turning point came when the small platoon, with Jim Russell as a BARMAN, seized and held the tiny point of land known as the "bird's beak" on D-Day. From that small point was launched the attack that would crack the elite Japanese forces. Wartime reporter Robert Sherrod said, "If we ever fought a battle in which courage was a dominant factor, it was at Tarawa."[39]

President Franklin Roosevelt awarded the 2nd Marine Division the Presidential Unit Citation, but perhaps the greatest tribute paid to the Marines who hurled themselves against the anvil of Betio came from several of the enemy survivors. Their comments are hauntingly similar to the praise the Japanese extended to the dauntless pilots of the torpedo squadrons in their suicidal attacks at Midway. When asked by debriefers if there was ever a time during the battle when their morale failed, they nodded and said, "It was when the dying Marines just kept coming and coming."[40]

FIVE
THE INVASION OF NORMANDY

June 6, 1944

Pvt. Kenneth Russell, 82nd Airborne Division
1st Sgt. Leonard Lomell, 2nd Ranger Battalion

Pvt. Kenneth E. Russell lay in his hospital bed in Nottingham, England, fighting a raging fever that left him flat on his back. He'd been in the hospital for four days, ever since he had been given his shots in the billeting area of the 82nd Airborne Division in Quorn, in Lincolnshire. While the shots had not affected many of his comrades, Russell and some other troopers, sensitive to the vaccines, had been put out of action by ensuing high fevers.

It was the last week in May 1944, and Russell strained at the leash to leave the hospital and rejoin his group. The rumors were everywhere that the great day was at hand. There was no hiding the excitement that everyone felt concerning the proposed cross-channel attack against the western wall of Hitler's Europe. It was the big day that had been anxiously awaited ever since 1940, when the German forces had driven the British out of France and conquered the French people.

Russell remembered those dark days and the disappointing news of the war in 1940. He had been in school, in Maryville, Tennessee, thirteen years old, and filled with the spirit of adventure. Two years later, at fifteen, he tried to enlist in the Marine Corps, claiming that he was older. The Marines gave him an application for his parents to sign, and young Ken stuffed it into the pocket of his overalls, intending to forge his mother's signature at the first opportunity.

Many of his older friends were going into the service, and he wanted to go with them. He had a limited knowledge of the service: He thought that when you joined the service, everyone went to the same place, all in one building, and he did not want to be left behind. But before he could practice his mother's signature and forge the papers, she discovered them sticking out of his overall pocket. She tore them up and that ended his career in the Marines.

But Russell was not easily dissuaded. A few months later, now sixteen, he watched an uncle join the service and leave town for the great adventure. He knew that he had to go, so he went to the Army recruiters, lied about his age, and became a fraudulent enlistee. He was assigned to the 35th Infantry Division for training.

Ken Russell was a strong, fast kid. As a sophomore, he had been penciled in on his school football team's roster as the starting tailback in their single-wing offense. He had no ability to throw the ball, but running was another story, and some sportswriters picked his school to win the championship in the fall—which they did, minus Ken Russell.

By that time, he had left the 35th Division, volunteered for the airborne, and was taking jump training at Fort Benning, Georgia. Adventure had attracted him to the airborne, just as it earlier had attracted him to the Marines. He was ideally suited to be a paratrooper, and in January, he was sent overseas, to Ireland, to join the 82nd Airborne Division—the All-Americans. He also learned that he was not the youngest man in his company: Two other troopers were, in fact, junior to him.

He trained in Ireland for two months, and then, in the spring of 1944, moved to Quorn, in the English countryside. He endured the grueling training and exercises and became part of the elite division training for what everyone knew would be the great invasion day. But now he was confined to bed, weak as a baby, and running a fever that would put him out of action. If the invasion went off in the next few days, it would go without Ken Russell, just like the football team that had won the championship without him.

Ken Russell's path to the brink of Invasion Day had been the result of five years of war in Europe. After Hitler's forces had overrun France, the führer toyed with the idea of invading England, but could not wrest control of the air from the Royal Air Force to make an amphibious invasion possible. Abandoning that plan, he then turned to the east, and the great spaces of the eastern Soviet Union, and launched his blitzkrieg into Russia in 1941.

After two years on the Eastern Front, first as a victor, and then as the leader of a retreating army, Hitler looked again to the west and recognized it as the source of the greatest possible danger to Germany. During his two years of waging war against Joseph Stalin and the Red Army, the British and American Allies had not been idle. They had defeated German forces, first in North Africa, and then in Sicily, and in 1944, they were driving up the boot of Italy. More important, they stood a mere 25 miles away across the English Channel from the Pas de Calais, in northern France, and had gathered a mighty army, hopeful of hurling it across the channel onto the Continent.

Adolf Hitler had no illusions. "If the enemy here succeeds in penetrating our defense on a wide front," he said, "consequences of staggering proportions will follow within a short time."[1] A simple geographic examination of the northern French coastline was enough to explain Hitler's concerns. The Pas de Calais was only 300 miles from the Rhine, and only 600 miles from Berlin. Again, on March 20, 1944, Hitler sounded the warning to his generals: "The destruction of the enemy's landing attempt . . . is the sole decisive factor in the whole conduct of the war and hence in its final result."[2]

But it was not at the Pas de Calais that the Allies planned to strike; They would attempt to cross at the widest part of the English Channel. Their eyes were on a 60-mile-wide assault area in Normandy, between the Orne River to the east and the Cotentin Peninsula to the west.

The plan was developed in maximum secrecy while the force gathered in southern England, and Gen. Eisenhower and his staff planned a direct frontal assault against Hitler's defending forces. While the defenses around the Pas de Calais were almost impregnable, even to Allied strategists, Normandy was more remote and less heavily defended.

For the attack to succeed, Eisenhower needed surprise, and he needed to keep the great German reserve forces away from the battle area for as long as possible for the invasion to have a chance. To that end, the plan was simple: Drop paratroop forces on both the east and west flanks to prevent reinforcement of the battle area, and then land the force across five selected beaches on the Normandy coast and gain lodgment. From there, break out and pour more troops and equipment into the attack, until the German forces had been neutralized and then defeated.

The logic of the plan was simple and the tactics were sound, but the difficulty was in the execution, which caused Eisenhower great worry. This would not be a landing on a far-removed battlefield where enemy resupply and reinforcement would be difficult, as the landings in North Africa and Sicily had been. This was the continent of Europe, and the Norman coast was less than 200 miles from the great reserves of the German Fifteenth Army at the Pas de Calais.

Eisenhower was also very aware of the difficulty of a frontal assault against a fortified position. Most amphibious assaults attempt to land in an undefended spot to allow lodgment, after which the invading forces would seek out the enemy forces. That philosophy had changed at Tarawa, and he knew the difficulties that the Marines had experienced there. On that small island, there had been no Japanese second line of defense, no reserves to bring in from other positions, no supporting arms and logistics from other areas, and, despite that, the Marine assault had incurred horrific casualties and almost failed on the first day.

At Normandy, Eisenhower would not be attacking a small Pacific island defended by isolated soldiers. This was Fortress Europe, as Hitler called it. The Germans could easily reinforce a threatened area; they could rush men and materiel to the battlefield, and they could mass artillery and armor against the Allied force. If they succeeded in pushing the attack back into the sea, the Allies could not resort to an alternative plan to, perhaps, bypass the area, as was sometimes a viable alternative in the Pacific war. If the Normandy attack did not stick, Hitler would not again be threatened by the British and Americans in the west for at least another year. His dilemma of fighting a ground war on two fronts would be eliminated.

On June 1, Pvt. Ken Russell was still in the hospital. Rumors were all around that the great invasion was to happen any day. He stopped nurses and doctors and tried to get someone to release him to return to his company. Company F of the 505th Regiment had become his home, and the camaraderie he had with his fellow paratroopers had been his greatest experience. If he was to go into battle, he wanted to go in with them.

Finally, when he had just about given up hope and had started to plan an escape from the hospital, a sympathetic doctor signed him out. He returned to his company area in Quorn just in time to see his buddies packing all their noncombat belongings in barracks bags to be stored. He had made it in time.

He rushed to his area and packed his bag. No sooner had he submitted it for storage than the order came for the company to move out to the airfield at Cottersmore, where they were sealed in with the rest of the 505th Regiment. To young Ken, this marshaling area was an area of confinement. It looked like a concentration camp, surrounded by barbed wire. No one got in or out.

After the units had been sealed in and settled down, there began a series of briefings. Company F was called for a briefing, and the men were brought into rooms that had sand tables showing various areas of the French countryside. The amount of detail on these sand tables was remarkable. Russell's company was briefed about a town lying in the Cotentin Peninsula called Ste. Mere Eglise. Russell thought it was more a village than a town as he followed the briefer's pointer to the cluster of buildings on the sand table. The dominant building, rising high above the rest of the buildings, was the church; an ancient Norman structure, most likely close to a thousand years old.

The briefer spent time pointing to the countryside, strangely not mentioning anything about the hedgerows that separated one farmer's fields from another's and created natural obstacles to movement. The troopers of Company F could plainly see that many roads in the area led into the town. The 505th Regiment had been given the mission to capture and hold this town of Ste. Mere Eglise, and Russell's company, with the rest of the 2nd Battalion, would be responsible for cutting the road leading toward Cherbourg to the north.

They would be night-dropped to the west of town and, after gathering their forces, would make their way to their objective. Ste. Mere Eglise stood astride the main communications and transportation line from inner France to the port of Cherbourg. In addition to holding Ste. Mere Eglise, the paratroopers were to prevent any German forces from reinforcing the defenses that would confront the morning landings at Utah Beach.[3]

From this detailed briefing and subsequent briefings, Ken Russell thought he knew the area intimately, even though he had never set foot on French soil. He'd memorized the details every time he saw the sand tables, and Ste. Mere Eglise and the surrounding areas became very familiar.

When not at a briefing, he checked and rechecked his equipment. He zeroed his new rifle and packed his kit until he had everything just where he wanted it. He test lifted his pack and felt the enormous weight; he guessed that it weighed over 100 pounds.

He had packed a couple of changes of underwear and, more important, several changes of socks, a blanket, and enough rations for three days. But the main weight was ammunition and explosives. For his M-1 rifle, he carried 160 rounds of ammunition, along with four fragmentation grenades and two Gammon bombs. He also had a 10-pound Mark IV antitank mine. Throw in an entrenching tool, wire cutters, gas mask, canteen, reserve chute, and other odds and ends, and the finished product could weigh as much as the man.[4]

The Gammon bomb was popular with the American troopers. It had been invented by a British trooper named Jock Gammon in 1942. Consisting of two pounds of plastic explosive stuffed into a stockinglike bag with an appropriate igniter, it was particularly deadly. When thrown against a target, it would mold itself to the target and explode with an enormous force, capable of blowing shards of metal from the inside of a tank.[5]

Although the Gammon bomb was a wonderful supplemental weapon, it was a plastic explosive. Ingenious soldiers soon discovered that a small piece could be pinched from the bomb and lit with a match. It burned with intense heat, sufficient to warm coffee or rations. Despite all directives and orders not to use it for that purpose, it was irresistible and, over time, the size of the bomb would shrink until it was gone.[6]

The days in the marshaling area moved slowly. After checking and rechecking their gear and sharpening knives, there was not much to do. Makeshift theaters showed newly released movies; games of softball and pitch and catch were played constantly; troopers read paperbacks and played card games, often gambling their whole stash in one final attempt at an enormous purse. Religious services were conducted every day.[7]

On the afternoon of June 5, Russell and the men of Company F got the word to dress for battle. An order had been canceled the previous day, but they now knew that the great day was at hand. Mess halls were busy preparing the final meal before battle, with all the trimmings: steak, eggs, potatoes—everything imaginable.

Pvt. Ken Russell went through the line, his tray heaped with food, and searched for a place to sit. He saw a number of his buddies seated at a table, but somehow he gravitated away from them toward a trooper who sat alone. The man's name was Graves and he was known as a very devout Christian who always prayed and offered blessings for his food. To some of the macho troopers, this was enough to make them shy away from Graves, who consequently usually ate alone.

Russell classified himself as not very religious, but on this night, there was a certain magnetism that drew him to the solitary trooper. He felt that Graves had something that he didn't have, and he wanted to sit close to him. As he approached the table, he asked Graves if he minded his company. Graves smiled and invited Russell to sit, and then Russell asked if he could share in his blessing. The other trooper looked aghast, no one had ever asked to join him before. He had gotten the impression that most of the troopers thought that his habits were a little weird, but he collected himself and shared his blessing with Russell.

When the meal was over, Russell thanked Graves and went out to meet with a friend, Charles Blankenship. Blankenship was nineteen, two years older than Russell, and was also a devout Christian; his father was a Baptist minister. He sensed Russell's nervousness. Blankenship slapped Russell on the back and told him that he'd be okay.

"I'm the tough guy in this outfit," Blankenship said, "and I'll be around a long time, and I'll tell you what I'm going to do."

Russell looked at him, feeling better already.

"When I get home, I'm going to raise the chickens to pick the grass off of your grave."

Russell laughed and was grateful for Blankenship's reassurance, and they went off to prepare for the jump.

Around 2000, the men were ready and grouped around their commanders for a final briefing and pep talk. Two hours later came the order to "Chute up." Russell and the fifteen men of his stick, one plane of paratroopers, struggled and grunted into their harnesses and buckles. As the chuting-up process continued, the troopers began to look like inflated mannequins, bulging at every seam, as their huge loads were strapped into place. When the last snap was snapped, they could hardly move, waddling in short steps.

This scene at Cottersmore was repeated all over Southern England by the thirteen thousand paratroopers of the 101st and 82nd Airborne Divisions at places named Welford, Greenham Commons, Membury, Merryfield, North Witham, Upottery, Exeter, and Aldermaston. The troopers, with their faces blackened, some with mohawk haircuts, sharpened knives and overloaded their packs, then waddled out to the C-47s, the two-engine trooper carriers waiting to take them to France.

Ken Russell and the members of his fifteen-man stick went in single file to their aircraft, whose props were idling. Russell looked up, toward the fence that separated the field from the English countryside, and he could see townsfolk lined up shoulder to shoulder, waving and cheering. He struggled in labored steps toward the plane, where the first men were being pushed and shoved up the steps. In their gear they were unable to ascend the few steps into the aircraft and had to be boosted up. The first men aboard then turned and offered a hand to the man behind them. Like giant turtles they moved to the rear, filling up the web seats on either side of the aisle, from back to front.

Finally, it was Russell's turn, and he grasped the hand extended by the man in front of him and gratefully felt the boost from the man behind. He was aboard and sidled down to the middle of the C-47, plopping down ungracefully in his seat. He was in the middle of the plane. He would be the ninth man out. He watched the rest of his stick enplane, and finally he saw Lt. Harold Cadish, the stick commander, hoisted in. They were all aboard.

It was cramped inside, with no room to move, and the men sat facing each other, waiting for the next move. There was a static line running down the length of the aircraft attached to the overhead, and the door was left off of the aircraft to facilitate egress. Outside, Russell could again see the cheering gentry. Other men looked out windows, too, struck by the sight of the cheering crowds.

"They must know something we don't know," one man said. Ken Russell looked to his right and left. Across from him was Charles Blankenship, who had been such an encouragement to him outside the mess hall. Russell admired Blankenship. You could not help but respect him. Not many people knew that Blankenship had even made arrangements through the chaplain to have his tithe for his church taken out of his meager pay.

Further down the line, he could see Johnny Blanchard, Cliff Maughan, Panelo "Russian" Lozensky, and, all the way in the back, Sgt. Johnny Ray, who would be the last man out. Russell smiled when he made eye contact with Lozensky. Russell had sold him a $30 watch for $5 down; the rest to be paid later. Survival confidence was high.

Up forward were H. T. Bryant, Laddie Tlapa, Richard White, John Steele, Alfred von Hallsbeck, and Penrose Sherer next to Lt. Cadish. There were also a couple of new men, recently assigned, whom he did not know.

The C-47 revved its engines and slowly taxied forward, first turning one way, and then another. With each turn of the plane, Russell could see different scenes out of the door. First there was the fields, and then other taxiing aircraft, and then the cheering people, and finally a glimpse of other aircraft taking off, their invasion stripes clear against the gray skies.

It was 2300 as the aircraft began taking off, and two at a time, they lifted into the air. In all, seventy-one aircraft took off with the 2nd and

3rd Battalions of the 505th Regiment. Simultaneously, forty-seven more aircraft took off from neighboring Spanhoe Field with the rest of the regiment. The aircraft flew in a long formation to cross the channel.[8]

As they leveled off, there was some singing, but then the men quieted down, and Ken Russell fell asleep. His thoughts as he dozed off were not of worry. He'd never been in combat like some of the men, who had jumped in Sicily. He was just a boy, seventeen, and he remembered that this was graduation night for his class back in Tennessee. He wondered about them.

It didn't seem like he had been asleep for long, when he was awakened by a banging sound. He looked at his watch. It was after 0100, and they were approaching the coast of France. The banging sound was the sound of flak, fired from German positions on the Jersey and Guernsey Islands, hitting the aircraft.

Ken Russell sat up as tall as he could and looked out of the round window opposite him. It seemed that a fireworks show was on, with streaks of every color ascending from the ground. Again there was the sound as if someone were throwing rocks against the plane.

The C-47 made a left-hand turn, and Lt. Cadish's voice boomed over the outside sounds. "Stand up, and hook up!" Behind him, Russell could see that the red light had come on.

Fifteen bodies struggled to their feet and hands reached up and felt the wire above their heads and snapped the D-rings onto it. Fifteen metallic snaps rippled down the line, and each man turned to face forward, sandwiched between two others. They shifted their weight for position and held the nylon straps in their right hands, unconsciously tugging on them to assure that every ring was hooked.

"Count off for equipment check," came the next command, and all the way in the back of the plane, Sgt. Ray called out, "Fifteen, okay." That was followed by, "Fourteen, okay," "Thirteen, okay."

The count moved down the line. "Nine, okay," Russell shouted, and in seconds he could hear, "One, okay."

He ran over the sand table in his head. The drop zone would be easy to see, they had been told. It was bordered by the Merderet River to the west and the main road coming from Ste. Mere Eglise to the east, both prominent landmarks.[9]

Just outside, Russell could see a pattern of tracers floating up to him. They seemed to be moving in slow motion and were beautiful and hypnotizing. One of the floating streamers erupted into a white cluster just below the window, and the C-47 lurched from the concussion. High-pitched snaps coincided with the appearance of tiny holes in the floor beneath his feet.

They hurtled through space in their flimsy C-47 aircraft, packed like sardines waiting to jump into France as the spearhead of the invasion.

German ground fire searched for them, and twice, off to the left, bright explosions lit the sky. He prayed for the red light by the door to turn green so they could jump. Anything to get out of this flying death trap. He pushed up hard against the man in front of him.

The light turned green, and Lt. Cadish stood in the door, and jumped out. Someone shouted, "Here we go," and the packed line inched forward in a little hop-step motion so no gaps would develop between any of the men that would translate into hundreds of yards on the ground. Russell's heart pounded in his chest as he moved closer to the door, and then he watched the man in front of him go out, and he was right on his heels. The noise of the plane was suddenly replaced with absolute quiet as he tumbled into blackness.

The opening jolt of his chute hoisted him upright, and he looked around, fully expecting to see the familiar landmarks, but all he saw was the colorful streamers coming up to him. He thought that the whole German Army must be firing at him, and he tried to hide behind his reserve chute. Little tugs on the chute told him that rounds were piercing his canopy, and he looked up to see tracers making holes through the nylon above him. Every time a bullet hit, it felt as if it slowed his rate of descent.

His next thought was that he seemed to be too high. They were supposed to exit at about 300 feet, but he estimated that they had jumped at closer to 700 feet. For the first time, he looked past the tracers and saw that he was coming down in an area where there was a building on fire. The light from the fire lit the whole landing area. Next to the fire was, unmistakably, the most prominent building in Ste. Mere Eglise. He remembered it well from the sand tables: the church, towering above the landscape, and its bell was pealing loudly.

His stick had not been dropped on the outskirts of the village, as had been planned. They had jumped right over the town, and Russell could now see small figures below, running back and forth trying to fight the fire. He quickly calculated that his whole group would land right in the town square. God, they'd be sitting ducks.

He pulled on his parachute risers and, for the first time, searched the sky around him. He could see two other jumpers, their parachutes reflecting white in the glow from the light of the fire. He had no idea who they were as they drifted down with him. His eyes riveted back on the fire, and he now could see that there was a bucket brigade trying to douse the fire, which was raging out of control. German soldiers in the square were firing their rifles upward at the descending targets. A bullet came up and grazed the back of his hand.

His fixation on the fire was suddenly jolted by the sound of an enormous explosion. He looked to his right, toward the sound, and was horrified to see an empty parachute lazily floating down with no one in the harness. The canopy had started to collapse since there was no weight to pull on it. Russell had just seen the man a few seconds before and, in the time it took him to turn back, the man was gone. Had ground fire detonated his Gammon grenade?

Now there was only one jumper to be seen, and he was much lower than Russell. Again the young trooper's eyes went back to the fire, and it seemed that his chute was being inexorably drawn toward the flame. The air rushing to feed the blaze seemed to be pulling him ever closer. He pulled on his risers, trying to change his direction, but his course did not change.

The multicolored tracers continued to arch skyward, but now they were farther away from him, directed more toward the edges of town. He could see large flashes from the barrels of the flak guns ringing the village.

He was now much lower, and he again looked for the other jumper. At first he couldn't see him, but in a moment he saw the billowed top of his chute almost directly below him. Russell could see that the man was headed directly for the burning building. He watched him twist in his harness in a last attempt to avoid the flames, and

Russell tried to look away, but his eyes were fixed on the doomed trooper. The flames engulfed him as he sailed into the inferno, and Russell heard one horrifying scream—just one, and then nothing else. Despite the pounding of the antiaircraft guns, after the scream the only sound that Russell was aware of was the constantly ringing bell.

Ken Russell spiraled down to whatever fate awaited him. He again looked around, but he was now alone in the sky. A quick check of the fire encouraged him that he would not be sucked into it. He seemed to be sailing away from the blaze, but realized that he would impact on the towering church itself.

There was no avoiding it despite his frantic tugging on his risers. He hit the steep slated roof hard and slid down, cutting and scraping himself on the sharp shingles. He had one quick look and saw that his bouncing body would be hurled off the precipice of the roof to the ground below. The fall would most likely kill him.

As he went over the edge, he braced himself for the impact, but was, instead, yanked to a halt, and dangled like a puppet on a string, 20 feet off the ground. The collision with the roof had knocked the wind out of him and it took a few seconds to gather his wits, but when he did, he could see that he was snagged on the top of the church.

Looking up, he saw that his chute had snagged on a protrusion from the belfry. In the flickering light of the fire, it looked like a gargoyle; there was one on each corner of the belfry, and he was shocked to see that another paratrooper was snagged on an adjacent gargoyle. This man, however, had tangled himself on a much shorter tether. His lines had fouled so that he hung only a few feet below the gargoyle, a full 20 feet above Russell. The man made no movements, and swung lifelessly like a pendulum in the night. His head hung on his chest, and his arms swung limply at his side.

Russell's mind worked furiously. He could only think of cutting himself down, but that created a problem in itself. If he cut the lines supporting him, he faced a nasty two-story drop. It would be like sawing himself off the limb of a tree. But to remain hanging on the church like a side of beef was to invite target practice from the Germans.

He struggled for his knife, which was strapped in its sheath to his boot, but he could hardly reach it. In several tries he only succeeded in brushing his hand against the handle, and then his efforts were inter-rupted by the sound of boots scraping on the roof as Sgt. John Ray brushed the roof and landed on the ground next to the church. His chute collapsed in a pile next to him.

Just as Sgt. Ray struggled to get to his feet, Russell saw a German soldier coming around the corner of the church with his eyes fixed on the two troopers hanging on the belfry. His rifle was already being raised to his shoulder, and Russell had no illusions about his intentions. He would be killed, never having set foot on French soil.

The German soldier saw Sgt. Ray on the ground and immediately shot him in the stomach. Ray collapsed where he was. Then he turned his attention to the easier targets and aimed toward Russell, who could only draw up his feet and hold his reserve chute in front on him. As the German sighted in, Russell saw that Ray had struggled to his knees and was holding his .45 pistol, aimed at the German.

There was one loud crack, and the German soldier crumpled to the earth. Ray again pitched forward to the ground, and Russell again sought his elusive knife. Finally he had it in his hand and sawed the risers. Ken Russell crashed to the ground in a heap when his last riser was cut and, despite his two-story drop, he was up shedding his har-ness and getting his rifle from his pack. He then crawled over to Sgt. Ray, but Ray was already unconscious and breathing his last. He looked up at the lifeless body still on the belfry, and then moved away from his landing spot. More Germans must surely be close at hand, he thought.

His first attempt to leave the area brought him to the front of the church, in the courtyard, on the other side from where he landed. There was some sort of little monument there, and he crouched behind it. The fire lit the square as if it were daylight, and the enemy soon discovered the small figure crouching behind the monument and un-leashed a volley of fire at him. Russell retreated again to behind the church, and then ran across the street toward a grove of trees. Bullets followed on his heels.

He worked his way through the trees and toward the outskirts of the town. The further he went, the louder became the sound of flak guns firing. Planes were still flying overhead, dropping paratroopers, and the ground gunners kept up a steady volume of fire.

In front of him, he could see the flashes from one of the guns and worked his way forward until he could see the gun and the crew. His heart was pounding as he caught sight of the enemy. Mechanically, he reached for the weapon that he knew could handle this gun that was firing at and killing his fellow troopers. He found his Gammon grenade, raised himself on one knee, and threw it into the pit. It detonated against the gun; the jarring explosion blocked his ears.

Once again Russell was on the move. Fearing Germans would follow the sound of the explosion, he reversed course back toward Ste. Mere Eglise. At a gravel road, he paused and stepped back into the shadows at the sound of movement coming down the road. Two Germans on bicycles approached, and Russell handled them both with his rifle.

He moved into the underbrush near a hedgerow and sat down. He felt so alone. From the time he had jumped, he had seen only four men who were friendly: the man who was blown out of his chute, the one in the fire, Sgt. Ray, who was now dead, and the other trooper on the belfry. He was alone and very frightened and he sat breathing heavily in the dark.

He froze when he saw a shadow moving close by him, and he snapped his cricket, a small signaling device that clicks when pressed, while he held a grenade handy. A return snap was the most wonderful sound he had ever heard, and for the first time he was paired up with another friendly, a man from the 101st Airborne who was as lost as he.

When Russell asked if he knew where he was, he answered, "No."

"I don't know either," Russell said. "We'll have to find someone who does."[10]

The two-man team moved along the hedgerow and came upon another 82nd man, this one with a broken leg. Several others joined up. With each new addition, Russell's confidence soared, and finally someone asked the inevitable question.

"Well, what are we going to do?" Russell said that they had to get back to town.[11]

The small group worked their way back to Ste. Mere Eglise, just as the sky began to turn gray with the approaching day. In town, it seemed very quiet. Many of the Germans had obviously pulled back or had at least gotten out of the main part of town.

As Russell and one of the other men moved down the street, they turned a corner and ran into one of the men from Russell's stick. He was being led at gunpoint by a German officer walking behind him. It was Cliff Maughan. When Maughan saw the two friendly faces, he simply turned to the German officer and told him to give him his gun, so they could trade places and the German could now walk in front.

Maughan told them the details of his jump, and how he had landed on the roof of a house where this German officer was living with a French girl, and he ended up hanging in his harness in front of the window. The German dragged him inside, and then locked him in a shed. He was being moved when they ran into Russell.

The small band of troopers became larger, and finally a whole company moved into town and raised the flag over the mayor's office. Ken Russell became part of the force to hold the town. It was then that he saw what happened to the rest of his stick, which had landed on top of the square.

In the trees across the street from the church was Charles Blankenship, still in his harness, hanging from the limbs. The man who had promised that Russell would survive with him was dead. John Blanchard, who had landed close by, had cut himself out of his own tree and, in his panic, had cut off one of his fingers without realizing it.

Around the corner, down the street from the church square, were three telephone poles. Laddie Tlapa, H. T. Bryant, and Lt. Cadish hung from them as if crucified. Penrose Sherer was also found dead in a tree. The trooper who had hung from the belfry with Russell was no longer there, and Russell found his own parachute was now in front of the church. A large square section of the nylon had been removed. No doubt some French lady, having endured the many years of war, found a good use for it.

Richard White had survived, but missing were John Steele, Panelo

Lozensky, and Alfred von Hallsbeck. Someone said that they thought it was von Hallsbeck who had landed in the fire.

Twice that day, the Germans counterattacked to try to regain Ste. Mere Eglise. As evening came, young Ken Russell was part of the small force of paratroopers clinging to the strategic French town that yesterday had only been an obscure name on the French map.

For his action on D-Day, Ken Russell was awarded the Bronze Star. He would later fight in Holland at the Nijmegan Bridge, where he was again wounded and returned home.

Several days after the jump into Ste. Mere Eglise, friendly forces recovered Panelo "Russian" Lozensky, who had been wounded and captured. The Germans had taken the watch for which he'd given Russell $5 down. Russell never saw the other $25.

John Steele had been the trooper hanging from the belfry with Russell. He'd been shot in the foot and played possum until he was finally hauled into the belfry by some Germans and taken prisoner. As the Allies drove toward Cherbourg, they overran the area where Steele was being held. Steele was forever immortalized by the actor Red Buttons, who played his part in the motion picture *The Longest Day*. Of the fifteen men who had jumped from the C-47 over Ste. Mere Eglise only six survived, and those survivors had all been wounded.

At 0400, almost three hours after Ken Russell had hung on the belfry of the church at Ste. Mere Eglise, the anxious eyes of American Rangers tried to peer through the dark and gloom from their positions along the rail of the British transport HMS *Amsterdam*. The vessel had stopped in the rough waters of the English Channel to disgorge its human cargo into the assault landing craft bouncing alongside.

The men of the 2nd Ranger Battalion were anxious to leave the vessel that had been their cramped home for the last five days. They had all trained for months for their special mission and, now that the time was at hand, they brimmed with confidence.

As the loudspeaker barked, "Rangers, man your craft," 1stSgt. Leonard G. Lomell, the platoon commander of the 2nd Platoon of

Company D, loaded his team into LCA 668. The davits were swung outboard, and the boat was lowered into the choppy waters. Other Rangers performed this same debarkation procedure from two sister transports, HMS *Ben Machree* and *Prince Charles,* and soon the entire Ranger force was in the water.[12]

It had been five months since the idea of this special assault had been explained to the Ranger commander, Col. James Rudder. In January 1944, he had been called to Gen. Eisenhower's headquarters in London and had been escorted into a second-floor room shrouded in blackout drapes.

The gist of the briefing, which left Col. Rudder's mouth agape, was the necessity of neutralizing a small piece of land along the Normandy coast. If they failed, the entire operation in the American invasion area at Omaha and Utah Beaches would be thwarted.

There was an 18-mile gap between Omaha and Utah and, in that space, 4 miles west of Omaha, the Germans had constructed a fortified position on the high ground overlooking the English Channel at the prominence called Pointe du Hoc. The fortified position was centered around six 155mm coastal guns with a range of 25,000 yards.[13]

Pointe du Hoc was an ominous piece of land, named long ago when Gaul was part of the Roman Empire. Literally translated as "this" point, strategically it was "the" point. Of all the objectives assigned to the Allied forces on D-Day, both at the beaches and in the paratroop drop zones, the guns of Pointe du Hoc, which threatened two of the five beaches on which the entire American sector would land, ranked near the top in the order of importance.

As the D-Day plan developed, evidence of the critical importance of Pointe du Hoc to the Allies could be found in the priority for neutralizing fires: The brain trust usually had Pointe du Hoc at the top of their list. The heavier naval ships, including battleships, were to attack eighteen targets. Of those eighteen, Pointe du Hoc was number one. Pointe du Hoc would receive maximum attention in the aerial support plan also. Three of the four phases of the air support plan, which included bombardments by night heavy bombers, night medium bombers, and daylight heavy bombers, all listed Pointe du Hoc as their top priority.[14] To the planners of Operation Overlord, Pointe du Hoc was critical to success. Failure elsewhere might be overcome, but failure at "the" point could spell disaster.

The point jutted out into the English Channel and provided an elevated vantage point where the guns could deliver beaten fire on the Omaha and Utah invasion beaches as well as the transport and supply areas at sea. If the Germans could defeat the American attacks at Omaha and Utah Beaches, they could very well stop the entire Normandy invasion and consign Gen. Eisenhower and his Operation Overlord to the history of failed attacks.[15]

Looking at the imposing 100-foot-high cliffs, an intelligence officer remarked, "It can't be done. Three old women with brooms could keep the Rangers from climbing that cliff."[16] Even Gen. Omar Bradley, who was the Commanding General of First U.S. Army, had to admit that the task of knocking out Pointe du Hoc was the toughest of any task assigned on D-Day. In preparing for the mission, the Rangers had endured rigorous training on the cliff of the Isle of Wight. They had practiced cliff scaling, using mortar-propelled grapnels designed by British commandos.[17]

Intelligence showed that approximately two hundred German soldiers of the 2nd Battery, 832 Army Coastal Battalion would be the defenders of the Pointe.[18] Against this force, the Americans would send 225 Rangers of the 2nd Ranger Battalion.

The scheme was to land Companies D, E, and F in a cliff-scaling attack. Companies E and F would attack the east side of the Pointe, while Company D attacked the west side.

Pending success of this daring attack, Companies A and B, along with the entire 5th Ranger Battalion, would mark time offshore, awaiting a signal that the Pointe had been taken. When that signal was received, the whole Ranger force would follow in at the Pointe and scale the cliffs as reinforcements. If the signal was not received, the rest of the Ranger force would land at Omaha Beach and attack the Pointe from the rear.[19]

First Sgt. Len Lomell's LCA 668 lurched through the dark waters of the English Channel toward Pointe du Hoc. Lomell had become a Ranger through a series of strange events. After Pearl Harbor, the twenty-one-year-old college graduate wanted to go to one of the service

academies. But in applying, he was required to produce a birth certificate, and he could not. He discovered that he had been adopted, and
retained a lawyer to get a proper birth certificate for him. In the mean-
time, the draft board caught up to him, and he found himself a member
of the 76th Division, the Liberty Bell Division, where he rose to the
rank of platoon sergeant.

Lomell's adoptive parents were a wonderful elderly couple, and Len
had the responsibility to provide for them, and when the offer to join
the Rangers came to him, the offer also included promotion to the rank
of 1st sergeant, which paid more money than he made as a platoon
sergeant in the 76th Division.

From the first day of his association with 2nd Ranger Battalion, he
had been the 1st sergeant of Company D and was still the 1st sergeant
as he rode in the choppy seas toward Normandy, but on this day, he
was also the acting platoon commander of the 2nd Platoon.

Lomell looked over the sides at the waves. They seemed to be at
eye level, often crashing over the low-riding LCA. Already the mission
was not going according to plan. Shortly after the small flotilla of ten
LCAs had pulled away from the transports, one of the supply boats
had been swamped in the high seas and sank.

Now, there were eight more miles to the invisible shore, and Lomell
noticed that the craft carrying his company commander and another
platoon commander was falling behind the rest. The farther they went,
the farther the other craft fell behind. Water poured in over the sides,
and, despite heroic bailing efforts from the rangers inside, this craft,
too, faltered in the seas and sank.

Lomell suddenly realized that his Company D was now minus its
company commander and one of its platoons. One-third of the sixty-
five-man force of Company D was out of action without having had
any contact with the enemy. There was no stopping for survivors. The
nine remaining LCAs plowed on in a double column. The men were
seasick, and water poured over the gunwales; the Rangers were forced
to bail with their helmets in an effort to keep the boats afloat.

Finally land appeared through the dark, gray morning. The point
was directly in front of them, and the boat commanders began thinking
about the maneuver that would bring them to the base of the cliff for

the assault. First Sgt. Lomell looked to the west to see if he could make out his landing area, but the shoreline was not familiar, and its unfamiliarity made him realize that the land in front of them was not Pointe du Hoc.

Col. Rudder, in the lead boat, also realized the error and pointed it out to his coxswain, who turned the craft to the right. The other boats followed in column, and the small flotilla began a run parallel to the Normandy coast, staying 200 yards offshore. Lomell calculated that their objective was several miles to the west.[20]

Each of the LCAs was equipped with six rocket mounts positioned on either side of the bow, midships, and stern. Connected to the bottom of the rockets were ropes, and two types of rope ladders.[21] On top of the rockets were four- and six-pointed grapnel hooks. The rockets were to be fired, mortar-style, at a high angle, carrying the ropes in an arch to the top of the cliff. It was hoped the grapnels would snag barbed wire or some other obstacle and be pulled tight to allow the Rangers to begin their vertical assault.

The lightly equipped Rangers watched the imposing cliffs of Pointe du Hoc slowly take shape as they approached from the east. Each Ranger company was limited to grenades and rifles. Their heaviest weapons were four BARs and two mortars. Most of the men only had a pistol or rifle and two hand grenades. Each company also had ten thermite grenades distributed among its men.[22] Company D lost several grenades with the boat that sank, and all of their packs and extra equipment were at the bottom of the English Channel.

The ominous Pointe was directly ahead. Company D was supposed to land on the west side of the Pointe, but that had presumed an approach that would have hit the Pointe head-on. Their axis of approach was now from the east, parallel to the shore, and to break off and try to round the Pointe to the other side would have wasted more time and would have made Company D's attack separate from the other companies'.

Lomell decided to jam the remaining two boats of Company D between the landing spots of Companies E and F. As the first boats approached to within 35 yards of the cliffs, they fired their rockets with the grapnel hooks. All six of the ropes of LCA 861 and 888 fell short, and LCA 862 fared little better, with only one of six finding the top of the cliffs. But their luck improved as the succeeding six boats managed to put a variety of twenty-one ropes and ladders over the top.[23]

LCA 668, with 1stSgt. Len Lomell, ground onto the shale around 0730. The boat was short of the narrow strip of beach because of rocks that had fallen from the cliffs as a result of the shore and aerial bombardments. The ramp went down, and the twenty-two Rangers swam the last few feet to dry land.

Lomell rushed off the ramp and quickly became the first casualty as an enemy bullet ripped into the fleshy part of his side. It stung but did not put him down, and, with his team, he rushed to the cliffs and grabbed the first rope he saw.

In moments his team was up and rolled over the top onto the enemy-held plateau. The first thing he saw was not the enemy but a wounded Ranger officer whose hand had been almost shot away. There was no time to tend the wounded, and Lomell just told him to hold on and a medic would come later.

Rangers on the right and left of him were moving out in twos and threes, but Lomell ordered his men forward in a platoon rush. Their objective was gun emplacements 4, 5, and 6. The men charged hard and low, like football linemen breaking through the defense. Their rush took them into one shell crater and out to the next as soon as there was a break in the fire. The platoon rushed toward the guns as fast as their legs and enemy fire would allow.

Len Lomell rushed forward in this group, thinking, Find the guns, find the guns! He repeated it over and over to himself. The whole ground looked different from what he had memorized from the maps and sand tables. It was hard to get his bearings, but the platoon quickly came upon the smashed casemates of what should have been gun 4. Nothing was there. The positions that were supposed to house guns 5 and 6 were also bombed and smashed. There was no sign of any guns.

Lomell halted for a moment, breathing heavily. They must be somewhere, he thought. As he looked at the smashed casemates, he could understand why the enemy might have moved the guns. They had certainly not been destroyed on the Pointe.

The Rangers paused to see if they could hear the big guns. If they were nearby, they should be firing and would be heard, but after several moments they heard no sound other than the rattle of small-arms fire all across the area of Pointe du Hoc.

There was no time to stop and lament the absence of the big guns, and Lomell ordered his men toward their second objective, the road that ran behind Pointe du Hoc and connected Omaha Beach to Utah Beach. As they moved, there was sporadic mortar fire, but the 2nd Platoon pushed on. German soldiers popped in and out of fighting holes as the platoon swept on.

Directly behind the Pointe, along the road leading to the highway, was the billeting area for the German defensive force. As Lomell's force rushed down the road, the surprised Germans came out in various stages of undress and were sent scurrying back inside by the attacking Rangers. Nor did the Rangers stop to engage them in firefights. Quick bursts of fire sent the enemy to cover, and the Rangers raced straight for the highway.

When they reached the coast road, Lomell counted heads and discovered that he only had a dozen men out of his starting force. With that small force, he started to set up his roadblock and cut the communications on telephone poles along the road. It was barely 0800. Their second objective was secured. Lomell went a short way down the coast road, in the direction of Utah Beach; they were to interdict any traffic heading for Omaha Beach.

Scarcely had they begun to set up their position when they heard a loud clanking and noise as if a patrol were approaching from their rear, from the direction of Omaha Beach. The men took up positions, concealed in the brush of the ditch along the side of the road. In moments, the source of the clanking and noise came into view.

A German patrol of almost fifty men came marching along, noisily chattering. They were loaded with heavy weapons, mortars, and machine guns, and their equipment clanged together as they marched. They had no idea that there could possibly be Allied soldiers nearby.

The Rangers lay low in their ditch, and Lomell let the Germans pass. He was not eager to take on a heavily armed patrol, and besides, his orders said to stop anything going toward Omaha Beach; this patrol was going *away* from that direction.

The patrol went by, and the Rangers watched it turn into a field, heading away from the coast. When they were out of sight, the road-block was completed.

Having secured their position, Lomell and Sgt. Jack Kuhn began a two-man patrol. A short way from the roadblock was a small sunken road that ran between two hedgerows. There were no tracks on the dirt road, but, to Lomell and Kuhn, it looked as if the road had been used. It most likely had been used for farm wagons or equipment, which, over the years, had worn down the earth. But since the hedgerows afforded them concealment, the two sergeants proceeded cautiously down the rutted road.

Two hundred yards down the road, Lomell saw a small draw to the side, and there was camouflage covering it. The hedgerow was between him and what was being camouflaged, so he struggled up the hedgerow and peeked over the top, and could not believe his eyes.

There were the guns, all sitting in the proper firing positions, ammunition piled neatly, and everything at the ready. From his vantage point, he could see that the guns were aimed not at Omaha Beach, but at Utah Beach.

Quickly scanning the scene, Lomell saw that no one was manning the guns, but there was a group of soldiers, almost 100 yards away, in the corner of the field. There was a vehicle, and it looked like an officer was talking to the men. Lomell saw he had a golden opportunity. "Cover me, Jack, I'm going in there to destroy them."[24]

Gathering his own and Sgt. Kuhn's thermite grenades, he slipped through the hedgerow to the other side and quietly placed one grenade into the elevating and traversing mechanism of the closest gun, and repeated the procedure on the next gun. Pulling the pins, the grenades silently burned through the steel of the mechanisms. For good measure, Lomell smashed the sights.

Back through the hedgerow, he signaled for Kuhn to head back for the road, and the two men ran as fast as they could to the roadblock. Breathlessly, they gathered the remaining thermites from the rest of the Rangers and returned to the guns.

Again Kuhn stood guard while Lomell slipped through the hedgerow. He stuffed the remaining grenades in the mechanisms of the other guns and scrambled back to Kuhn. He could hear Kuhn whispering for him to hurry, and in just a few moments was back with him. As he slipped down the embankment and started to run, the whole place blew up. The sky darkened, and debris rained down on them.

The two men got up and ran for the roadblock. They figured that it had been a short round from *Texas,* which was firing in support of them. Much later they found out that the "short round" was, in fact, the detonation of the ammo dump, courtesy of another Ranger patrol led by Sgt. Frank Rupinski of Company E. Rupinski's patrol had found the main dump, and blown it.[25]

When Lomell and Kuhn returned to the roadblock, it was almost 0830. They were ecstatic. They had accomplished the two missions assigned to the Rangers: The guns were out of action, and the roadblock had been set.

Lomell asked for two volunteers, and Harry Fate and Gordon Luning stepped forward. They were to go by separate ways to the command post and inform Col. Rudder that the guns had been knocked out and the mission accomplished. The Rangers had become the first American unit to accomplish their mission on D-Day.

For their roles in the destruction of the guns of Pointe du Hoc, the Army decorated sergeants Len Lomell and Jack Kuhn. Lomell received the Distinguished Service Cross, and Kuhn received the Silver Star.

Lomell received a battlefield commission in October 1944 and would fight on at Huertgen Forest and in the Battle of the Bulge. In these battles, he was wounded three times and eventually medically discharged as disabled after the war in 1945.

But the action of Lomell and his 2nd Platoon on D-Day, especially the destruction of the 155mm guns, remained an untold story for almost forty years. Despite the fact that Lomell had been decorated for his action, that his citation was available for inspection, and that the guns themselves remained in their "welded" positions, in the same location until the end of the war, no one seemed to get the story straight.

Gen. Omar Bradley, whose memoirs were published in 1951 and

who had the disquieting habit of calling the place "Pointe du Hoe," came close. He had it that a Ranger patrol had killed the gun crews and destroyed the guns by blowing the breaches.[26] Any research on D-Day would certainly lead the researcher to Bradley's memoirs, and to his mention of the guns, so it is hard to understand why the story remained a mystery for so long, but it did.

The excellent book by Cornelius Ryan, *The Longest Day,* and the movie by the same name, also missed the story. Valiant Rangers scaled the Pointe, and the guns were not there. End of story. As the years went by, Lomell read one account after another that described the attack on the Pointe and its missing guns as "a cruel joke," "a suicidal mission," "an unnecessary undertaking," or "a valiant effort made in vain." No one ever came to interview him.[27]

Finally, in 1979, author Ronald Lane took the readers past the initial discovery of the missing guns. My own research at the Eisenhower Center led me to Len Lomell, and he gave me extensive interviews. His story is told in *Voices of D-Day,* and in Stephen Ambrose's *D-Day, June 6, 1944.* It is one of the great success stories of June 6, 1944.

Crew of plane 13. Bob Bourgeois on the far right.

Bob Bourgeois, fourth one to the left, after bailing out over China, shown with his Chinese guide, third from the right (also note man standing second to the right, with the jacket of a captured Japanese soldier).

F6F Hellcat of VF 1, preparing to take off from Yorktown on July 19-20, 1944, during Marianas Turkey Shoot. Note high hat near cockpit.

Wrecked TBF of Ensign Albert Earnest on Midway Island.

June 1942 aboard Hornet. George Gay is center of first row.

Flight Deck on Yorktown in July 1944. VF 1 "Highhatters".

Lt. Jack Bolt.

Blacksheep Squadron VMF 214 in Solomon Islands. Aircraft is Corsair, 1943.

PFC Joseph Herberski (right) and PFC James C. Russell (center).

Private Ken Russell.

1st Sgt. Leonard G. Lomell, 1943.

Vf-1 pilots prepare to leave the ready room to join in the Marianas Turkey Shoot, June 19, 1944. Abe Abramson in the foreground, George Staeheli and Ralph Wines stand, and Mad Dog Tomme in the background.

Lt. Lyle Bouck, 1945.

Private Jay Rebstock, age 19.

SIX

THE BATTLE OF THE PHILIPPINE SEA

June 19–20, 1944

Lt.(j.g.) Arthur Abramson, USN

Arthur Abramson was in the second grade in New Orleans in 1929. After two years of what he deemed confinement in a school he hated, he decided to run away to protest that he had been forced to go to school against his will. But running away, as a second-grader, was not for the faint of heart. Talking about it was one thing, but doing it required great bravery and determination. Seven-year-old Arthur Abramson knew he had both.

After morning formation one day, the teacher picked up the hand-bell and rang it loud and long. That was the signal to the rest of the students that the singing of "America the Beautiful" was over, as was the Pledge of Allegiance, and the school day should commence with a march to the classrooms. To young Arthur, that ringing bell was the signal to bolt for the front door and freedom on the other side. He would not spend one more day in this accursed place.

He ran as fast as his legs could carry him and hit the door in stride, only to have his way temporarily blocked by some meddlesome teachers intent on barring his freedom. He would have none of that. Small fists flailed away, making contact with some beefy bosoms of teachers unlucky enough to try and stop him. Soon he was free and in full flight for home, some four blocks distant.

Unfortunately, the first person he met on this day of freedom was his father, who had returned home to retrieve something he had forgotten. Mr. Abramson scooped the running boy up as he entered the house and demanded an explanation. Arthur explained the whole situation to his dad, who did not seem to understand the great bravery his son had just displayed and unceremoniously packed him into the car to return him to school.

The teachers, especially the two who had tried to stop him from leaving, immediately concluded that Arthur was, in some way, mentally deficient, and placed him in the class with the mentally retarded. He spent the rest of the year cutting and pasting.

Fortunately, his dislike for school gave way to better habits. He finished high school at sixteen, and the next year Hitler invaded Poland. Arthur went to work, mostly as a gofer, for $25 a month. It was at that time that the service seemed very attractive, and he had a desire to one day be a Navy pilot. War was not in his mind, but flying was, and he was so enthralled with the prospect of it that he mentally planned a career as a naval pilot in the peacetime Navy.

In 1940, as he worked his way through two years of college at LSU, the government had introduced a program called Civilian Pilot Training (CPT) that would teach flying and eventually give the candidate a civilian license. Additionally, this government program issued aerial students a set of khaki coveralls with some LSU purple-and-gold wings. That uniform made Arthur feel "nine feet tall." He only had one change of clothes, so at every opportunity, he'd get into his khaki uniform and walk proudly across campus. The girls liked the uniform, and Arthur liked the girls.[1]

On the day that Pearl Harbor was bombed, Abramson and his friends gathered to discuss the situation, and like most other young Americans, they had an immediate reaction: Some said they were going to join the paratroopers, while others opted for the Navy.

Six months later, Arthur Abramson was in the Navy at the Naval Air Station in New Orleans as a seaman second class and, after opting for flight training, went to Pensacola, Florida, where he was commissioned as a Naval Aviator in January 1943. Advanced training took him to Chicago, and the freezing cold. In February he underwent carrier training on *Wolverine* in Lake Michigan. The training carrier was an old paddlewheel boat that had been converted to include a flat deck up top that was used to train young carrier pilots. Each hopeful pilot was required to make eight takeoffs and landings on it.

Training on *Wolverine* was unusual at best. To make these required landings, the aviators were once again placed in their advanced trainer aircraft, which they had used during earlier phases of their training. But these aircraft had no tail hook with which to catch the arresting wires on deck and stop the airplane.

Naval ingenuity, however, had solved that problem. A hook had been attached to a rope and run from the tail of the aircraft, up over the top of the tail assembly, to the cockpit, and inside the aircraft. To accomplish this, the cockpit had to be left open. This was not unusual as the cockpit was left open during training for safety purposes, but what was unusual was that the rope, with the hook, was in the cockpit. There was little place to put it and the pilot couldn't just hold it. It was cumbersome, and the pilot needed both hands to fly and land the aircraft. Usually it was just hung over some handles or an instrument knob that he wouldn't be using.

After takeoff, with the cockpit open in the frigid Chicago air, Abramson would circle the aircraft for the inevitable landing, and it was then that the young pilot would throw the hook out of the cockpit with the hope of engaging the arresting wires. The hook flapped in the wind behind the aircraft, and despite some anxious moments, worked pretty well.

But the hook was less of a problem to Abramson than the stabbing cold, with the wind whipping through the open cockpit. He had never been issued any winter clothes, so he and the rest of the pilots flew in the same khaki uniforms they had used in Florida. Later they would joke how it had been perfect training to deploy to the Pacific.[2]

• • •

One year later, dawn launch in the Philippine Sea on June 19, 1944, was no different than thousands of other carrier launches that had been conducted by ships of the U.S. Navy during the two and a half years of war in the Pacific since Pearl Harbor. On this day, the carrier *Yorktown* turned its bow into the wind along with the other three carriers of Task Group 58.1 and prepared to send its fighters and bombers into the sky. The mission today was to support the Marines who had invaded the twin islands of Saipan and Tinian three days earlier in an attempt to wrest control from the Japanese. Of the two islands, Saipan was the most heavily defended, and the strategic, 14-mile-long island in the Southern Marianas was defended by 32,000 determined Japanese soldiers who had proven themselves formidable foes.

Early progress reports of this landing indicated that the struggle would be as savage as had been the battle for Tarawa in November 1943. Twenty-thousand Marines and Army forces landed on June 15 on the western beaches the first day at Saipan and, by nightfall, more than 10 percent of the American invasion force had been killed or wounded.

By June 19, the two Marine divisions, with more grim casualty statistics, had joined up and began to swing toward the north, a move that they hoped would crack the Japanese defensive line and bring the campaign to an end. But there was still hard fighting ahead, which required support, particularly air support. Some of the aircraft from Task Group 58.1 were detailed for that mission.

Task Group 58.1, with its four carriers, four cruisers, and eleven destroyers, was only the tip of the enormous iceberg known as Task Force 58. This monstrous naval force was an armada of four carrier groups and one battleship group. The force counted fifteen carriers, seven battleships, twenty-one cruisers, sixty-nine destroyers, and 891 carrier aircraft.

The mission was to capture Saipan, Tinian, and Guam, as well as defend against any naval attacks from the newly formed Japanese naval force known as the Mobile Fleet. The Mobile Fleet was centered on nine carriers, five battleships, thirteen cruisers, twenty-eight destroyers, and 430 carrier aircraft. It had recently been sighted operating 300 miles to the west of Saipan.[3]

To Lt.(j.g.) Arthur Abramson, who sat in the cockpit of his F6F Hellcat on the rolling deck of *Yorktown,* this grand picture of opposing, maneuvering fleets was unknown. He was not concerned with grand strategy. The only thing that he knew was that the wind was whistling down the deck. The launch officer, known as Fly One, with his flag snapping in the breeze, had just given him the go, and he pushed the throttle full forward. It was now his job to get the 2,000-horsepower, 12,000-pound, armed-and-loaded Hellcat into the air. His mission that day was to bomb and strafe targets on the island of Guam and, like the hundred other combat missions he had flown since becoming a naval aviator with the fleet, that was all he needed to know.

There were thirty aircraft on the mission to Guam.[4] Once his mission was completed, his job was to bring his aircraft safely back to the carrier, be debriefed, and stand by for his next assignment.

Flying with Abramson were other aircraft from his own squadron, VF-1, and there were separate flights from the three other carriers of Task Group 58.1, *Belleau Wood, Bataan,* and *Hornet*. Both *Hornet* and *Yorktown* were named for the carriers sunk by the Japanese in an effort to confuse the enemy and possibly deny him the knowledge, and satisfaction, that the originals had sunk.

The missions assigned to the aircraft from Task Group 58.1 were varied. They included supporting the troops fighting on Saipan, bombing and strafing the enemy airfields at Rota and Guam to the southwest, and conducting air strikes to "soften up" Guam, which was next on the invasion list. The remaining aircraft, still on the carriers, provided carrier and task force defense.

After launching, Abramson flew close to the water to avoid radar detection as he began the 200-mile flight to the target area. He was twenty-two years old, but his youth belied his experience. He was a veteran of a hundred combat missions and was flying with the oldest and most prestigious fighter squadron in the Navy—the Highhatters of VF-1.

As the force flew to Guam, young Abramson studied his instrument panel and navigational data, and finally reviewed his target assignment. He carried 2,400 rounds of .50-caliber ammunition that would feed the six machine guns in his wings. Today, he also carried a 250-pound bomb under his right wing, which he hoped to deliver to a particular antiaircraft position at Agana, on the Orote Peninsula, on the western end of the island.

He would unleash the .50-caliber ammunition on the fuel and repair facilities on the Japanese airfield and, if lucky, on a Japanese Zero who might venture up to challenge the force. He had a score to settle with the Japanese and their Zeros.

It had been seventeen months since commissioning, and this combat mission to Guam was a long way from home, college, family, and the special girl he hoped to one day marry. Flying close to the water, Abramson watched the whitecaps pass rapidly beneath him. The war in the Pacific was a seducing war indeed. He had gazed out over the miles upon miles of open water, which was deep blue and spectacularly beautiful. He marveled at God's work in the breathtaking beauty of the cloud formations that jutted into the sky. It was hard to believe that a war was taking place. There were none of the signs of war one might see on land, no shattered buildings or bombed-out villages. There were no craters and twisted railroad tracks or burned vehicles pushed to the side of the road—lifeless relics of earlier battles. There were no fields with rows of white crosses interspersed with Stars of David. There was just water, the sun, and the crystal-clear majesty from 20,000 feet.

Even in aerial combat, he realized, the killing was sanitized. In a small, cylinder-shaped space rising from the water to 15,000 feet, aircraft would swirl and dive in a ballet of death. Planes and pilots plunged inside this cylinder, often to their flaming deaths, but when the dogfight was over, the area was again peaceful and serene—no broken aircraft or bodies littering the battlefield—just the Pacific Ocean in all its beauty.

Guam came into view, and Abramson rose to attack altitude and swung his Hellcat to approach the area of his target, easily identified by the Orote Peninsula and the town of Agana. As he had done so often before, he placed the fighter in a glide bomb run and lined up the area of the suspected antiaircraft position in his sights. At 425 knots, his right thumb pressed the red bomb-release button on the tip of the control stick.

The 250-pound bomb released, telegraphing its departure with a slight uplifting of the aircraft, and Abramson pulled out of his glide. He gained altitude and banked to the left, looking back for the explosion. A dirty cloud was all that he could see from the spot of the impacting bomb. His second, third, and fourth runs were strafing runs, and his .50-caliber wing guns shredded storage, maintenance, and fuel areas on the airfield. Fires sent black smoke into the air and some ground fire followed him as he pulled out of each run.

Other aircraft in the strike force engaged Japanese Zeros that challenged the attack, but those engagements were brief. Again, he had no opportunity to confront the accursed Zero aviators. Out of ammunition, and with just enough fuel to return home, he headed for the rendezvous point where his squadron would meet for the return flight to *Yorktown*.

What a difference this mission was compared to his first combat mission seven months earlier. He had entered the war zone on the small jeep-carrier *Nassau*, which had never been designed to handle the F6F Hellcat. It was so small that it looked like the training ship *Wolverine* on Lake Michigan. The only difference was that he didn't have to throw the hook out of the cockpit when he landed. Flying on the tiny carrier was nothing like being on the big fleet-carrier *Yorktown*.

Back then the squadron was inexperienced. They been told that their mission was to bomb and strafe Tarawa in support of the invasion. The puzzled pilots looked at each other and asked, "Where?" They scratched their heads as they opened their maps in the ready room and ran their fingers across the vast blue area, searching for the strange-sounding place. Some asked for a hint of where to look. When they were told that it was in the Gilbert Islands, that was even less help. "Where the hell is that?" they asked in one voice.[5]

They finally found the tiny speck that was Tarawa. In the days before the Marine invasion, the squadron flew bombing and strafing runs. The battle itself was a three-day slaughter. VF-1 provided air cover, but there were no Japanese aircraft to contest control of the skies. On D+1 they were pressed into service to deliver close air support for the embattled Marines pinned down by the resolute and unsurrendering enemy.

It was more of the same on D+2, and D+3; on D+5, the squadron was ordered to land on the newly captured airfield, even though the last remnants of the Japanese force were still fighting on one end of the island. If the young, unbelieving pilots of VF-1 had thought life on the jeep-carrier had left something to be desired, they were soon to discover that their new life on Tarawa would have them begging to return to *Nassau*.

On Thanksgiving Day, November 25, Arthur Abramson and VF-1 roared in on Tarawa and bounced down hard on the compacted coral runway. They were greeted like saving angels. Abramson had hardly brought his Hellcat to a stop when he was surrounded by over a hundred bedraggled Marines, cheering his arrival to the terrible island. The cheering Marines were soon flat on the ground as the whine of snipers' bullets zipped overhead, and Abramson found himself standing upright, alone. A bellowed order to get his "f——ing ass" down was quickly obeyed.

The following day, with part of the island still unsecured, he and another pilot went souvenir hunting. The first souvenirs were the ghastly remnants of bodies strewn all over in various stages of disfigurement. Their wandering brought them to the main blockhouse, which was piled three high with bloated corpses. The stench was overwhelming. There were no souvenirs, but the grisly task of scrubbing decomposing remains from their boots later left a lasting memory.

They had been assigned to the island because there were no Marine squadrons to call upon for close air support, and so VF-1 was it. Their original task was to provide air cover for Tarawa and to begin flying combat patrols to the north for the next leap forward into the Marshall Islands. They began flying monotonous four-plane patrols over the shattered island, day in and day out, never seeing one Japanese plane. In addition to monotony, their new enemies became dysentery and dengue fever. One by one they succumbed to the diseases, the result of exposed, unburied, rotting corpses in the tropical sun, and the blue-green flies that happily flitted everywhere. In death, these former Japanese soldiers were still inflicting casualties.

Life on Tarawa was devoid of redeeming qualities. Comfort was measured by new standards—comfort was keeping most of the swarm-

ing blue-green flies off your food and having your daily ration of dis-
tilled seawater flow into your canteen only slightly hot, and hoping that
the water intake was not too close to a decomposing Japanese body
bobbing in the lagoon.

To the parched and sunburned Marines on the island, this precious
water was swallowed, despite its awful taste, in long gulps to slake the
never-ending thirst. Happiness was dreaming of a long drink of iced
water, and imagining what a wonderful thing it would be.

But what started out as wishful thinking soon became a reality, and
the pilots of VF-1 found themselves the answer to those dreams. It
started slowly, first one Marine and then another. Soon there were long
lines of Marines, each with his one canteen, in a water-soaked cover,
waiting his turn to approach the pilots to have them hang it in the
fuselage for high flight: The cold of the high altitude chilled the water
to near freezing and, upon landing, the pilots were greeted by men
waiting to reclaim their iced water. It was only one step from heaven.

But there were few heavenly things about Tarawa, and sickness
and dysentery became a way of life. Sickness did not stop the necessity
to patrol; sick or not, each pilot flew his turns. The flesh melted off
their bones. After two months, Arthur Abramson's 155-pound frame
had shrunk to 123 pounds. The parachute riggers would tease him and
say, "Mr. Abramson, you'd better never jump out of your plane, because
you don't have enough meat on your butt to deploy the chute."

When the Army took the nearby island of Makin, VF-1 started to
fly north, escorting bombers to the next island, and then to the one
after that. Each one had an equally unfamiliar name: Kwajalien, Eni-
wetok, Wotje, Mili, Maloelap, and Jaluit. The dysentery and dengue
fever never let up, nor did the combat patrols. Oh, for the clean sheets
and tablecloths aboard ships, especially the jeep-carriers, instead of the
rot of Tarawa.

The daily scene at the flight line bore a contorted resemblance to
a dusty bar in an Old West saloon, but instead of a bartender serving
whiskey in shot glasses to red-eyed, worn-out trail hands, two corpsmen
served the exhausted fliers shots of medicine in paper cups: paregoric
and bismuth, ladled from gallon jugs set up on a makeshift table. Like

the trail hands, the pilots were red-eyed and gaunt-faced, and tossed down a couple of jiggers, hoping the magic elixir would quell their raging intestines.

It usually didn't work, but like punch-drunk fighters, they lined up every morning, tossed the liquid down, staggered to the aircraft, and flew the daily missions. If, during the flight, the pilot suffered an attack of gut-wrenching cramps, his only relief was in his seat. It was not uncommon during a flight to see the cockpit open and the pilot's shorts come flying out.

As the weeks and months went by, each man finally accepted his fate, the realization that he would spend the rest of the war not as a glorious, carrier fighter pilot on a majestic ship, but as wasted warrior in a hellhole named Tarawa.[6]

On one of the high-cover missions protecting Army bombers in the lower reaches of the Marshall Islands, Lt. Abramson finally got his first encounter with a Japanese Zero. It was not at all like he expected.

He was flying as wingman for the squadron executive officer, who did not possess great fighter-pilot skills and who rode herd over the junior officers as if they were recruits. On this mission, with no warning, young Abramson saw the exec's external fuel tank fall away, which is the maneuver when going into combat. Immediately he bent down and reached for the release of his own tank, but when he looked back up, he was alone. No sign of the exec.

He had no idea of even where to look, so he continued his patrol, on which he was to provide cover at 25,000 feet. Suddenly two Japanese Zeros came across his front from his right as he flew in a left turn. They were at least 2,000 feet above him, which put his Hellcat in a very disadvantageous position. No one had ever told him what to do in a situation when he faced the enemy alone. He thought for an instant, and then did what he'd been trained to do in the face of the enemy. He attacked.

His attack forced him to try to climb the additional 2,000 feet while still continuing his turn, and engage the speeding enemy in a full-deflection shot. His other option was to attempt to get behind for a zero-deflection shot. Despite his bravery and resolve, the maneuver he was attempting was impossible. He was also too green to recognize that the Jap planes were decoys, flying this tempting pattern in the hope of luring an American airplane into attempting his exact maneuver. Abramson took the bait.

As he began firing in his steep climb, his aircraft began to shudder, and he knew instantly that he was shot. Two other Zeros zoomed down on him from a high dive. Their 20mm cannon fire smashed his right aileron and he felt the stick between his knees go dead. The plane did not respond to his command. He looked in the rear mirror and the tail seemed okay, but a quick look to the right revealed a soccer ball–size hole in the wing.

With the aileron shot away, the plane went into a deep spiral, and the Zeros followed, pouring cannon fire into the stricken Hellcat. Abramson placed both feet on the right rudder and pulled the stick all the way back in an attempt to get the plane to respond, but it continued to fly in its deep, descending spiral.

In his rearview mirror he could see the two Zeros, even see the faces of the grinning enemy pilots as they hammered him. He radioed a Mayday as he watched more holes appear in his wings as if some giant were stabbing them with a huge icepick. His instrument panel was shattering before his eyes, and he could feel the thuds as the rounds impacted the armored plate in the back of his seat. He hunkered down as far as he could.

Using both feet he pushed his entire 123 pounds against the rudder, wondering how long the aircraft could remain up with the pounding it was taking. Just when he thought it couldn't get any worse, one of the Japanese pulled off for an oblique shot and sent rounds into the propeller. When the rounds hit one of the blades, they made a zinging sound like a ricocheting bullet in a Wild West movie.

With the propeller nicked, the aircraft began severe shuddering and vibrating, and the panicked aviator could now see completely through the wings in some spots. He had endured ten minutes of battering and had lost altitude. At the lower altitude, he managed to get the wing over somewhat to slow the spiraling, and he now flew in a flat turn, going nowhere but in a circle. A quick glance at his watch told him it was time for rendezvous. In a few minutes, the aircraft of his squadron would assemble and return to Tarawa. He'd be left alone.

Again he felt the sickening thuds of the Japanese rounds impacting the rear of his seat, and he wondered why they hadn't tried to make a high-side run, which would kill him or cut the plane in half. The Japanese seemed content to stay behind and pound on him. Perhaps by now they were wondering what was holding this aircraft up and were like a cat with a mouse, tossing it in the air before killing it.

Abramson knew that the plane was finished, and thought to try and bail out, but knew that the Japs would strafe him, so he stayed put. Even if he made it to the water, he knew that the possibility of making it to land was remote, and anyway the land belonged to the Japanese, which meant capture and torture and, most likely, death. The thought of digging his own grave and kneeling before it while some bastard with a sword decapitated him and then kicked his scrawny, 123-pound ass into the hole after his rolling head kept him in the cockpit.

Minutes later, he opted to jump. Despite the grim possibilities of jumping, one fact was sure! Death was certain if he stayed in the Hellcat. At the first lull, he would jump. They must be close to being out of ammunition by now and most likely low on fuel.

He went through the checklist for jumping. All straps and cords were free. It would be a disaster to jump and suddenly find yourself snagged on the doomed aircraft like a cowboy fallen from his horse with one foot stuck in the stirrup. The aircraft would fly around, dragging him on the outside, until it made its final dive to the ocean with Arthur in tow.

Straps free, he said to himself, now breathe deeply from the oxygen bottle, jettison the canopy hood, make sure the survival kit is in the backpack, and stand up. He would jump out the left side since that was the direction of the turn. He had one foot out when the Japs fired again, this time hitting him and flinging him back into the cockpit. He could feel his own blood running down his back and reached back to discover the fluid was clear and tasted like water. His survival pack had absorbed the bullet.

Arthur Abramson now resolved to die with his aircraft. He carved out in his mind the plan for a victory, even though it would be a small one. He would deprive his attackers the thrill of returning to their officers' club that day and bragging how they had killed an American. It wouldn't change the outcome of the war, but it would be his own private, personal victory. He would keep the plane up until they had to go, and he would determine when he would die, even if that was only a minute after they left.

With that resolve, he felt a sudden calm come over him, and he was at peace. He marveled how the Hellcat continued to fly against the odds and his thoughts now turned to his girl, Toni, thousands of miles away, who would never know what happened to him. He put her picture on the shattered instrument panel and leaned back to spend his last moments with her. Instinctively, his feet and hands still fought to keep the plane aloft.

At the lower, denser altitude, some of the controls began to work and he had minimal control over the aircraft. He flew closer to the water to keep the Japs from making a high-side run on him—25 feet off the water, a plane trying that maneuver would crash into the ocean.

Finally the Zeros broke off. He'd sent them home without a confirmed kill. He'd won. They'd drink no saki over him tonight.

He limped in the direction of Makin. Reaching into his survival pack, he found a handheld compass and plotted a reciprocal course. The aircraft was a mass of metal, shuddering and vibrating in its death throes, threatening at any second to plunge out of the sky.

His radio periodically emitted static as the jiggling wires occasionally made contact, and although there was some comfort in that, he knew that his comrades were long gone. He resolved to continue with his one-man war.

Suddenly a voice came over the radio. "Hold on, I'm coming." Someone had heard his original Mayday, and shortly, on his left, the welcome sight of another Hellcat appeared. The pilot was giving him the thumbs-up. It was his closest friend, Norman Duberstein, who had not joined the rendezvous but had come searching for him. They flew on for forty-five minutes, like a Seeing Eye dog leading a blind man, but at least now, Abramson knew that if he had to ditch, someone could report his position.

His hopes soared when the island of Makin came into view, but this joy was short-lived when the control tower informed him that the runway was closed because of crashed aircraft. That meant another seventy-five minutes to Tarawa. Certainly his aircraft would disintegrate before then. But somehow, the Hellcat stayed in the air, and Abramson found himself making his approach, more crablike than straight, to the 50-foot-wide, 2,700-foot-long airstrip. His wheels were down, but he didn't know if they were locked, and he could not get the wings level. With both feet on the right rudder and the stick jammed to the right, he came in listing 30 degrees.

On either side of the narrow strip, other aircraft were parked like dominoes. He knew that he would smash into one side or the other. His long, unbelievable flight was still going to kill him. To his front he could see men running from the airfield.

The first part of the aircraft to touch the runway was his left wing tip. It flipped the plane up on its two wheels and, instead of smashing into the parked Hellcats, Abramson suddenly found himself rolling straight down the coral strip. He came to a halt at the very end and stood in his cockpit on legs of jelly. Vehicles and men raced to him as he stepped out onto the wing.

Climbing out, he inspected the pile of junk, just as if he were going to return it to the Navy for future use. In the space behind the cockpit he found more than thirty 20mm cannon bullets that had bounced off his armored seat and fallen to the deck. The ground crew stopped counting holes at 275, and a bulldozer came and pushed the wreck off the strip.[7]

Abramson shuddered as he flew back from the attack on Guam and reflected on his narrow escape seven months earlier. In the distance he could see *Yorktown* on the horizon. What a joy to call the big carrier home. After three months flying from Tarawa, his time in hell had ended as abruptly as it had begun. One day the CO announced that they had been relieved, and would go to Hawaii for one week's leave and to be assigned to a carrier.

The squadron was jubilant. They left Tarawa hoping never to see the place again.

As their week in Hawaii came to an end, they saw a huge carrier pull in and anchor at Ford Island. It was *Yorktown,* and no one had to tell them that this was it. They knew it: VF-1 had been assigned to the Fighting Lady.

Abramson and his friends walked down to the dock and looked at the monster 850-foot ship and smiled. He knew that his lifelong dream was to be fulfilled at last.

Within weeks, he was at sea on the Fighting Lady, and now, seven months later, his flight of four aircraft, returning from their strike on Guam, flew head-on to *Yorktown.* They flew down the starboard side of the ship, spaced in an echelon column in preparation to land. He was third in line and, as the first plane passed the ship, Abramson began a slow turn to bring himself astern to approach the flight deck. Several seconds later, the second plane broke from the column to make the stern approach, and then Abramson broke so that he could arrive to land just as the flight deck had been cleared.

Already he could see the first plane had landed and was rolling forward, folding its wings. The second plane made his approach, correcting his path and attitude from signals from the landing signal officer (LSO) who stood to the left on the stern. First his arms were level, then tilted, then level again as he signaled the pilot the attitude of his plane on approach. At the last moment, the LSO whipped his right paddle across his chest indicating to cut power, and the second aircraft dipped its nose, pulled it back up, and slammed the Hellcat down hard, catching one of the fourteen arresting wires.

Abramson approached as the deck crews fought to clear the landed plane from the deck. The deck of the 33,000-ton carrier pitched and bobbed, and was anything but stationary. He had the LSO in view and adjusted the flight of his plane to the arm movements of the man with the paddles. He held his altitude at 105 feet and was gliding for the deck when, suddenly, the LSO gave him a wave-off. For some reason, he could not land and Abramson pushed the throttle forward to gain airspeed. He pulled the nose up and flew over the deck and saw there was a problem getting the second plane free from the arresting wire. He banked to the left for a second approach.

Again, he flew down the starboard side of the carrier and watched the fourth plane land, indicating that whatever had been the problem was now corrected. In less than a minute, Abramson was down and walking toward the island and the eventual debriefing below.

The whole ship was buzzing with activity. Everyone was cheering and slapping one another on the back, the atmosphere was like New Year's Eve. What had happened? What was all the fuss about? When he finally was able to get one of his friends to calm down, he learned that he'd missed the greatest naval victory since Midway.

While Abramson was on his mission to Guam, the Japanese Mobile Fleet had launched four attacks against Task Force 58. Each had been annihilated by the American planes. Those few enemy aircraft that had broken through the phalanx of fighters had met the withering fire of the American antiaircraft guns. The Navy had lost only thirty aircraft while shooting down more than 350 of Admiral Ozawa's Zeros.

One young American pilot quipped, "This was like an old-time turkey shoot." Some member of the press picked it up and the battle was forever named the Marianas Turkey Shoot.[8]

Abramson and the thirty aviators from the Guam mission were delighted with the victory, but inwardly were very disappointed to have missed the great battle. They had been part of the force from the beginning, and to be left out of the glory now and miss the chance to strike the great blow against the enemy was more than frustrating.

The next day, *Yorktown* settled to a very light schedule, with the morning flights flown by some of the new replacement pilots. They were off at 0400, after a full breakfast of steak and eggs, and all the trimmings, which was a Navy tradition for the early flight since it always had the heaviest casualties. The big breakfast came jokingly to be called the condemned man's last meal.

The veteran pilots found spaces to hang out and relax. Some wrote letters home in the ready room, others read in little corners or worked crossword puzzles. Most enjoyed the light day but knew that tomorrow would bring more of the life that had become their own. They were convinced that this war in the Pacific would go on forever. There were thousands of islands between them and Japan, and they had seen the Japanese fight for every inch of terrain. When the island hopping was over, there was still the Japanese mainland itself to invade.

The favorite hangout on light days was the officers' wardroom. Most pilots described it as an oasis where they could return to civilization. The room gleamed with clean, starched white tablecloths, polished silver, and sparkling crystal. Meals were served by white-jacketed Filipinos with white gloves. The food was delicious, the coffee hot, and the tea ice cold. It was a place of civility and elegance, the reward for service at Tarawa.

At 1400 on this lazy day in the Pacific on June 20, the lounging men were jarred back to reality by the grating voice over the PA: "All pilots and crews, report to the ready rooms."

Most everyone figured that they would get an update on yesterday's climactic battle, and shuffled off to the ready rooms with their unfinished letters and crossword puzzles in hand. Ten minutes after assembly, the ship's intelligence officer came on.

"The long-range search planes have located Ozawa's fleet fleeing northwest for Japan." They were escaping to fight another day. There was no way that Task Force 58 could catch them. They were already 240 nautical miles away and increasing the distance, and the pilots knew that they would have to fight them again another day. The word quickly spread that with the enemy in full flight and out of range, Task Force 58 would cruise slowly and refuel. It was a promise of, perhaps, a few more days of light duty.

An hour and a half later, at 1545, came the shocking word over the PA: "The Task Force commander has decided to launch a maximum attack against Ozawa's fleet. Strike in forty-five minutes. Stand by for general quarters!"

In the ready rooms, there was dead silence. Only the clicking Teletype broke the pall. No one had to tell the squadron that if an attack was launched at 1630, it would be dark three hours later. No one had to announce that the extreme distance to the target meant that the strike force could not return to the carrier after the attack. Still, the aviators scribbled on their boards figuring the data they needed for their flight.

The squadron commander, Lcdr. Bernard "Smoke" Strean finally spoke. "Okay, gentlemen, we have our orders. I'll lead the entire strike. We'll be first in to find the target."[9]

The only noise was the scribbling on the plotting boards. Slowly the names of those who would go were called and marked on the blackboard. Arthur Abramson's name was assigned to one of the two standby aircraft—ready to replace one with mechanical problems.

No one asked, "Why me?" Those who were called knew why. It was because they were there.

Then came the details of the flight. Hellcats would be rigged with the external 150-gallon tank to bring the fuel capacity up from 250 gallons to 400. The bad news was that instead of running the engines lean, which would consume the precious gasoline at a rate of 35 gallons per hour, the force would have to catch the retreating Japanese Fleet, and that would require a power setting that would consume close to 100 gallons per hour.

Abramson rechecked his calculations. No matter how he figured it, the result was the same. His night splashdown in the ocean would still be 150 miles short of home.

Twelve pilots from VF-1 were designated to go. Four hundred were scheduled to launch from the entire Task Force. The chance to annihilate the fleeing enemy fleet overrode the concern for the safety and well-being of the men involved in the attack. The importance of the mission made them expendable.

The squadron commander instructed the selected men to refresh themselves on the techniques for night bail-out and water landings. It was all matter of fact, no drama, no emotion. It was warriors following orders, and training and discipline took over. Those officers not flying the mission went topside to watch the launch. The others donned their flight gear.

Abramson approached his aircraft, and the three members of his deck crew were standing waiting for him. They were three Navy enlisted men, a radioman, an ordnance man, and a mechanic. They had a special relationship with their pilot—they considered the plane theirs and only lent it to the pilot for a mission, and they expected him to return it to them. As with most deck crews and pilots, the relationship was informal. No stiff salutes or anything like that. In fact a breezy touch of the cap was more in order, and when the aircraft went to the line, the deck crew usually gave the machine a loving pat as if it were a pet.

Today was different. They helped Abramson into the aircraft and made sure he was buckled, and the tug on his straps seemed somewhat loving. In moments, the deck crew had retreated from the plane. With goggles down, the young pilot watched the three men straighten to attention and snap a salute and hold it. Tears welled in his eyes, and when they snapped the salute away, he was glad his goggles made his eyes invisible. He knew they were telling him good-bye.

Engines coughed to a start, and the whole deck became a scene of whirling propellers. The first aircraft was off at 1627. Abramson waited, wondering if he would be needed and realized that the 240-mile estimate to the enemy fleet was wrong. The flight would be longer. *Yorktown* had turned into the wind to launch, and that was east. The Japanese Fleet was to the west. He also realized that if, for some miraculous reason, they did make it back, most of the pilots had never made a night carrier landing. He had made a couple, and it was sheer terror.

First it was necessary to find the ship, and the only way to do that was to fly to the spot where it was thought to be and look for the telltale phosphorescent trail that all vessels make as their props churn the water. After finding the biggest trail, which would indicate the carrier's path, the pilot had to make an approach from the stern in the pitch dark, trusting to fate that the ship was there. If he found the LSO, in his pink and yellow fluorescent suit with his fluorescent paddles glowing in the dark, he would look like some ghost or underworld specter. When he gave the signal to cut power, the pilot had to slam the Hellcat down. Only when the aircraft hit the deck would he be sure that the carrier was beneath him. It was a complete act of faith. Why worry about a night landing? he thought. There was no way to make it back anyway.

He sat in his cockpit with engines idling and watched his friends roar down the deck and into the air. He checked once again that his flaps were lowered to the proper position, just in case. Only a few planes left to launch—all on a one-way trip.

A banging on the plane's fuselage startled him. It was his signal to go, and within seconds, he sent his Hellcat racing down the deck. He became part of the first wave of the strike force of eighty-five fighters, seventy-seven bombers, and fifty-four torpedo planes.[10]

The carriers brought the second wave of aircraft up from the hangar decks to launch. On board *Lexington,* Adm. Marc Mitscher's flagship, a radio operator rushed to the admiral and handed him a message. Mitscher read it and was dismayed. He gave orders to stand by to recall the flight while he studied the chart. When he was finished, he canceled the second-wave launch but did not recall the aircraft now flying west, into the setting sun, toward the Japanese.

The message had come in at 1605, but by the time it had been copied and decoded, it arrived on the bridge after the last of the first wave was gone. There was a mistake. The corrected report placed the enemy fleet 60 miles farther away. It was not a 240-mile flight; it was 300 miles. Two hundred sixteen aircraft flew into the setting sun.[11]

Shortly before sunset, the aircraft from Task Force 58 saw the first ships of the fleeing Japanese Fleet. Two oilers plunged along in the ocean far below, and several planes attacked, sinking both. Forty miles later, the main body came into view. Cdr. Strean led the diving attack on a large carrier, which placed three bombs on target.[12]

In the setting sun, the appearance of the bursts of antiaircraft fire took on beautiful colors, puffs of red and yellow and orange. Also in the bright sun, nasty black puffs appeared, but these exploding rounds made the sky over the battle area look like fireworks.

In fifteen minutes the attack was over, and the aircraft from the strike force turned for home. All external tanks had been dropped, and fuel gauges showed tanks more than half empty. They flew to the east and into the night.

Everyone was on his own, and most of the flight flew in small groups. The pilots leaned the engines back as far as they could without killing them. Abramson teamed up with Ens. M. M. Tomme, an all-around nice guy who never let anyone know what M. M. stood for, and insisted that everyone call him Tommy. Yesterday had been a red-letter day for Tomme. He had scored his first two kills in the Turkey Shoot.

Abramson and Tomme flew at 15,000 feet and set their flight path on a slight descending angle. That would ensure the greatest conservation of fuel and allow gravity to stretch out the distance covered. Radio silence was broken, and there was chatter among the planes as they "held hands" on the return flight.

After an hour, the first aircraft began to call out longitude and latitude in preparation for ditching. These were the aircraft that were damaged or those that had burned the most fuel in high-power settings in the target area or had carried more weight in bombs. Some time later the radio crackled with, "I'm going in." As the miles increased, the calls increased. There were ingenious techniques for ditching. Some decided to ditch together rather than individually crash after fuel ran out, and the radio crackled with, "Here we go," or "The Navy's losing its best fighter pilot. I'm going in."[13] As the miles increased, the bombers splashed into the ocean.[14]

The Hellcat fighters had a great advantage. They had been able to carry extra fuel whereas the torpedo bombers and dive-bombers were not afforded that luxury because their load was the bombs and torpedoes they carried.

Tomme and Arthur flew on. More and more planes ditched, and Abramson suggested they refigure their fuel. It was 2115 and pitch dark as the two aviators scribbled separately in their cockpits. Abramson calculated twenty-two minutes left. Tomme figured twenty-three. They decided to take Tomme's estimate.

Their altimeters showed they were at 4,000 feet. They had glide-flown to stretch every mile, but they knew the end was near. Both men were silent, engrossed in their own thoughts for the next fifteen minutes. Abramson visited Toni, whose picture was in front of him. Who would tell her he was missing and presumed dead? Where on the ocean would they point to his grave?

At 2130, an excited voice crackled over the radio, shaking the two pilots out of their melancholy thoughts. "Lights! Lights, at ten o'clock!"

Anxious eyes snapped to that bearing and, sure enough, on the horizon was the glow of lights reflecting in the night sky as if a city were there. Every aircraft headed for the illumination.

After Adm. Mitscher had launched the flight in the afternoon, he had turned the Task Force to the west and ordered a maximum-speed pursuit. For four hours, he had been proceeding at flank speed to try and shorten the return distance to save his pilots and planes. Now he chanced lighting the fleet, disregarding the possibility of a submarine attack.[15]

The fleet was lit as if in daylight. Running lights, truck lights, and searchlights stabbed into the sky. Star shells were fired from guns to mark the way. The carriers were attacked like a swarm of hornets by the frantic aircraft, parched for fuel. The first arrivers landed easily, but the ensuing stampede caused the LSOs to wave off many. Some aircraft, so short of fuel, could not stay airborne with a wave-off and were forced to ditch. Other ships moved to rescue them.

Pilots landed on the first carrier they could find. Some pilots committed the court-martial offense of ignoring the wave-off and crashed onto the decks, resulting in destruction and death. On one carrier, two planes landed simultaneously, miraculously not crashing into each other.[16] Some aircraft discovered, as they came in on their final approach, that the ship they were approaching was not a carrier but a cruiser or destroyer that had its truck lights burning. Some of those who pulled off the mistaken approaches then ran out of fuel trying to find the carriers.[17]

Tomme and Abramson found *Yorktown* and made their approaches. They promised to meet in the ready room as soon as they landed for some of the medical officer's "prescription." Abramson went in first. He could already taste the brandy.

He was never so glad to see the LSO signaling him that his wings were level and he was on course. When the signal officer gave the cut-engine signal, he chopped off the throttle and put the Hellcat on the deck. In a moment he had taxied forward, while crewmen folded the wings. He followed parking instructions, signed the yellow sheet, and jumped to the deck. He ran to the island.

He looked back to see Tomme set his aircraft down and catch a wire. In the next moments, he, too, was rolling past with a big grin and a big thumbs-up. Abramson stepped through the door and down the ladder to the ready room. Doc's "prescription" was almost in his hand.

As he went down the first flight, he heard the telltale sound of a crashing airplane and wondered who it was. Was it a VF-1 plane or a plane from a squadron off another carrier who had found *Yorktown?*

He burst into the ready room to wait for Tomme so they could be debriefed, but the assembled pilots seemed strange. There were no smiles on their faces—none of the expected exhilaration. Something was wrong.

And then they told him. Tomme was dead.

This was some kind of joke. He had just waved to him on deck, and he'd be down in a minute. Come on, fellows. But the shaking heads confirmed it was no joke.

A pilot had ignored a wave-off and set his 13,000 pound Hellcat on top of Tomme's plane. The prop ripped into the cockpit and killed Tomme instantly.

Abramson sank into a chair and buried his head in his hands.

The next day, Arthur Abramson served as one of eight pallbearers for Ens. M. M. Tomme's funeral. Tomme's body was wrapped in a canvas bag and lay on a board next to the edge of the flight deck. On either side four of his friends faced one another. Each man's somber stare spoke volumes of deep emotions buried inside. They wore their flight suits and vests.

The chaplain prayed, taps were played, and the board, under the American flag, was tilted until Tomme's body slid off and down into the deep. The eight men then manned their Hellcats for the next mission.[18]

EPILOGUE

The Battle of the Philippine Sea, June 19–20, 1944, was a crushing defeat for the Japanese Navy. Admiral Ozawa lost almost 350 aircraft and their pilots. He also lost three carriers and two others were damaged. The Mobile Fleet was driven from the Marianas, and the Allied occupation of the island chain was ensured. The juggernaut American Navy now set its sights for the next chain, the Bonin Islands, and its gemstone, Iwo Jima, a close base from which to begin the air attacks necessary for the eventual invasion of the Japanese homeland.

It was the last classic carrier battle of the war. The Japanese could not replace the planes or pilots or ships to venture out again as a challenge to the American Navy.

The day following the dramatic night mission, ships from Task Force 58 steamed westward in search of the downed pilots. Almost eighty aircraft had splashed into the ocean on the return flight, and the next day, half of those pilots were recovered along the path of their flight.[19]

In the battle of June 19–20 Ens. Tomme had downed two enemy aircraft. In later action, Abramson would shoot down four Zeros. When his combat tour ended, he was credited with four kills and two probables, but those probables would deny him the official status of Ace. Arthur Abramson was awarded the Distinguished Flying Cross for his action while a member of VF-1.

SEVEN
THE BATTLE OF THE BULGE, LANZERATH, BELGIUM

December 16, 1944

1st Lt. Lyle Bouck, 99th Infantry Division

The 99th Division made its landing onto the Continent of Europe at Le Havre, France, in the gray evening of November 4, 1944. The flat, beach landing area, suitable for LSTs, had provided a port for newly arriving divisions of GIs fresh from the States. It was less than 50 miles east of the now famous Overlord beaches, which had been stormed in June. Unlike the fierce fighting of D-Day, the landing of the 99th was an unopposed, administrative landing. The short November days were damp and overcast, and there was a chill of winter in the air.

First Lt. Lyle Bouck, who commanded the Intelligence and Reconnaissance (I&R) Platoon of the 394th Regiment of the 99th Division, walked among his men as they bent to the task of probing for mines left behind by the retreating Germans with their bayonets. The ground was an open field that would serve as their bivouac area. The occasional sound of distant shots had the new men anxiously looking to the east, but the shots were explained as "sporadic resistance."

Once the field was proved to be clear, the men of the 394th pitched their shelter-halves, set security, and spent their first night in France on the muddy ground. Lt. Bouck was the second-youngest man in his platoon, somewhat baby-faced, small in stature, and just twenty years old. His sparkling blue eyes signaled a confidence much admired by his men, and his small, muscular stature denoted his athleticism. Few, however, would have guessed that this young officer was already a six-year veteran of the armed forces.

He had been born on December 17, 1923, in St. Louis, Missouri, and had attended grade school and one year of high school. In August 1938, at his father's suggestion, fourteen-year-old Lyle and his older brother, Robert, who was nineteen, joined the National Guard. Their father, a veteran of WWI and a former guardsman, knew how the system worked. The National Guard offered a chance for young men to go to a two-week camp, where they would get a dollar a day and three good meals. It was generally recognized that after the two-week camp, anyone wanting to could get out. The Guard really only needed bodies for their summer maneuvers.

Lyle's father took the boys down to the armory, and, in short order, they both signed papers. The elder Bouck was known there, and no one asked any questions; there was no need to. Young Lyle never lied about his age—no one ever asked him. When they placed an application in front of him, he signed it. On August 3, 1938, he became a fourteen-year-old National Guardsman in the 138th Infantry Regiment of the 35th Division. The division was made up of men from Missouri, Kansas, and Nebraska.

Bouck went to camp at Camp Clark in Nevada, Missouri, for his two weeks and served as a messenger. On one occasion he was ordered to deliver a message from Regimental Headquarters to the 1st Battalion, and he eagerly set off in the night. The technique to find the way from one switchboard to another was to grab the wire and simply follow it through the woods until it led to the next switchboard.

Bouck was moving through the trees, crouching to hold the wire in his hand while he held the message in the other, when he suddenly found himself on the ground, with a strange metallic taste in his mouth. He scrambled to his feet and felt numb all over, but he was most concerned that he could not find his message.

He got on hands and knees and rustled through the leaves. Finally finding the paper, he grabbed the landline again and continued on his mission. The wire finally led to the communications center of the 1st Battalion, but when he arrived, he discovered that a crowd was milling around the tent, and there was excited conversation.

He walked into the center to find that the operator was dead, killed by lightning that had struck the switchboard. That ended the maneuver, Lyle Bouck's first Army experience, and the shocked teenager moved out of sight and cried over the terrible experience.

But when the two weeks were over, Bouck realized that he had enjoyed the camaraderie of camp and the athleticism. The food had been good, and the dollar a day had been better; so he stayed in the Guard. He would have to drill, one night a week, but he would get a dollar for each drill period. It was wonderful to be handed thirteen dollars every thirteen weeks. In 1938, this was more than a young man could hope for.

Although war was threatening in Europe in 1939 and Adolf Hitler was constantly in the news, young Bouck was not aware of any of it. What he was aware of was the rumor that there might be a coal miners' strike in Kentucky. His outfit had been alerted that they might be issued picks and shovels and sent off to some mine somewhere. This excitement lasted for a while, but the strike never materialized, and when it was over, so was the major threat of the year.

But something was happening, and the Army was changing before his eyes. Suddenly there were new positions created, mostly new non-com positions. There were some promotions, and Bouck found himself with the title of Armor/Articifer. He had never heard the word *articifer*, but found out that it meant that he had skills to care for the weapons, which, of course, he did not. But he prided himself on being a quick learner.

He ended in the supply room and when the supply sergeant was moved, he was the only one who knew anything about supply, so they made him a sergeant at the ripe age of sixteen. This put him in the same rank, and pay scale, as many of the men who were in their twenties and thirties.

On December 23, 1940, his National Guard unit was mobilized for a year. Now his pay jumped to an incredible $60 a month. The draft was instituted, and despite his mother's concern over her son being mobilized, Lyle comforted her by promising that after the year he would come back and finish school. He explained that he would most likely get drafted, in which case he would only be paid $21 a month instead of the $60 he was now making. Mrs. Bouck relented.

He went to Camp Joseph T. Robinson in Little Rock, Arkansas, and his year was scheduled to end on December 23, 1941. Everyone was anxious to go home, but two weeks before their mobilization ended, the Japanese ended all possibility of going home soon. The year-long order was now amended. Their new commitment was for "the duration of the war, plus six months."

His unit was detached as a separate regiment and, within two days of the attack on Pearl Harbor, they were moving west, toward the Aleutians. At Bellingham, Washington, they dug foxholes and put up barrage balloons in anticipation of a Japanese task force rumored to be headed for the Pacific Northwest.

When that didn't happen, Bouck was sent to Dutch Harbor, which he thought was the most dismal place on the face of the earth. This was followed by other assignments to places named Umnak, Cold Bay, and Kodiak. It all chilled his bones. The weather was so bad and constantly cold that he searched for any means to escape.

He applied to Officers Candidate School (OCS) and also to the Air Corps, the paratroopers, and the infantry; anything to get out of Dutch Harbor. The Infantry accepted him, and in May 1942, he was in Class 57 at Fort Benning. Ninety days later, he had finished fourth in his class of 208 and was commissioned a second lieutenant in the Army of the United States.[1]

One hundred and ninety-eight of the new lieutenants went their way to different commands, but the top ten graduates were held as instructors by order of Gen. George Marshall, who needed to expand the Infantry School for the two-front war.

Bouck spent the next two years at Benning as a tactical officer, spending every hour with the candidates, weeding out and teaching tactics. He taught defensive small-unit tactics at the platoon level and, because of his excellence, was sent to the advanced course, which was mostly reserved for field-grade officers. As a first lieutenant, the youthful officer raised several eyebrows.

In February the war was over two years old and, except for the year of active duty and his original deployment to the Pacific Northwest in anticipation of a Japanese attack, Lt. Bouck had only been an instructor and a student. But in April, he was given command of a weapons platoon at Camp Maxey in Paris, Texas, with the 99th Division.

His regiment, the 394th, participated in the Qualify Corps Maneuvers, the training program to see if a unit is ready. After the maneuvers, the air was filled with apprehension: Something was very, very wrong. Bouck had no idea what had happened, but the regimental commander was relieved. The rumor was that the I&R Platoon had made a major screwup.

The new regimental commander sacked the Intelligence Officer (S-2), along with the entire I&R Platoon, and brought up a decorated combat officer, Maj. Robert Kriz, to take over. Kriz knew Bouck and reached out and grabbed him, telling him that "a new I&R Platoon had to be formed."[2] Kriz also told him that he had been given great latitude to handpick the members for this new platoon.

There were many men in the 394th who were Army Special Training Program (ASTP), trained as engineers, pilots, navigators, and so on. Most of these men had recently been on college campuses and had not expected that their services would be needed, but they now found themselves called up for the war's final pushes against Germany and Japan.[3]

The ASTP soldiers afforded Kriz and Bouck a pool of excellent prospects. They decided to pick the brightest, most athletic, and physically fit of all the men. Additionally, each man had to be an expert with the M-1 rifle. They interviewed almost seventy men, but the final criterion was the decision of the man himself. Each man was asked if he wanted to be in this platoon. The result of the rigid screening was the creation of an elite unit.

Maj. Kriz laid out an exacting training program, and Lt. Bouck conducted it. All aspects of intelligence were stressed: map and compass reading, scouting and patrolling, observation posts, stealth, and all the other skills necessary to make the I&R Platoon an effective force. The training became very physical, and Bouck led by example. He never had to order the men to the obstacle course, he just told them he was going, and they all followed. The platoon jelled as a team. Competition bred on itself.

For their final selection as to who would be the platoon sergeant, Kriz and Bouck selected a non-ASTP soldier who was a little older and a little rougher, and who could push the men. Any rough spots would be handled by twenty-four-year-old Sgt. William Slape.

For the entire summer of 1944, this elite platoon acted as aggressors for the training of the platoons of the regiment. By October, the 394th was ready for combat.

After a cold night on the ground in Le Havre, the 394th struck camp and the GIs boarded trucks to bring them to the front. The truck convoy bounced through France, and on Armistice Day, November 11, Bouck was in Butenbach, and the day after in Hunningen, Belgium. The local crowds cheered, waved flags, and tossed fruit and other food to the arriving Americans.

The 99th relieved the 9th Division on a very quiet section of the front and tied in with the veteran 2nd Division on the right, which occupied the Schnee Eifel, a prominence overlooking the German-Belgian border.

But as this American repositioning was taking place and Bouck and his men were getting settled into a pretty comfortable house next to Regimental Headquarters, there was a change in the enemy disposition. Hidden from their eyes by the forest, which looked every bit like the winter wonderland they had seen in Currier & Ives pictures, was a massing of German forces. The fog, mist, and snow of the Schnee Eifel camouflaged the greatest massing of forces the Germans had ever undertaken.

From the end of November to the second week in December, the Germans had managed to haul five hundred trainloads of equipment, fuel, and ammunition across the Rhine and had staged these massive stores near the front. More than fifteen hundred troop trains delivered 300,000 soldiers, formed into twenty-five divisions, nineteen hundred pieces of artillery, and almost one thousand tanks and armored assault guns.[4]

The plan of attack had been outlined by Adolf Hitler. He envisioned an attack that would exploit the long Allied supply lines. Since the Invasion of Normandy, the Allies still only had the deepwater port of Cherbourg, some 350 miles to the west, to supply their massive armies. The port of Antwerp was a recent prize of the Allies, but Hitler intended to deny them the use of that prize and to split the American and British Armies with a counteroffensive of his own.

For his attack, he had selected an area that did not offer good roads, but was concealed from much observation because of the dense forests. Most important, though, the attack area was defended by a thin American line. A surprise attack with massive force and overwhelming numbers could break the American line and allow a German rush to Antwerp, with the annihilation of many Allied forces along the way. "It will be another Dunkirk," he had boasted to his generals.[5]

The selected area was large, more than 80 miles wide. The Sixth German Panzer Army would deliver the main blow between an area bounded by Monschau on the north and Prum on the south. The Fifth Panzer Army would also attack, to the south of the Sixth, with its northern boundary at Prum and its southern flank on a line from Bitberg to Bastogne. The Seventh Army, the third attacking army, would attack south of the Fifth Panzer and sweep north of Luxembourg to the Meuse.[6] Both the Fifth and Sixth Panzer armies were to race to Antwerp.

The plan called for infantry, preceded by artillery fire, to break the Allied line. Once the breach had occurred, armored columns would roll, like a flood through a broken dam, stopping for nothing, to the Meuse River. Once across the Meuse, it would be a race for Antwerp.

The commander for the main attack of the Sixth Panzer Army was an old-line Nazi, SS Gen. Joseph "Sepp" Dietrich. While his lofty command was the result of his long friendship with Hitler, Dietrich had no illusions of military genius, and he was served well by his subordinates.

One of those subordinates was the commander of the spearhead of his armored column. Lt.Col. Jochen Peiper commanded the 1st SS Panzer Regiment of the 1st SS Panzer Division and was notorious for getting the job done at all cost. Violating the accords of war was not unusual for this fiery commander. An action on the Eastern Front credited him with burning two towns to the ground and killing all the townspeople. That savagery had earned his unit the nickname the "blowtorch battalion."[7]

Peiper was a twenty-nine-year-old regimental commander and one of the youngest in Hitler's army. He was from an old-line Prussian family and was the quintessential graduate of SS Officer Training School—cold, efficient, and ruthless. Despite his high acclaim, the German High Command did not reveal the details of the offensive to him until December 14, two days before Null Day (D-Day).

Peiper had a hint that something big was brewing when Gen. Kraemer confronted him, on December 10, and asked him whether a tank regiment could cover 50 miles in a day. Peiper left nothing to chance and took a German Panther behind German lines for a test run. Under the cover of darkness, he easily pushed the panzer 50 miles in the allotted time, but warned that an entire tank regiment could not cover that much ground.

On December 14, he got his formal briefing and, when all the commanders had received their attack routes, Peiper examined his and groaned. He told the briefing officer that the roads assigned to him were "not for tanks, but for bicycles."[8]

While Jochen Peiper was conducting his tank test on December 10, Lt. Bouck met with Maj. Kriz and received orders to prepare to move his platoon from the Regimental Headquarters at Hunningen to a new position on the right flank of the regiment at a little village called Lanzerath, which had no more than ten houses. The reason for the move was a 1,700-yard gap in the line. The new division to their right had not occupied all the previous positions.

An examination of the map revealed to Lt. Bouck that this move would be unusual. Their new position was outside of the regiment's and the division's boundaries and, more incredibly, outside of the Corps' boundaries.[9] The I&R Platoon would be situated on terrain assigned to VIII Corps.

In the early afternoon of December 10, the small platoon moved to their new position, on the high ground, several hundred yards to the northwest of Lanzerath. The remainder of the day was spent improving a position that had been dug by some previous outfit. They also scouted the terrain for possible avenues of enemy approach. Fields of fire were selected and cleared, and the platoon dug in for the early night, which came around 1630.[10]

For the next five days, the platoon improved its position. Bouck ordered the foxholes to be covered with logs, so trees were cut down and the logs laid, Alpine style, over each hole. Two were laid on the ends of the foxholes, then more logs stacked across the hole, to form a pyramid. Inside the holes, two men could stand side by side, their eyes level with the slit openings. Each position provided support for an adjacent one. The pyramid was packed with dirt to seal the cracks and camouflaged with fir branches. After a snow on December 13, the I&R position was virtually invisible.[11]

Whereas the platoon had run patrols from their position in Hunningen, at Lanzerath, they did not. They remained concealed since their mission was to be the eyes of the division and V Corps. From their position on the high ground, they could see for miles.

The 99th Division commander placed an artillery forward observation post in Lanzerath. This four-man team, from C Battery, 371st Field Artillery, commanded by Lt. Warren Springer, occupied the second floor of Anna Christen's house on the edge of the town, and was in position to interdict any German column that might come from Losheim. The scarcity of foliage on the trees actually gave the team a view of Losheim, several miles to the east.[12]

Sgt. William Slape ran telephone wire to the only other friendly forces in the area, a tank destroyer platoon, known as Task Force X. It consisted of fifty-five men and four towed guns of the 14th Armored Cavalry Regiment. They occupied the small town of Lanzerath.[13]

Lanzerath itself was not a place to be defended. It offered little in the form of defensive positions since the few houses were made of wood, and it was dominated from the northwest by the high ground now occupied by the I&R Platoon. Except for the fact that it lay 300 yards south of an important fork in the road, it was unimportant. The left fork ran toward Buchholz Station, to the rear of Bouck's position, and paralleled the hard-surfaced road to Hunningen and the 394th Regimental Headquarters. The right fork ran to Losheimergraben, and then to the northwest to Hunningen, Bullingen, and Butgenbach, and finally, west toward Liege and the Meuse River.[14]

Maj. Kriz came to the position on several occasions and each day someone from the platoon went to Hunningen on supply runs or for mail. On one of the runs, information was brought back that Marlene Dietrich was due to perform on December 17. One man from the platoon would be allowed to go.

From the evening of December 10 to December 15, Bouck saw no enemy movement in the area. Every hour the I&R Platoon made contact with the cavalry in Lanzerath, who in turn passed the hours sometimes playing cards with the local townspeople. The forward observe (FO) team, in Anna Christen's house, had no movement or targets at which to shoot.

On one of the runs back to Hunningen, Bouck managed to "appropriate" a .50-caliber machine gun, pedestal-mounted on a jeep, and quickly dug it into a defilade position behind his line. In addition to the .50-caliber, Bouck's armament consisted of one .30-caliber machine gun and one BAR (Browning automatic rifle). The rest of the men carried M-1 Garrands, and Bouck and Slape carried carbines. The platoon also carried seventy-five grenades.[15]

As darkness set in on December 15, most of the men put the thoughts of Christmas and home out of their minds for a while. Bouck briefed his men that they would be on 100 percent alert. The 2nd Division, which had previously occupied this section of the line, would be attacking to the north, through their own 99th Division. That attack might precipitate some sort of "spoiling" attack, or counterattack, by the Germans, so everyone would be awake and ready. Their thinly held line on the southern boundary might invite such an attack.[16]

The long night produced a variety of strange noises and rumblings to the front, and the men were anxious for dawn. The reflecting snow in the black night gave the whole area an eerie look. On the second floor of Anna Christen's house, the FO team observed many lights in the German-held village of Losheim. Sgt. Peter Gacki reported that Losheim was "lit up like a Christmas tree."[17]

At 0530, the hills to the north suddenly twinkled like thousands of fireflies. Seconds later, the spectacular twinkling became the roar and crashing of a monstrous artillery barrage. The earth convulsed and trees split as Bouck and his men retreated to their covered holes. Although the position was showered with hot shrapnel, no one was injured. Their covered positions protected them from anything but a direct hit.

Fifteen-year-old Adolph Schur was awakened as the artillery bursts split the air and made the ground tremble. He ran to the window, but could see nothing, and then lay on the floor as the rounds first hit close, and then rolled farther to the south, and then back again. For two hours, this incredible bombardment rolled back and forth over the Belgian countryside.[18] None of the buildings in Lanzerath were hit, but the people were badly shaken.

Finally, the bombardment lifted and where there had been two hours of a deafening roar, now there was dead silence. Bouck and Slape came out of their holes to survey the damage. It was still dark, but it didn't take long to find out that all of their communications wires had been cut. There were no landline communications to regiment, Lanzerath, or the cavalry.

Bouck told Slape to try and reestablish communications and, along with Cpl. John Creger, the sergeant followed the wire from their command post toward the battalion on their left flank. The wire had been severed in so many places that repair was impossible. The two-man team then followed the wire toward Lanzerath and found it cut at the fence that bisected the field in front of their position. They were able to splice it.[19]

Meanwhile, Bouck was on the radio to regiment, only to find that the shelling was all across the front, not just in his area. By 0800, the first gray of dawn broke the black winter sky. In the valley, only the tops of the few houses in Lanzerath were visible above a heavy, billowing fog that obliterated the roads and the woods.

In the village, Adolph Schur ventured out of his house and, despite the thick fog, was able to make out the figures of some of his neighbors.

What they saw was a shock to them. The bright, white snow of the previous evening had turned black. All around, the thick blankets of snow were black with cordite and explosive residue, as if some giant chimney had belched soot onto the countryside.[20]

Up on the hill, as the land became brighter, the I&R defenders also saw the transformation of the snow: The whole slope was dirty. Bouck crouched over his radio requesting orders from regiment. He was told to get a patrol into Lanzerath and find out what was going on. As he prepared the patrol, he observed the cavalry unit revving their engines and their vehicles moving out of town, heading north. They passed in front of his position and turned west toward Buchholz Station.

Sgt. Slape and Cpl. Creger, who had just finished repairing the wire to the tank destroyer unit, were joined by Bouck and his messenger and point man, PFC William James Tsakanikas. The four men proceeded down the slope and into town. Tsakanikas was nineteen and the only man younger than Bouck in the whole platoon. Everyone called him Sack.

The patrol followed a circuitous route so as not to give away their position to any observing enemy. They first moved north, toward the fork in the road, where they passed a forward three-man position manned by Aubrey McGehee, Jim Silvola, and Jordan Robinson. Then they went south, keeping to the ditch on the side of the road leading into Lanzerath.

When they reached the house that had been the headquarters of the cavalry unit, they sprinted inside and up to the second floor. They burst into the room and surprised a civilian talking, in German, on the phone. At the point of his bayonet, Sack encouraged the man to drop the phone. Bouck stopped any further confrontation, and the scared man ran down the steps.[21]

From their elevated positions, the four men could see, through the trees, all the way to Losheim, to the east. What they saw was not encouraging: A long column of German soldiers was moving out of Losheim, and their route was going to take them either to Manderfeld, to the south, or into Lanzerath. Through his field glasses, Bouck could see the distinctive helmets of German paratroopers. It was 1000, and the Germans were on the move.

Bouck told Slape and Creger to stay as long as they could, to determine if the column would continue to the village or deploy and possibly enter the woods and outflank his position. He further cautioned them to abandon their position if the Germans got too close and return to the platoon on the hill. Slape and Creger had the landline for communications, and Slape ran another line to the FO team in Anna Christen's house.

Bouck and Sack raced down the stairs and retraced their steps back to the three-man position, stopping only long enough to brief McGehee, Robinson, and Silvola. They then raced up the hill to their main line, where Bouck was immediately on the radio back to Hunningen.

The conversation was frustrating. Bouck screamed for artillery support and reported his target to be a long column of German paratroopers advancing on the open road toward Lanzerath. Obviously the officer on the other end doubted the existence of such a lucrative target, because in the next instant, Bouck was telling him, "Don't tell me what I don't see! I have twenty-twenty vision. Bring all the artillery you can on the road south of Lanzerath!"[22]

But the artillery did not come and, as anxious minutes passed, the anticipated sight of American shells blasting the German column vanished. Instead, the Germans got closer to Lanzerath. Then the phone from Lanzerath rang. It was Slape, and he spoke in a whisper.

Slape and Creger had taken up a position in the attic and had an excellent view to the north. They could see the crossroads well, as the road bent toward Buchholz Station. The wooded area to the east was less visible. The Germans had entered the town from the south, through a draw to the east that ran through the backyards of the village houses, and it was only when Creger walked to the window on the south side of the room that he discovered that the Germans were in the streets. The column was moving at sling arms, carrying their rifles on their shoulders by the sling, not at all in any tactical formation, and certainly not expecting to launch an attack.

Slape and Creger prepared to leave the house, but before they could escape the attic, they heard the front door being kicked in. Slape tried to call the FO team, but there was no answer. He cranked the phone to Bouck and told him that the Germans were on the first floor. He requested fire on the village, to distract the Germans and to allow himself and Creger to escape.[23] By this time the Germans were on the second floor. The Americans crouched in the attic, and Slape could hear Bouck's voice telling him, "We'll get you out."[24]

Bouck ran down the hill to the three-man position, accompanied by PFC Risto Milosevich, and ordered the three men to cross the road and go toward town and place fire on the building to try to rescue his other two men. The team crossed and fired on the building. The rounds cut through the roof, just over Slape and Creger crouching in the attic.

The startled Germans, on the second floor, ran outside, and soon had McGehee, Robinson, and Silvola under fire. The three men returned fire, and began a slow retreat to the north. Slape and Creger used the distraction to run down the steps and out the back door. They first ran to the barn and hid under some cows, then gathering their wits, they raced across an open space in the snow and into the trees. Once in the cover of the trees, they moved to the north, in the direction of the friendly fire. When they had reached a spot across from the three-man position, Slape sent Creger across the road first. He could see Bouck and Milosevich waiting for them.

It was now Slape's turn, and as he raced across, he looked to his left and could see German soldiers on both sides of the road, a good distance away. They fired at him, and one of the bullets tore the heel from his boot. His feet went out from under him, and he fell heavily on the icy road. He felt pain in his left side and in his chest, but a quick inspection revealed he was not hit, and he joined Bouck to return to the hill.[25] There was no sign of the three-man patrol.[26] Although Bouck had lost those three men, he had picked up the four-man FO team, who had abandoned their position as the Germans approached and retreated to the I&R position on the hill.

This small skirmish must have seemed to the Germans to be only a scattered fight from a retreating enemy. When the Americans were no longer in sight, quiet settled over the contact area, and the Germans occupied the town in force.

At his house the teenager Adolph Schur watched the Germans force their way in, demanding food, cigarettes, and chocolates that they knew the Americans would have left behind. The soldiers frightened the young boy, and they were bragging that now that they were back, things would be different. Many were fanatical in their tone, and Adolph kept away from them.[27]

The I&R Platoon was now back in their defensive positions. Again Bouck requested artillery fire through the newly joined FO team, but the answer was that artillery was committed elsewhere. No amount of pleading changed that.

The German column was the vanguard of the 9th Parachute Regiment of the 3rd Parachute Division, commanded by Col. Helmut Hoffman, and its job was to punch a hole in the American lines. Once that was accomplished, the Panzer force under Jochen Peiper, waiting in the rear, would roar through on its way toward Antwerp. But the paratrooper column hardly looked like a disciplined force as it marched down the road through Lanzerath. Their rifles were at sling arms, and no flank security was out. The men chatted with each other and some were even singing.

Bouck and Sgt. Slape watched the march from their concealed position on the hill, and the lieutenant gave the order to hold fire until he signaled. Slape drew a bead on one of the lead figures, but Bouck told him to let the first group pass, in hopes of bagging a larger force.

In the farthest hole forward on the slope, Tsakanikas watched the tightly bunched troops come up the road. He thought to himself that a mortar team would have a field day. He reported their movement to Bouck, but a few of the houses masked the advancing column, and Bouck told him to hold fire.[28]

The first thirty men went by and took the fork to the right, toward Losheimergraben. At least they would not be on the left fork, which would threaten the rear of the platoon. Part of a larger group now appeared, and in their midst three figures stood out since they were consulting maps. One of them must be the commander. Bouck nodded and raised his arm to signal Slape to open fire. Sack had drawn a bead on the center officer, and the rest of the weapons of the platoon were trained on the multiple targets presented to their front. Each man held his breath and tightened his finger on his trigger.

As Sack increased the pressure on his trigger, he saw a figure out of the corner of his eye and looked up to see a little blond girl, with red ribbons in her hair, dash out of a house. She spoke to the German officer and pointed toward the I&R position. The German officer shouted and the column on each side of the road jumped into the ditches. The chance for the ambush was gone, and the I&R Platoon opened fire, raking the ditches. The stunned Germans returned fire against an unseen enemy.[29]

After the initial exchange of fire, the Germans seemed to regroup and within forty-five minutes, close to noon, launched a frontal assault up the hill toward the I&R Platoon positions. The paratroopers struggled through the snow toward the crest with the towering trees, and Bouck's men held their fire. When the attacking Germans hit the fence that bisected the field, they began to climb over. Then the Americans opened fire and cut the attack to pieces. The Germans were stopped in their tracks.[30]

In addition to the small-arms fire spitting out from each of the firing slits, Sgt. Slape had mounted the jeep and was firing the .50-caliber machine gun into the close ranks of the Germans pinned at the wire. Two German machine guns, delivering covering fire for the attacking force, proved to be no match for the .50 caliber. German mortar fire was ineffective against Bouck's dug-in force, and the attack was over in thirty minutes.[31]

From far below, Bouck saw a white flag flutter in the breeze, and the Germans asked to attend their casualties, which he allowed. Two hours later, the Germans attacked again. Again it was a frontal assault up the hill, and again the attackers hit the fence and were mown down as if a great scythe had cut through them.

During the attack, Lt. Springer, the artillery FO, radioed frantically for fire from C Battery, but he was answered that the guns themselves were under fire.[32] Meanwhile, Tsakanikas was everywhere. He fired the .50 caliber relentlessly.

PFC Risto Milosevich hammered away with his .30-caliber machine gun, and the German bodies piled in front of the fence and their position. All along the treeline, the I&R positions delivered devastating fire into the attacking Germans. When the survivors finally retreated down the hill, Bouck and Slape were able to inspect their own positions. This time they were not unscathed. Several of the men had been wounded by fire, and Pvt. Lou Kalil had been hit in the jaw by a rifle grenade that did not explode. It had broken his jaw in four places and drove five teeth into the roof of his mouth. Kalil was knocked unconscious, and Sgt. George Redmond administered first aid as best he could. He rubbed snow onto Kalil's face, gave him a few sulfa pills, and wrapped gauze over his mouth.[33]

Bouck surveyed his flanks, sure that the Germans would try to get behind him, but saw no evidence of that. He reported to regiment and sent a message at 1550: "We are holding our position. Enemy strength 75. They are moving from Lanzerath NW to railroad. We are still receiving enemy artillery fire. Ammo OK."[34]

Bouck then asked what he should do, and the answer was hold at all cost. "We'll try to get you out," was the terse answer from regimental headquarters. Before he could say anything else, a German bullet shattered the receiver in his hand, and their last communications link was gone. Gone, too, was the artillery radio, destroyed in the last attack.

Exploding mortars signaled the start of the third attack, and again the Germans surged up the hill. Again they hit the fence, and again the I&R Platoon opened fire. Even Pvt. Lou Kalil was at his post. Having regained consciousness, with his shattered jaw packed with snow and bandaged, he fired through the slit of his position.

This third German attack had the support of a panzer, far down the road past Lanzerath. It was bogged down in the mud, but it lent its machine-gun fire and tank gun to the assault.

Sgt. Slape could see the tank and two other destroyed tanks, compliments of the small minefield placed in previous days by the I&R Platoon, which blocked the road. He raced to the .50 caliber and neutralized the panzer, but a German round hit the receiver of the gun and put the .50 caliber out of action.

Down the line, Milosevich called for help. He was single-handedly operating the platoon's remaining machine gun. He fed the belt and fired, then reloaded and fired again. When his gun jammed, he picked up his M-1 and continued to fight. Slape raced to him and joined him in his foxhole. Milosevich fed the gun while Slape fired, and the team fired and fired until the gun was so hot it became a runaway gun, and Slape had to break the belt to stop it. Smoke poured off the weapon, and the sergeant could tell that the barrel was burned out as it now bent in a gentle arc.[35]

They removed the ammo from the belt to load into their rifles. The Germans were within 50 yards of their bunker when the attack was finally stopped. Bouck and Slape raced between positions checking the men and distributing the dwindling supply of ammunition.

Most of the men had now been wounded, and T/5 Billy Queen of the FO team had been killed. Bouck decided to send two of his men toward the rear to get help. Cpl. Sam Jenkins and PFC Robert Preston slipped out of their position from the rear of the trees and headed toward the 3rd Battalion line at Buchholz Station.[36]

Lyle Bouck now faced a dreadful decision: He had little ammunition left and no communications, and his last order had been to hold until relieved. His platoon had stopped three German attacks, and they could do no more. The I&R Platoon was down to twelve men, and the FO team was down to three. His .50-caliber and .30-caliber machine guns were out of action.

He thought about the last order he had received. The FO team, which had joined him, had previously been ordered to fall back, and the cavalry was long since gone. Surely if he could talk to someone, and tell them his plight, they would order him to fall back also.

Having exhausted the strength and firepower of his command, and having decided that he would answer for his next action, he decided to send the men out the back of the position in twos and threes. He would gather the wounded, break contact, and slip out the rear under the cover of darkness.[37]

Daylight was failing fast, and snow swirled down in Lanzerath. Young Adolph Schur peeked out of the side window into the alley that came from the main street. He could see German soldiers were forming next to his house, talking excitedly and checking weapons.

He estimated that there were 150 soldiers, and he watched as they marched away, in the gathering darkness, around the back of the house, toward the hill. Adolph knew that the path would bring them to the right flank of Bouck's position. This was a new approach since all the other German forces had moved frontally against the hill from a position farther down the street. Col. Hoffman now ordered a flanking attack.

As the soldiers disappeared down the path, Adolph's grandfather summoned him and his cousin to follow him to the top floor. They followed the older man to the top of the stairs, and then to the window in the attic, which faced out of the back of the house. They huddled together peering out into the evening gloom.

In the snow on the slope, they could see hundreds of dark, lifeless forms sprawled in contorted positions—the results of the three failed frontal attacks of the day. German artillery began pounding the hilltop again and, to their left, they watched the German force that had assembled next to their house launch its flanking assault.

The soldiers fired and maneuvered, unlike the other attacks, in which they had charged in a line up the slope into the murderous fire of the dug-in Americans. They advanced up the hill in small groups, first one, and then another. Adolph's grandfather, who was a veteran of the Great War, pointed to the assault line and said, "There you see what is real war. Take a look."[38]

Adolph and his cousin could see the back of the German line as it surged forward in the gloom. Suddenly an explosion hit near the house, and the elder Schur grabbed the boys, closed the window, and took them downstairs.

The artillery crashed among the foxholes in the I&R position. Before Bouck could act on his plan to evacuate, the German fire covered his position. It was the heaviest since the huge bombardment from early morning.

Bouck shared a hole in the center of the line with his messenger, Sack. Turning to the young soldier, he said, "Bill, my orders are to hold the hill at all costs, but you take as many of the men that want to go, and take off."[39] One part of Sack's mind had already picked out the escape route, through the woods to the rear, and he turned in the covered hole as if to see to the rear, but just as suddenly, he turned back and told his commander, "Bouck, you stay, we all stay."[40] Nothing more was said, and both men turned to the firing slit, and commenced firing at the targets that again began to appear on the slope of the hill. The mortar shells exploded outside.

Several holes away, Slape and Milosevich were making their last stand. They were out of clips for the M-1 rifles, but Milosevich loaded some from the belt of the machine gun and gave them to the sergeant, who fired as fast as he could at the swarming targets. His M-1 became so hot that its barrel, too, began to bend, and the tracer rounds exited the weapon looking like corkscrews, spiraling toward the advancing Germans.[41]

All down the defensive line, the attacking Germans rolled up the flank of the I&R Platoon. One by one the positions fell, and soon it was only Bouck and Sack firing their last rounds. Grenades exploded all around their hole, and suddenly, Bouck saw the ugly black barrel of a German burp gun, named for the sound it makes, appear through the firing slit. He reached for it and pushed on the barrel, but the weapon fired a burst, and Sack was hurled to the bottom of the hole. It was over. In the beam of a German flashlight, the lieutenant could see that his young messenger was gravely wounded. The side of his face was a red pulp, and the sickening scene of one eye hanging out of its socket made Bouck cringe.[42]

For Tsakanikas, the end came in bright flashes of color, like looking in a kaleidoscope. He barely heard the "brrrp" of the deadly gun, but felt himself being lifted upward and backward, before being dumped to the bottom of the hole. There was no pain and, as if in a dreamworld, he could hear Bouck's reassuring words, "You'll be all right, Bill. I'll get you out of here."[43]

He felt several hands dragging him and felt the cold blast of winter air as he was pulled outside the hole. In his dazed state, he heard a German voice order, *"Nein! Nein!"* Presumably the commander was signaling for his men not to shoot the now-defenseless Americans. As he approached the terribly wounded Tsakanikas and saw his shattered face, he exclaimed, *"Ach, mein Gott!"*[44]

Sack lost consciousness and slumped to the snow. He vaguely knew that a German medic was bandaging his wounds and sank into blackness again. In perfect English, the German asked, "Who is the commandant?" and repeated his question. Bouck indicated that he was the commander.

The firing was still going on and the German shouted, "What are you going to do?"

Bouck answered that his men were out of ammunition, the firing was all the Germans. Just then, he went down with a bullet wound to his left leg. The German questioning him was also wounded before the firing stopped. The German medic wrapped Bouck's leg in brown paper, and then helped lift Sack to his feet. With a German soldier helping him on one side, and Lt. Bouck helping him on the other side, Sack started down the hill. A second German soldier walked behind, with an automatic weapon trained on the two Americans.

Bouck and Sack went down the slope, which was littered with the bodies of dead Germans. As they trudged several hundred yards, Bouck heard Sack mumble something through his bandages. He could not make it out, and Sack repeated it.

"Let's take them," the wounded private mumbled, and inwardly the lieutenant had to laugh, realizing that Sack was delirious. In Sack's mind, he was convinced that they could overpower the one German holding him, take him as a hostage, and make the other German surrender his weapon. Again he muttered, "Let's take them," not realizing that the only reason he could stand was because of the two men supporting him.[45]

The wounded Americans were led past the house of Adolph Schur, who watched as the prisoners passed his window. He never went outside, and, in minutes, it was dark as night fell over Lanzerath.[46]

When they reached the main road, they turned to the right and went to the Scholzen Cafe, which had become the headquarters of Col. Hoffman, of 9th Paratroop Regiment. Bouck and Sack were placed on a bench, just inside the door to the right, and others were laid on the floor. Other German wounded were also brought in. Sgt. Bill Slape was led in and stood toward the back of the cafe.

Lyle Bouck supported Sack, who leaned his head on the lieutenant's shoulder. In the light of the cafe, Bouck could see Sack's left nostril and his left eye. He could also see that the dressing was not like the gauze of an American dressing. This bandage was like brown paper, very stiff and not absorbent. The blood seeping from Sack's wounded face slowly dripped onto Bouck's field jacket, soaking it through.

Bouck looked around the room. The Germans huddled around a dresser with maps on it, and there was excited talking. Suddenly, from the far wall, a cuckoo clock signaled the hour. It was a strange sound in the midst of war, but it reminded the young lieutenant of an old aunt who was supposed to possess some gift of clairvoyance and could read palms. She had told him, years earlier, that if he could live past his twenty-first birthday, he would have a successful life. At the stroke of twelve he would be twenty-one, but he was not sure if he would make it.

His thoughts were broken as he caught Slape's eye; the sergeant was definitely trying to communicate with him. He was signaling with his eyes toward the back door, indicating a way for them to get away when the opportunity presented itself. Bouck shook his head and signaled that there were wounded that needed them. Again Slape tried to communicate with his eyes and subtle motions, but an alert German saw him, and Slape was taken out of the room.

The evening wore on, and Bouck became aware of the sound of idling engines just outside the cafe. They sounded like tank engines, and for hours they broke the silence of the night.

Finally, the cuckoo clock struck twelve, and Lyle Bouck turned twenty-one. Despite his dreadful situation, the thought ran through his mind that now there was no way for the Germans to kill him.[47]

An hour later, some Germans came and took Sack and laid him on the floor of the cafe. Bouck was relieved. He had supported the young soldier for hours—his jacket was blood-soaked—and he felt as if an enormous load had been lifted from his shoulders. He knew as well that the young private had to be better off lying down.

But his relief was short-lived, as the front door slammed open, and a fiery officer strode into the room, barking orders. From his tone, Bouck could tell that he was very agitated. He shouted to everyone around.

Jochen Peiper wanted to know what the delay was. He ran back and forth, first questioning one officer, and then another. Throughout the cafe there was much upheaval, and Bouck watched it all from his position on the bench. He was very frightened and wondered if perhaps he would survive past this birthday.

Col. Jochen Peiper unfolded his maps and, using two bayonets, stabbed them to the wall of the cafe. What is the holdup, he wanted to know, tracing his fingers over the route he should have been barreling down on the way to his objective, the Meuse River.

With his panzers idling their engines, he had waited all day for the infantry to tear a hole in the American lines so he could roar through the gap. As the hours stretched on, the news got worse. His original route, which was from Losheim to Losheimergraben and on to Hunningen, had been jinxed from the start. A bridge over railroad tracks leading into Losheim had not been repaired, so his tank column, instead of racing for the Meuse shortly after the initial bombardment, did not even get to Losheim until 1930. By that time, he was already twelve hours behind schedule.

At Losheim, the fiery SS commander received even worse news. A second bridge on the road to Losheimergraben was also blown, and the town itself was still in American hands. An order from his division commander told him to abandon his originally scheduled route and detour to the southwest, toward Manderfeld, and then resume his northwesterly route through the little town of Lanzerath.[48]

The new route was no cinch. The road to Lanzerath was clogged with stalled columns, and well-placed American mines cost him five panzers. He was in a foul mood when he finally stormed into the Scholzen Cafe, an hour after midnight, on December 17.

Still seated on the bench, Bouck watched the noisy confrontation. He spoke no German and had no idea what the subject of the animated conversation was, but was thankful that no one was paying attention to him or his wounded men.

The subject was, What is the holdup? Col. Hoffman, the commanding officer of the 9th Paratroop Regiment, told Peiper that the woods to the northwest were heavily fortified and full of fighting Americans. The German bodies on the snowy slopes were proof of that. No, he'd not seen the fortified position himself.

Peiper then questioned each commander on down from the regimental commander, and each verified the ferocity of the fighting, but no, no one had actually seen the heavy fortifications responsible for such a slaughter. The reports had come up the line.

Peiper became furious and ordered the regimental commander (actually his senior) to give him one of his battalions, whose soldiers would mount his panzers. He would personally lead the breakthrough. By 0400, Peiper was ready, and his panzer juggernaut shifted into gear and attacked forward, toward Buchholz Station. Of course, there was no resistance.

"Strangely enough," Peiper said, "we broke through the area without firing a shot and found it completely unoccupied."[49]

As he pulled away from the Scholzen Cafe, Jochen Peiper had no way of knowing that those few, pitifully wounded soldiers lying on the cafe floor were the fiercely fighting American battalion he expected to encounter in heavily fortified positions. He had hardly paid them any attention.

The German column roared off, toward Buchholz Station. Peiper's eyes were set on the Meuse.

Inside the cafe, Lt. Bouck listened to the rumble of the panzer engines as they rolled by. The sound of them seemed endless, and they kept passing by until he was ordered out of the cafe at dawn, four hours later.

The wind was howling and the snow swirling in the air, when suddenly the door opened and Tsakanikas and Kalil were brought out, wrapped in blankets, and hoisted into the back of a truck, along with four wounded German soldiers.[50]

Bouck pressed Sack's Bible and two pictures of his girl into the wounded man's hand and told him that they were being separated but would get together later. But as he watched the truck pull off, he knew, in his heart, that he would never see either man again.

The Germans formed the rest of their prisoners into a column and marched them east, through Losheim. The whole way, they passed one continuous column of German tanks. German soldiers pelted them with insults and snowballs as they trekked to the rear.

Lyle Bouck was in a downward spiral. He was devastated that he had failed and he and his men had now been captured. But as he walked those feelings of self-pity changed to feelings of anger. His job now was to snap out of it and tend to the men around him. They would have to look out for one another. Escape must now occupy their thoughts.[51]

December 18 found the POWs in the basement of a railroad station. The Germans ordered them out, and they faced a long line of forty-and-eight boxcars; their name derived from their rated capacity—forty men or eight horses.

Into these forty-man cars, the Germans loaded seventy-two American prisoners, and they were stacked in like cordwood. In addition to the remaining eleven men from the I&R Platoon, most of the men on the train were from the 106th Division.

Despite the shocks and stresses these soldiers were experiencing as POWs, leadership took over. Someone said, "We've got to get organized." And then came the order to "Count off." Bouck was number seven.[52]

The train rumbled off toward the east. There were two tiny metal-framed openings high on the end walls, and the freezing air whistled in, mixing with the body heat generated by the crammed bodies of the men inside. Initially everyone stood, but a close examination revealed that, with a plan, some would be able to sit and a few could lie down. The plan was put into effect: two men lay on the floor, a few others sat cross-legged, and the rest stood. Periodically, someone pulled himself up to the tiny windows to see where they were, but the signposts were meaningless, until the train pulled into Koblenz.

On December 23, the train clanked on toward Limburg, Belgium, and arrived just as the British bombed the city's outskirts. Several of the cars on the train were hit. The one in front of Bouck took a direct hit, and his car was knocked over and fell on its side. Throughout the night, the dead and wounded were pulled from the wrecked cars, and sentries with dogs were called out to ensure none of the prisoners escaped.

German engineers somehow put the tracks back together, righted the overturned cars, and reloaded the prisoners. By daylight, they were rolling through the marshaling yard bound for Nuremberg. For these seven days, the men existed in their confined quarters with no food or water. Some of the men were wounded and received no medical care, and there was no consideration for sanitary facilities. Conditions became indescribable.

Still, discipline prevailed for the most part. In the rotation from a standing position, to a seated one, to one lying down, each man eventually found himself directly beneath one of the small windows. The cold air mixed with the warm breath of the prisoners formed frost on the metal parts of the window.

When a man was in such a position, he was "authorized" to scrape the frost off the metal frame and bars and eat it. No one but that man had that privilege, and it amounted to his only source of water. Finally, after a seven-day-long, start-and-stop journey, the train pulled into Nuremberg on Christmas. The prisoners were placed in a compound on the outskirts of the city and moved into sheds with straw mats on the floor. The compound was surrounded by wire, and the straw mats were full of lice.

On January 3, 1945, the Royal Air Force bombed Nuremberg during the night, and when daylight came, U.S. planes flattened the city. By mid-January, the prisoners were again loaded on trains and moved to the prison at Hammelburg. This time, they traveled in more sensible numbers. In fact, there were only twenty-five in the boxcar with Bouck.

The prison at Hammelburg was a permanent facility. Life at the prison was not easy. The prisoners were counted each morning and each evening. Their subsistence consisted of meager portions, usually served once a day, of watery turnip soup, some hard, black bread made from potato peelings, barley, and sawdust. On a good day there was cooked beet jam. On a bad day, they got nothing or a broth made with dehydrated vegetable tops that they dubbed the "Green Hornet," garnished with floating maggots.[53]

After an initial period of confinement, the prisoners resorted to tweaking the Germans even at the risk of mistreatment. At morning roll call, two men were assigned to hide and miss formation. This naturally led to great consternation among the guards. The camp commander would be notified and hurriedly come out to make his own count.

By the time the commandant began his count, the two missing prisoners were, of course, in formation. When the count was now right, the commandant fumed at the guards and stormed off in a huff. The threats from the guards to the practical-joking prisoners were always severe, but they did not stop the giggling Americans. When asked why they resorted to that risky type of humor, Bouck said, "There was nothing else to do."[54]

The most important possession of the prisoners at Hammelburg was a radio, smuggled in by an air force prisoner. Few knew where it was, and the Germans knew nothing of it, but the grapevine kept the inmates informed on the progress of the war. The BBC provided a gigantic lift for the morale at Hammelburg, and the men knew that the Allies were on the move. By spring, the whole camp knew that the Rhine had been crossed. Thoughts of liberation were hard to contain.

Then, on March 27, the unexpected happened. An armored column broke through and opened the prison. While the prisoners thought that this was the front lines, it was, in fact, only a spearhead of Gen. George Patton's 4th Armored Division, which was 60 miles ahead of the Allied lines. Its commander, Capt. Abraham Baum, led the 350-man force in a daring attempt to liberate Lt.Col. John Knight Waters, Patton's son-in-law.

The POW commander met with Baum, and they decided that only 350 men out of 1,500 prisoners could be rescued by the force. Field-grade officers (majors and above) would be allowed to go; the rest could try to make their escape to the American lines, 60 miles to the rear, or stay at the camp. In the compound next to the Americans, Yugoslavian prisoners, who had endured four years of captivity, took off for the woods.

Bouck turned to a second lieutenant whom he'd known from his days at Fort Maxey, and told him that he was promoting him to the rank of major. The surprised officer looked quizzically at Bouck, who then instructed him to now promote him to the same rank.

"Now let's get on a tank," Bouck said, and they mounted an armored vehicle.[55] The tankers gave them helmets and two Thompson grease guns.

By 2200, the column was ready to leave. They rolled out of the compound, and traveled for forty-five minutes toward the American lines.[56] Suddenly, the first tank blew up, and lighted the countryside with its blazing fire. A German antitank force had hit the lead tank, and now, the tank column tried to swing around and retrace its path.

Bouck and the other newly promoted major jumped off the tank and attacked the enemy position with their grease guns, wiping out the force. They ran back toward the other tanks, telling them that they could proceed, but it was too late; the tank column was moving in the opposite direction. The two officers jumped on the last tank but, in moments, the new lead tank was also hit, and the column turned around again, placing Bouck again in the lead.

It was hopeless. The Germans had the column cornered, and the tankers retreated to a farmhouse. They placed a Red Cross flag on the building and brought the wounded inside. Capt. Baum went along marking every other tank with chalk, designating those that would be siphoned for gas, so half the column would be able to break out. The riding prisoners were told they were on their own. Bouck and his friend stayed at the farmhouse.

At daylight, the armored column departed, but were hit by a combined air and ground attack and wiped out. The surviving tankers now joined the rest of the prisoners at the farm. They were conspicuous in their tankers overalls and were told by the other prisoners to take them off and try to blend in, because the Germans would be looking for them.

The Germans arrived and asked who were the tankers. No one said anything, but the Germans went along, pinching cheeks, to see who had flesh on their bones. The new tankers were easily culled out and separated, and everyone else was marched back to the prison.

The next day, Bouck was again herded on a train and taken to a new camp, this time the prison at Moosburg, near Munich, and became one of the twenty-seven thousand inhabitants there. His confinement, however, was short. On April 29, the camp was liberated by none other than his old outfit, the 99th Division, who learned, for the first time, that he and his men were not dead. Bouck's body, however, had shrunk from 180 pounds to a jaundiced 112 pounds.

EPILOGUE

Lt. Lyle Bouck was nursed back to health and released from active duty at war's end. He pursued a career of chiropractic medicine in St. Louis and was not aware of the enormous contribution that his I&R Platoon had played in the entire outcome of the Battle of the Bulge.

Unbeknownst to him, or to any of the other defenders of Lanzerath on that December 16, their action had cost Jochen Peiper, and his armored spearhead, the opportunity of reaching the Meuse River and moving on Antwerp, dooming the entire Sixth Panzer Army, the main strike force of Hitler's counteroffensive, to failure.

Peiper rolled out of Lanzerath in the dark hours of the morning and, on the morning of December 18, was approaching Trois Pont, 25 miles west of Lanzerath. He had encountered little resistance along the way, and his eyes were still on gaining the Meuse, despite the eighteen-hour delay at Lanzerath. Trois Pont was the final bridge that barred him from the Meuse.

But by 0800 on December 18, a force of engineers, just having arrived at the bridge site, was in position to destroy the structure that was vital to Peiper's advance. In the face of Peiper's lead tanks, the bridge was blown, forcing him to turn away from his main route. Eventually his attack was contained, less than 5 miles from Trois Pont. Peiper himself was bitterly disappointed with his inability to cross the key bridge: "If we had captured the bridge at Trois Pont intact . . . it would have been a simple matter to drive through to the Meuse early that day." He said, "If our own infantry had broken through by 0700 as originally planned, . . . I think we might have reached the Meuse in one day."[57]

It was not until twenty-three years later that Bouck's actions were investigated, beginning with a phone call from John Eisenhower, who was trying to put the pieces of the puzzle in place. He had researched the German and American records, and especially Peiper's testimony, and was trying to determine which battalion was blocking Peiper's way. The only forces he could find at Lanzerath was the small, eighteen-man I&R Platoon.

In 1981, thirty-seven years after their action, the I&R Platoon finally received their long overdue recognition and were awarded the Presidential Unit Citation. Additionally, four members—Bouck, Slape, Tsakanikas, and Milosevich—were awarded the Distinguished Service Cross, the highest award the Army can give. Five Silver Stars and nine Bronze Stars were also awarded, making the I&R the most decorated platoon in the war. A recommendation for the Medal of Honor for William James Tsakanikas was approved by the U.S. House of Representatives, but soon ran afoul of the Army's bureaucracy, which was guided by the rules that said that the recommendation must be presented within two years of the action—an impossibility in this case.

William James Tsakanikas did not die as Bouck had thought he would as the truck pulled out of Lanzerath with his body wrapped up in the back. He was taken to a German hospital on the west side of the Rhine, and there doctors operated to save his life. On March 26, 1945, he was liberated and eventually returned home. Over the years, Tsakanikas endured a life of pain and underwent thirty-seven operations to repair his shattered face. He died in 1977 as the result of complications from the final operation.

William Slape served thirty years in the Army, and was a finalist for the first position of Sergeant Major of the Army.

PFC Risto Milosevich returned to civilian life and started two construction companies.

Jochen Peiper was tried as a war criminal at Dachau and sentenced to death for his participation in the infamous Malmedy Massacre. Later, because of mitigating circumstances, his sentence was reduced to life in prison. He was released in 1957. On Bastille Day, July 14, 1976, Peiper was assassinated at his French villa by a group calling themselves the Avengers.

EIGHT
NAMKWAN HARBOR, CHINA
The Eleventh War Patrol of USS *Barb*

JANUARY 23, 1945

CDR. EUGENE B. FLUCKEY, USN

Eugene Bennett Fluckey was born on October 5, 1913, at the home of his parents in Washington, D.C. Two days after his birth, President Woodrow Wilson pressed a button from the White House, signaling the opening of the last section of the Panama Canal, and crowds in Panama watched the waters of the Atlantic and Pacific oceans meet, swirling together for the first time in the newly cut channel through the isthmus.[1]

As time passed, it seemed that this occurrence's proximity to his birth must surely have had an influence on young Eugene, because the boy was fascinated with mathematics and engineering, and he admired those who overcame enormous obstacles in the pursuit of their goals. Early in life, he believed that there were no such things as problems—just solutions.

His determination and work ethic were most likely passed down from his parents, who were both schoolteachers and demanded excellence. The most important man in Eugene's life was his father, a hard-working man of German extraction and a great model. "He was like Abe Lincoln," Eugene Fluckey remembered. "Honest, hardworking, and would walk a mile to pay a penny if he owed it."[2]

But the young boy also had the genes of his ancestors coursing through his veins, and they seemed to be a pretty hearty and undaunted people. One of his paternal ancestors came from the Alsace-Lorraine along the French-German border, and had made his arrival in North America as the thirteen colonies of Great Britain were struggling to become the United States. His arrival can only be described as less than dignified.

The Revolutionary War was in full swing, but to the German gentry of Alsace-Lorraine, that war in far-off America meant little. To Jorge Flocke, who was content to mind his own business, there was no thought of the struggle going on in the British Colonies. Nearer home, however, Hessian troops had been recruited to fight for the British and, as they made their way to embark for America, the British Crown paid a nice bonus for every additional soldier who could be shanghaied by the Hessian troops along the way.

Jorge and his horse were on the road at just the wrong time, in just the wrong place, so off they went, in the column of Hessians, with nary a chance to tell anyone good-bye. At journey's end, he landed on Staten Island and found himself fighting for the British. He was in the action at the burning of Philadelphia, and in the Battle of Trenton, where Washington crossed the Delaware, when the war was going badly for the revolutionaries. Washington's troops surprised the Hessians, and Jorge Flocke, and gave the Americans a much needed victory.

Young Jorge finally deserted, met a young Dutch girl who was an emissary of Washington, changed his name to Fluckey to avoid any possible encounter with the hangman, and began the Fluckey lineage in America.

One hundred and fifty years later, Eugene Fluckey was ten years old, and a student at a Washington, D.C., grammar school. He loved to listen to his radio crystal set, and on one particular afternoon, he tweaked the tiny device in an attempt to tune it and was able to pick up a radio station in Pittsburgh. His eyes twinkled with excitement when he heard that President Calvin Coolidge would be making a speech. "Silent Cal" was never known for long speeches, so this must be important.

The president's address began, and the young boy strained to hear his words. They were the most electrifying words he had ever heard. "Press on," the president said, challenging America to achieve greatness. "Nothing in the world can take the place of persistence." The young boy's ear was glued to every word. He listened as the president explained that talent, genius, and education would not, of themselves, guarantee success. Fluckey swelled with pride. "Nothing is more common than unsuccessful men with talent," Coolidge lectured, and, "Unrewarded genius is almost a proverb," he scoffed. As for education as the means to guarantee success, the president dismissed that thought by saying, "The world is full of educated derelicts." Eugene Fluckey listened for the president's final words, and they were the best. "Persistence and determination alone are omnipotent," the president concluded. And then his speech was over. The young lad determined that day that the president had been talking to him, and he was so excited and impressed that he named his first dog Calvin Coolidge.

Fluckey applied what he had heard that day to every aspect of his life, and when he was only fifteen, he graduated from high school. His father realized that the boy was too young to start college, so he enrolled him in Mercers Academy, an advanced school for bright students, and made him work his way through.

But at Mercers, Eugene met a professor who would have a profound effect on his life. The professor wanted Eugene to enter the annual local Original Math competition and told him that he could win, but the boy deferred, knowing that the exam was hard and, most likely, above his level. He didn't want to fail, but the professor persisted and told him that he had bet fifty dollars that Eugene could win.

Seeing the confidence that the older man had placed in him, and flattered that he was held in such high esteem, Eugene entered, not wanting to disappoint the professor. As expected the exam was a brain crusher. There were four problems and, after eight hours, the youngster had answered one and half of another. He would always remember that exam as the hardest of his life.

He went to his professor, crestfallen, and confessed that he had done poorly and had been a failure. The elder man bucked him up, and told him that the important thing was that he had tried and done his best. He patted him on the back and told him that he was very proud of his effort.

Still, Eugene was not happy with his performance until the results were released. After the final grading, he won the competition. No one else had completed even one of the four questions.

When he was finally of an age to attend college, he took the examination for Princeton, and passed, but a neighbor told him about the Naval Academy, and so he took that exam also, finishing number one in the entire country. His credentials were so strong that he eventually received three offers for appointment to Annapolis and six to West Point. He chose Annapolis, and entered the class of 1931, at the age of eighteen.

But as a 2nd class midshipman, in his third year, Fluckey's eyes failed him. His physical exam revealed that his eyesight had deteriorated to eleven-twenty, which meant that he was only able to read the letters on the eye chart at eleven feet when he should have been able to read them at twenty feet. This change in eyesight threatened to wash him out of the Academy, but Fluckey would have none of that.

He decided to take a course by Bernard McFadden called "Sight Without Glasses." He experimented with a prescription that he thought would help, but could not get it filled. Finally he brought it to the Naval Academy ophthalmologist, who examined it, determined it could do no harm, and signed the prescription.

When it was time for his reexamination, Fluckey went to the surgeon general's office, along with a number of other midshipmen whose careers were on the line. When it was his turn, he stood in front of the chart and began to read the letters. The examining doctor slowly shook his head as Fluckey read all the letters wrong. He stopped him and asked, "Can't you see the big E at the top?"

Fluckey informed him that he was reading the bottom line, which was virtually invisible. The doctor stepped closer to the chart and, indeed, the young midshipman was reading the last line. By that standard, he had thirty-six–twenty vision. He was passed and was back in the Academy, where he graduated in June 1935.

His first assignment was on the battleship *Nevada,* but he didn't like it and managed to transfer to destroyers. The destroyers of those days had no sonar, and Fluckey thought they would be sitting ducks for submarines in a war, so he decided to apply for submarine school at New London, Connecticut, in 1938. Upon completion he was sent to the USS *Bonita* in Panama.

Life on *Bonita* was not easy. Fluckey quickly learned that the sub, which had been built in 1925, had great difficulty diving. Any dive angle greater than two degrees resulted in loss of control of the boat. A two-degree dive angle meant certain death in any conflict with a destroyer, which could pounce upon the descending sub long before it could reach the safety of deep water.

To attempt to correct this problem, the Navy recalled the men who had originally been with the boat and, at one point, the average age of the petty officers on board *Bonita* was sixty-two. They were certain, as Fluckey tried more and more steep dives, that they were all doomed. Eventually, the maneuvering problems were solved, and when the Japanese bombed Pearl Harbor, Fluckey found himself on a boat with the responsibility of guarding the canal that seemed linked to him since birth. Fluckey made five war patrols on *Bonita,* certain that the canal was high on the Japanese target list, but they all proved to be "no soap" patrols, and the enemy never attacked.[3]

After Pearl Harbor, the U.S. Fleet had been reduced to a few precious aircraft carriers and 150 submarines. The submarines went on the offensive on the very first day. Four submarines were off on simulated war patrols and received the word that they were at war while at sea. They began an immediate search for Japanese targets, but found none.

Four other boats were dispatched to the Marshall Islands, but those patrols were futile as well. Three more boats were sent to the waters off the Japanese homeland, in the hopes they could bag the enemy in his home waters, but they too came up empty. A month after the devastating attack at Pearl, the U.S. submarine force still could not claim a victory against the Japanese to help ease the pain.

Then, during the second week of January 1942, the submarine *Gudgeon* scored the first kill for the United States by sinking a man-of-war. The rival Japanese submarine *I-173* was its victim.[4] But victories like that were to be few and far between.

For two incredible years, the U.S. submarine fleet experienced first one setback and then another—the result of the poor quality of its ordnance. Torpedoes exploded prematurely, failed to explode at all, or ran at erratic depths, passing harmlessly under the bottoms of their targets. Depth settings for 10 feet found the torpedo actually running over 20 feet deep. Magnetic exploders were notoriously flawed and were abandoned for contact exploders, but then the contact exploders didn't work. "Dud" became the most frequently used word to describe the performance of torpedoes fired at Japanese ships.

Morale among the submarine skippers reached rock bottom as, one after another, they watched certain kills steam away unscathed. One hapless submarine commander had identified and tracked one of Japan's biggest tankers and closed in for the kill. In an hour and a half, he systematically fired fifteen torpedoes at the huge target, eleven of which were duds.[5]

The result of the ordnance snafu was total frustration among the commanders, testy charges and countercharges at the highest ranks of the Navy, and low morale among sub crews. The Japanese merchant fleet became the recipient of this unexpected good fortune caused by the flawed American ordnance. Its ships sailed on, unaffected by the scores of torpedoes that passed harmlessly under their hulls or bounced noisily off of their sides.[6]

Finally, in October 1943, after almost two years of war against Japan, the Navy developed a reliable torpedo, and submarines began to score. In that month alone, twenty-six Japanese merchant ships went to the bottom, victims of the modified torpedo. More important, no duds were reported. In November, forty-eight enemy merchantmen and three men-of-war were sunk.[7]

During those two years of frustration in the Pacific, Eugene Fluckey endured his own frustrations on the other side of the world. Five war patrols out of Panama were uneventful, and he could not get assigned to action in the Pacific. Instead of action, he was sent to the command school in New London, Connecticut, after which he was finally ordered to Pearl Harbor, in January 1944. His expectations for combat rose to a cautious high.

But he was destined not to see action again. Instead, he was assigned to inglorious duty on a tender repairing the combat subs returning from patrols against the Japanese fleets. His service on the older boats in Panama and his lack of combat experience had sealed his fate. He was told that his new assignment would last at least two months, and then he might be sent on patrol with a seasoned skipper.[8] Eugene Fluckey was very disappointed.

He retired to his cabin on the sub tender, thinking only thoughts of rear echelon duty and of spending the war in a noncombat role. He fell asleep but was awakened at 0200 by a knock on his door. Sleepily, he invited his unexpected visitor in. In the small light of his cabin, he greeted a longtime acquaintance from his days in Panama, Lcdr. Johnny Waterman, who had commanded the old submarine S-45. Waterman was the present commander of the newer *Gato*-class sub, *Barb*.

Waterman had a worried look on his face. He had been *Barb*'s skipper since the sub had been commissioned in 1942 and had made six war patrols on her—five in Europe and the most recent one in the Pacific. During those patrols, *Barb* had not been credited with sinking a single vessel, and in just a few days, she was to embark on her seventh war patrol.

Fluckey listened to his visitor, and Waterman whispered that he had bad vibes about this upcoming patrol and a premonition that he would be sunk. It was to be his last combat patrol before he would be assigned to noncombat duty, and he was just plain scared.

Fluckey did not know what to say and wondered how he could help the dejected skipper. Waterman said that he knew Fluckey's record, and his excellence in engineering and torpedoes, and he would feel very much relieved if Fluckey could sail with him and act as a "joint commander." It would just be between them: Waterman would run the boat in the day, and Fluckey would command at night. At the end of the patrol, he would recommend Fluckey as his relief.

The exhausted skipper looked to Fluckey for an answer and, after some hesitation, received an okay from the newly arrived officer. Despite this left-handed opportunity, Fluckey saw a chance to escape his assignment on the sub tender—a chance for a command and for combat—and accepted the strange offer.[9]

The seventh combat patrol of *Barb* began in January 1944, and Fluckey was able to observe the tactics employed, which were from an earlier time: The boat was positioned in a known shipping lane, submerged, and the captain kept the surrounding seas under observation through the periscope, which barely poked out of the water. If a ship came by, then an attack would be launched, and the sub would dive to the bottom for protection.

Fluckey felt these tactics were too passive. He preferred to surface during the day and search the enemy out using the high periscope, which gave him a 200-square-mile visibility from its 50-foot elevation above the water.

On his watches as skipper, he employed bolder tactics, and on many occasions came within sight of land, much to the consternation of the older skipper, who preferred the open sea. But Fluckey's tactics paid off, and *Barb* finally sank its first ship, and then teamed with a sister submarine on a daring, double-shore bombardment using its deck guns. For the crew, which had never experienced the exhilaration of sinking a ship, much less the sight of American shells blowing up installations on the Japanese homeland, the effect was electrifying.[10]

But mostly, Fluckey was bored to tears on that seventh patrol. The junior officers shared his frustration and the days dragged by in inaction.

One night, the captain reported that Gen. Jonathan Wainwright, who had surrendered at Corregidor, was known to have been moved to Formosa, well within striking distance. When the captain suggested a rescue, Fluckey's eyes lit up and he immediately volunteered to take a rubber boat and look for the general. The skipper looked at the eager officer and smiled, but Fluckey was dead serious. The captain had to admit that he was just joking. But Fluckey was desperate for action, and pressed on. He asked to take one of *Barb*'s scuttling charges and blow up a railroad bridge on Formosa—anything to attack the Japanese—but he got a thumbs-down on that also.

When they returned from patrol, Waterman was true to his word.

He recommended Fluckey as his relief, and the latter became commander on April 28, 1944. The new skipper would always remember that date as a "red-letter" day in his life.[11] It would also be a red-letter day in the life of the submarine *Barb*. The boat that had not been credited with a single sinking of an enemy ship suddenly became the scourge of the seas.

On its eighth combat patrol, from May 21 to July 9, 1944, *Barb* sank five Japanese ships in the Sea of Okhotsk, north of Hokkaido. The ninth patrol, in the South China Sea between Formosa (Taiwan) and the Philippines, lasted for two months, between August 4 and October 3, 1944, and Fluckey's boat again scored big. This time the tally was four ships, including a prized escort aircraft carrier and a remarkable rescue of fourteen British and Australian POWs who were adrift at sea, facing certain death, after the Japanese ship transporting them had been sunk by an American submarine.[12]

Barb was given only three weeks to rest before departing on her tenth war patrol. This time the area was in the East China Sea, adjacent to the island of Kyushu and the Japanese homeland. On October 27, 1944, the sub departed Majuro Atoll in the Marshall Islands. Ten days later they were in their assigned waters and prowled the area for targets. It didn't take Fluckey long to add to his impressive total of ships sunk: He sank another three vessels, including a cruiser and two merchantmen during a three-day period.

That patrol ended on November 25, one month after it started. *Barb* had become the darling of the submarine fleet, and its daring skipper had earned the Presidential Unit Citations and three battle stars for his boat. For his own heroism, the Navy awarded him three Navy Crosses—the highest award the Navy can give.

On January 1, 1945, Eugene Fluckey commanded *Barb* on her eleventh war patrol. He opened a new logbook and made the first entry. He wrote that *Barb* had celebrated the arrival of 1945 as, hopefully, the last year of the war. The boat was now in its assigned area in the East China Sea, near the Straits of Formosa and the China coast.

But *Barb*'s luck seemed to be running out. For the first eight days of the patrol in enemy waters, there had been only one sighting. There should have been lots of cargo traffic since the fighting in the Philippines was reaching a climax, so Fluckey concluded that convoys must be hugging the China coast. In the shallower waters there was no threat from attacks by submerged submarines.

Fluckey's conclusion was correct, and shortly after noon, on January 8, Barb's lookout sighted the smoke of a convoy, seemingly coming from the shallow waters of the China coast. Fluckey looked through the high scope and could count five separate wisps. No masts were in sight, only the wisps. Then from the bridge came the report of seven smoke columns, and Barb bolted ahead at flank speed in an attempt to get ahead of the column.

Fluckey gave orders to close on the convoy until he could make out masts and funnels of the ships, and then to race ahead and try to "end around" from the port side of the convoy to the starboard side in order to attack and drive the ships away from the shallow waters of the China coast.

The end around was a tricky maneuver, requiring the sub to race ahead until it was 20,000 yards, or 10 miles, ahead of the convoy. It would then cut across the approaching path of the ships, get on the opposite side, and lay in submerged ambush.[13] On this particular maneuver, Barb was attempting to drive the convoy out into the waiting arms of two other subs operating with her as part of a wolfpack.

The race was on. Barb cut through the waters at flank speed of 20 knots, slowly putting distance between her and the slower moving convoy. Through the high periscope, Fluckey kept an eye on the ships.

At 1500, he turned the boat for his end-around run from port to starboard. The sub cut across the path of the convoy, 20,000 yards ahead, and one hour later had completed the maneuver.

Fluckey had made the daring move following the long-ago exhortations of Calvin Coolidge to "Press on." He was now taking a great risk to achieve a great victory. He had entered Barb into waters in the Formosan Straits that were designated as a "blind bombing zone." Translated, that meant that U.S. aircraft were permitted to attack and bomb any target in that zone without first identifying it as the enemy. Submarines entered the zone at their own peril.[14]

The Japanese convoy plodded on a southwesterly course toward the straits in three columns of ship. The convoy commander had them placed so that the starboard column consisted of a cargo and troop ship, followed by two tankers. The center column contained the most important ship of the convoy, containing troops, supplies, and kamikaze pilots. It was surrounded by four escorts. Following the escorts were two freighters. The port column consisted of a passenger/freighter and a tanker.

At 1612, Fluckey gave the order to "Man battle stations, torpedoes." The crews manning the six forward tubes and four stern tubes raced to their stations. Four minutes later, Fluckey ordered, "Take her down," and *Barb* dived below the surface.[15]

Securely submerged, Fluckey headed the sub in toward the convoy at full speed. He knew that he could easily get into the center of the convoy and create havoc among the ships, like a shark in the middle of a school of fish, but he knew that he would scatter the convoy after he fired his torpedoes. He wanted to bag the whole convoy by bending it out toward the other subs of the wolfpack after his attack and while he reloaded.

He chose the large troop carrier leading the center column as his first target. The four escorts were astern of her. He would fire three of his six forward torpedoes at the big ship, and the other three torpedoes at the first ship in the starboard column nearest himself. He'd then wheel the sub around for a stern-tube shot at the second ship in the starboard column.

The plotting for the attack took almost an hour and, at 1710, they were ready. Fluckey ordered "Up periscope," for a four-and-a-half-second look at the target, and then it was, "Down periscope, open outer tube doors, forward!"

In the forward torpedo room, the outer doors were opened and, at each tube, a man positioned himself with his hand over the firing pin in case the automatic firing control should malfunction.[16] In the conning tower, the sub's command center, the orders now came fast and furious.

Fluckey squatted on the deck next to the periscope well and ordered, "Up scope," grabbing the handles as soon as they came clear of the well and rising with the scope so that when it broached the surface, his eye would already be looking at the target. The periscope was out of the water for only a second or two, and Fluckey placed the hairline sight on the middle of the leading ship in the center column and ordered, "Down scope." The scope receded into the well, and all hands waited.

Then came the most exciting moment in this deadly game of hunted and hunter: It was the final setup before shooting.

"Set torpedoes for eight feet," Fluckey ordered, "divergent spread from aft forward; 50 yards between torpedoes." Trained hands set the appropriate data, and Fluckey crouched to the deck again. "Up scope." The periscope rose from the well and, again, Fluckey had the handles as soon as he could reach them and pressed his eyes against the rubber cushions on the sight.

Rising with the scope, he barked out the final orders. "Angle on the bow, 70 starboard; range, 2500 yards."[17]

He only had a few seconds to look before he ordered the scope down, but in those moments above the water, he saw that he had brought the submarine in at a perfect attack angle. Not only was he set up for a high percentage shot on the large ship leading the center column, but he had the bonus of a full overlap on the large freighter leading the port column.

It was a captain's dream. Any torpedo that might miss its selected target would strike a second vessel trailing in the line of fire. For the unsuspecting ships, it was a devastating situation. It was more than the legendary maneuver of "capping the T," it was the naval equivalent of enfilade fire. Enfilade fire engulfed enemy infantry by arranging the long axis of the beaten zone of fire to correspond to the long axis of the troop formation, resulting in an inescapable killing field. Capping the T involves positioning the broadside of friendly ships to cap the T of the column of enemy ships, bringing guns to bear on the long axes of enemy vessels. The enemy can only fire to the side.

"Bearing, mark," Fluckey ordered, as the hairline on the scope bisected the target ship. "Down, scope." He stood back as the periscope receded.

Within seconds, the operator of the torpedo data computer had locked in the final bearing, and the computer set the firing angle on the torpedo. "Set!" the operator exclaimed.[18]

There was no hesitation. "Fire one, fire two, fire three," Fluckey ordered.

The torpedo officer hit the firing plungers in succession with the heel of his hand to initiate the firing. Air pressure, compressed at 600 pounds per inch, propelled the 20-foot-long, 3,000-pound torpedoes from the firing tubes. They were away, at 1724,[19] almost three and a half hours after the first sighting of the convoy.

As soon as the first three torpedoes cleared the sub, Fluckey had the scope up again, giving a new setup for the second three-torpedo attack. He fixed the hairline on the lead freighter in the starboard column, gave range and angle, and ordered, "Bearing-mark." The scope was down again. Another "set," from the operator, and Fluckey ordered torpedoes four, five, and six fired. The sub's hull shuddered as the second set of torpedoes was expelled.

Throughout the confined quarters of the submarine, the only confirmation to the crew that an attack was actually under way was the welcome whooshing sound and the shudder of the vessel as the torpedoes exited the tubes. The men in the conning tower, near the captain, were privy to the conversation of battle. They could hear the sonar operator report the course of the torpedoes with words like, "hot, straight, and normal" or "one torpedo running left of course." They could see the captain raise and lower the periscope and bark out commands. On occasion, someone else got to look through the scope.

But except for those in the small command center in the conning tower, the rest of the men at their battle stations throughout the sub were blind and could only respond to relayed commands. They fought their battle, never seeing the enemy or the results of the attack. In the hot, sweaty world of the submerged submarine, they could only listen for the results of the attack, and cheer if they heard an explosion, and wait for the officers above to fill them in. If an enemy destroyer attacked, they were informed to rig for depth charges and held on to endure the jolting explosions threatening to seal them all in their 312-foot steel casket. Their world under the water during such an attack was one of breaking lightbulbs, rupturing cans, and water rushing in through broken pipes and seals. The sub pitched and rolled under the force of the explosions, and men and loose objects were thrown around.

Near misses were deafening, and men prayed and sweated as the attack continued with little letup.

Up in the conning tower, the silence was broken as the quartermaster counted off the running time to the target: "Forty-nine, fifty, fifty-one . . ."

At the time when the first torpedoes should be hitting, Fluckey raised the scope and watched as two large geysers and explosions erupted on the port side of the transport in the center column. The third explosion was enormous and the shock wave pushed *Barb* down over 20 feet from its 60-foot attack depth. Lightbulbs burst, and the men scrambled to grab on to any support to prevent being knocked to the deck. Sonar reported the sound of high-speed screws indicating destroyers prowling. Fluckey rigged for depth charges and silent running, but there was no counterattack. Twelve minutes later, he returned to periscope depth for a look-see.

The sight was unbelievable. The large transport was down by the bow with its stern 30 degrees above the water. The lead freighter in the starboard column, the target of the second set of torpedoes, had disappeared. The enormous explosion had left no sign of the ship, not even debris.

As a bonus, Fluckey could see that the first ship in the port column was on fire—the recipient of the third torpedo, which had missed its target ship. The whole convoy had turned and stopped, taking it out of range of Fluckey's intended stern-tube attack. *Barb* reloaded her six bow tubes for further action.

It was dark when the convoy reformed the remaining six ships and the four escorts into two columns and steamed in the direction of Formosa. *Barb* surfaced and followed, 10 miles astern, and sought opportunity to attack again.

Fluckey maneuvered, on the surface, toward the starboard column and inched his way to a position, 2,000 yards astern of the last ship. He planned a daring attack on that trailing ship. If successful, he would move up and try to pick off the next one, and so on, for as long as he could.[20] He reasoned that if the rear ships fell, the head of the convoy would steam on without disruption, like a running herd of zebras, when a trailing animal has fallen to a lion. The convoy would be in full flight.

As Fluckey moved closer to the trailing ship, he slid to the right to set up his shot. In the dark, *Barb* was unseen, and on radar she blended in with the escort ships.

Again the outer doors of tubes one, two, and three were opened, and the hairline in the periscope was fixed on the middle of the target. When he was in position so that he also had an overlap on the trailing ship in the port column, Fluckey gave the order to fire three torpedoes, then set up on the next ship.

There was only a fifteen-second torpedo run before the 668-pound torpedo warheads detonated against the flank of the target. One hit forward and the second hit midships, sending the ship into a nosedive. A third explosion detonated on the overlapped ship in the port column, engulfing it in smoke. Three shots; three hits.

It was 2015, just over seven hours after the original sighting of the convoy, and *Barb* hustled forward to set up a shot on the next ship in the starboard column. She had fired nine of her twenty-four torpedoes and had sunk three ships and damaged two others. She had joined the convoy and become a wolf in sheep's clothing in the middle of the flock. *Barb* maneuvered among the enemy escorts, some less than 600 yards distant.

At 1,500 yards from the next ship, the crew opened the outer doors to tubes four, five, and six. Torpedoes were set for 8 feet, and the hairline was on the middle of the target.

"Fire four, fire five, fire six," Fluckey barked, and the torpedoes whooshed on their way. All three struck the doomed tanker. A colossal explosion erupted. Fluckey thought the explosion resembled a "gigantic phosphorous bomb."[21]

The exploding ship became a volcano, lighting the area for miles. Flying debris hit *Barb*'s hull, as the lookouts ducked. The enemy ship had been transporting precious aviation fuel.

At 2219, *Barb* broke off the attack and set course for her lifeguard station, which had been assigned for the following day along the known aircraft route to possibly rescue downed fliers conducting air attacks in the Philippines. She'd sunk four ships and damaged another two. She still had twelve torpedoes left.

For the next ten days, *Barb* patrolled toward the north, hugging the 10-fathom, or 60-foot, curve. It was the minimum depth in which a sub could dive. She had to dive often to avoid patrol planes, and intermingled with fishing fleets of Chinese junks for cover, but found no targets. There was nothing in the deeper water, so Fluckey concluded that shipping must be hugging the coast in waters too shallow for submerged subs to attack.[22]

Puzzled by the lack of targets, Fluckey asked if a channel, close to the coast, had been dredged, permitting ships passage close to the Chinese coast. A reply from Commander Naval Group China informing him that such a channel had been dredged and major ships, including battleships, were using it shocked him.[23]

The convoys traveled during daylight, when a submarine surfacing in shallow waters could be detected. At night the convoys would hole up in a safe harbor to preclude such a surface attack.

Fluckey knew that the chances of finding targets under such conditions were slim, unless he could find a way to get *Barb* on the surface to make an attack more like a torpedo boat than a submarine. His recent successful attack on the surface at night emboldened him to creative thinking.

On the morning of January 22, Fluckey moved *Barb* in among more than two hundred junks, bobbing and fishing in the choppy seas and solid overcast. He planned to mingle with them as they fished and to reverse course with them in the afternoon as they headed toward the shore. He hoped that, surrounded by his camouflage of junks, he could move several miles inside the 10-fathom curve for a better look for a reported convoy.

If he found the convoy, his options were limited. An attack on the surface during daylight was out of the question, unless there was poor visibility and few escorts. He would attack at night if the convoy was under way. Ships at anchor usually meant the presence of minefields, so an attack without details on the minefield was out.[24]

At noon, the junk fleet began its movement toward shore. *Barb* followed, sometimes waving at the junk crews. The overcast was welcome to minimize the possibility of air intruders.

The depth soundings showed the water becoming more shallow. At 1421 the sounding showed only 48 feet, when one of the lookouts on his perch above the bridge sighted small wisps of smoke on the horizon.

Through the high periscope, from 9 miles away, Fluckey could see the masts of at least six ships, traveling south. Four miles inside the 10-fathom curve, *Barb* stopped in 42 feet of water. The junks plodded on toward the shoreline. The convoy moved on, and *Barb* tracked it by radar as the smoke disappeared. At 14 miles, Fluckey could still see the radar contact on the ships. The captain then reversed course and headed out toward the deeper water. He'd seen what he wanted to see.

He plotted the course to intersect with the convoy as it exited the dredged channel to the south. That exit was 100 miles away and, at flank speed, *Barb* would arrive an hour after dark.

At 1830, *Barb* was at the 10-fathom curve. It was dark as the sub moved through the local junk fleet and advanced into the shallower waters, navigating by radar. A lone junk appeared in front of the sub and became a welcome shield for possible mines.

An hour later, *Barb* was in 30 feet of water and only 2,000 yards from the channel. She remained stationary, hoping that any escort ship would mistake her for just another rock among the many that jutted above the surface. In this position, she was ready to shoot the passing convoy like targets in a shooting gallery. They would be in formation, passing in review.

But no ships passed the deadly ambush. There was no sound, no movement, and it was pitch black. Nothing was on radar. After more than an hour, it became evident that the convoy had given them the slip or had anchored. A disappointed Eugene Fluckey took his submarine back out to the deeper water, retracing his steps to avoid mines.

But he wasn't through. Spreading maps on the wardroom table, he and his officers examined the charts. A radio message had informed them that there were no reported minefields to the north of their position.

At 2200, with eight hours of darkness to work with, Fluckey plotted a daring surface patrol. He would turn to the north, parallel the coast, and move between the 10- and 20-fathom curves. Twenty-five miles from his present position, he would turn in again toward land and continue the patrol along the 10-fathom line. The convoy had to be nearby at anchor.

His men looked at him as if he were crazy, but he reassured them. "I know no sub has ever done this before. That's our great advantage— surprise!"[25] He then moved through the length of the boat and, at each station, the men gave him a thumbs-up. They were with him.

But how to find the anchored convoy was the question. Just as *Barb* hoped to blend in with the rugged coastline and the many exposed rock formations and remain invisible to radar, the convoy had a similar advantage.

The solution was to trace the coastline—and rocks, and islands, and anything else that appeared on the navigational charts of the area— onto a piece of Plexiglas that fit on the radar scope. Any strange blips would warrant further investigation.

Three hours later, at 0112, on January 23, the plotting room reported pips at an extreme range of almost 15 miles. *Barb* moved cautiously forward, dodging an occasional junk. At 7 miles, radar reported a contact circling counterclockwise around a prominent 150-foot-high island named Incog Island.

The radar continuously painted Incog Island and the circling blip for more than an hour. The operator's eyes were glued to the sweeping light, and he finally reported that the blip must be an escort. He also reported that radar was sweeping from the escort as well as several other locations. The operator watched the circling blip as it went round and round Incog Island. It took twenty-one minutes to disappear to the other side.

Fluckey now knew that a convoy must be anchored in a safe harbor on the other side of Incog, and ordered *Barb* ahead, up the line. There was no moon, and the overcast was heavy. Radar now identified two other escorts several miles to the north. The operator watched them until the circling ship reappeared on the screen. She was only 3 miles away, and her circling route moved her track right into the path of the entrance into the harbor. On the charts it was named Namkwan Harbor.

At 0300, the circling escort again disappeared behind Incog Island, which was now to the left of *Barb*'s position on the 10-fathom line. As soon as the ship disappeared from the radar scope, Fluckey ordered the sub forward at emergency speed. The sub surged forward and followed a curving left path around Incog and into the harbor entrance. Fluckey called the maneuver "the revolving door treatment."[26]

At 0320, radar counted thirty ships jammed into the safe haven. Low whistles could be heard in the conning tower as eyes fixed on the saturation of blips as the circling light painted them on the radar screen. The ships were anchored in three lines parallel to the coast, with 500 yards between the lines. Fluckey ordered *Barb* ahead and switched on the intercom to brief the anxious crew below.

"We've got the biggest target of the war in front of us," he said. "Make ready all tubes . . . Man battle stations, torpedoes."[27] Cheers and gongs resounded in the hull.

Fluckey had twelve of his twenty-four torpedoes left, but only four were in the forward torpedo room, which had six tubes, leaving tubes five and six empty. The other eight were in the less-used after torpedo room, which had only four tubes. There would be no time to reload.

Fluckey marked the firing position at 3,000 yards from the inboard ship line. This was 6 miles inside the 10-fathom curve, and 25 miles to the 20-fathom curve, which offered safety to a diving submarine.

The captain planned to fire the four bow torpedoes first and then swing around for a four-torpedo shot from the stern tubes. The maneuver would have him facing the harbor entrance after his final shot, and it would be all ahead, flank, for a run to the deep.

His best calculations projected an hour and a half run to safety. He plotted his retreat course through an area marked "Unexplored." The chart showed "rocks awash" and "rocks—position doubtful," but, despite the obvious danger in traversing such waters, Fluckey hoped that the Japanese had the same charts and would balk at hot pursuit. His course would also take him through the area of the local junk fleet— hopefully another barrier to a chasing escort.

Stepping to the periscope, Fluckey placed the hairline on the big ship, just to the left of the center of the first line. His first target was marked. He then selected the largest ship to the right of center as target number two, and marked it for the stern-tube shot.

This unbelievable target in front of *Barb* was 4,200 yards of continuously overlapping ships. Any torpedo missing the front line would surely strike a ship in the second or third lines.

Fluckey spurred *Barb* ahead at two-thirds speed and inserted 150 percent spread to preclude too many torpedoes from hitting the same ship. This greater spread launched the torpedoes at wider angles to cover more of the target area. "Open outer doors," he ordered. The outer doors of the four bow tubes opened as he took his final bearing. "Fire one, fire two, fire three, fire four!"

The torpedoes sped toward their anchored targets. Fluckey swung the sub around and added 300 percent divergence to the spread for the stern torpedoes. Two minutes later, it was, "Fire seven, fire eight, fire nine, fire ten!"[28] Off they went toward their anchored prey. On the bridge, those who were privileged to observe the attack fixed binoculars to their eyes and focused on the sprawling merchant fleet in front of them. Fluckey awaited the "rape of solitude."[29]

At 0406, two torpedoes hit the first ship and settled her to the bottom. A third torpedo hit a ship in the second line, behind the main target. A minute later, a ship in the third column exploded in flames that flared and quickly went out—a sure sign that it sank. The four bow torpedoes had all scored.

Then the stern torpedoes hit. Two hits in the first line on the target freighter, with enormous geysers and clouds of smoke. Seconds later, a hit in the second column that blew out the entire side of the vessel, sinking her immediately. Seven out of eight hits. Not bad.

And then the eighth torpedo hit. With a deafening roar, a munitions ship anchored in the third line exploded, casting projectiles into the air before it sank. The explosion sent shock waves over the submarine.[30]

Barb bolted for the deep, leaving Namkwan Harbor to explode. The circling escort was still behind Incog Island and missed the fireworks, but the two other escorts picked up the sub and began closing on her. The closest was at 6,000 yards. *Barb* was in for a race. To her stern, Namkwan was in a pall of smoke. One hour earlier, it had been peaceful and quiet, and dark and safe, but that was before *Barb* had entered the "revolving door."

The fleeing sub churned the waters and had a bone in her teeth, but despite her high-balling pace, the next report was distressing. One pursuing destroyer had closed to 4,200 yards. With each turn of the screw, it closed on the slower submarine. In the aft torpedo room, the crew was ordered to load the last four fish (torpedoes) into the stern tubes. The deck gun crews stood by in the control room for action in an unthinkable last stand.

Barb streaked across the uncharted waters. Eleven minutes into her run, the closest destroyer had closed to 3,600 yards. Fluckey pleaded for more speed from the engine room, but was told that the engines were at top speed and any increase would activate the governors, which would cut the engines off. All engines have governors to prevent a runaway engine and overheating. They interrupt the fuel flow to keep the engine within a certain rpm range.

"Tie down the governors," Fluckey barked out, "and put 150 percent overload on all the engines!" The governors were disabled.

The destroyer was now at 3,200 yards and still closing, but not quite as fast as before, as *Barb* raced forward at almost 24 knots—unheard of for submarines. The increased rpms were not without their toll: The engine room reported the bearings were overheating. In the aft torpedo room, a frantic crew had reloaded tubes seven and eight.

Fluckey had originally plotted his course to come within 3,000 yards of the area marked "rocks" and "rocks awash." He now cut that distance in half in an effort to discourage the pursuing destroyer. At the speed he was traveling, he knew that the destroyer could only engage with his bow gun. To turn for a broadside, it would have to swing away and fire an illumination round to light the submarine. Fluckey expected that maneuver would happen when the pursuing ship had closed to 2,000 yards.

The moment the destroyer fired the illumination, *Barb* would fire her two stern torpedoes and then swerve to the left, even closer to the dangerous rocks. If the destroyer swerved with her, either to fire a broadside or to avoid the torpedoes, Fluckey hoped it would pile into the rocks or hit a submerged obstacle.

Barb raced on in full flight. The situation in the engine room with the overheating bearings was only getting worse. The Japanese destroyer closed the gap with each turn of its propeller. No one spoke. Every man held on.

The spell was broken when radar suddenly reported that the junk fleet was only 900 yards to the front. There was no chance to avoid them and the sub plowed on. The destroyer was at 2,700 yards. *Barb* maneuvered wildly through the fleet and within minutes the race was over as the escorts opened fire on the junks. Obviously, they were unable to distinguish, on radar, the difference between junk and sub.

At 0446, *Barb* slowed to flank speed, offering the howling bearings some relief. Thirty minutes later, just before dawn, she crossed the 20-fathom line. When radar picked up an approaching aircraft, Fluckey took her down to 150 feet and ordered the crew to sleep. Everyone collapsed. In the distance, explosions and depth charges and bombings continued as the Japanese searched in vain for the unseen attacker. It would continue for hours.

In the ship's log, Fluckey made the final entry, closing the attack of January 23, 1945. He simply wrote, before retiring, "Life begins at forty—fathoms,"[31] and then he slept.

For his conspicuous gallantry and intrepidity, above and beyond the call of duty, Cdr. Eugene Bennett Fluckey was awarded the Medal of Honor for his actions at Namkwan Harbor.

EPILOGUE

Eugene Fluckey took *Barb* back to Midway, arriving on February 10, and to Pearl Harbor, arriving five days later to the red-carpet treatment. The sub was scheduled to go stateside to Mare Island for refitting and overhaul. The crew was overjoyed.

At Pearl he was debriefed before the Navy brass. He shocked them by reporting that on no day during the entire patrol was *Barb* submerged for eight hours. Five hours had been the longest they'd been submerged and that was in the first attack on January 8 and during the resulting enemy destroyer attacks. His actions had shattered all conventional thinking on sub tactics. All his other torpedo attacks had been launched from the surface. Here was a skipper who had turned a submarine into a surface man-of-war.

More incredibly, Fluckey had made his shots count. He had sunk seven ships and heavily damaged five others, with twenty-four torpedoes, twenty-two of which had been hits. His crew called him Dead-Eye Fluckey,[32] and he richly deserved the name: In January 1945, the average American submarine expended sixteen torpedoes for each kill.[33]

Navy psychologists had determined that after four patrols, a submarine commander should be relieved, since the strain of combat had worn him down. Fluckey objected and demanded a fifth patrol, despite the tradition that Medal of Honor recipients need not be placed in unnecessary danger. He was adamant, professing that he had new tactics he wanted to try that would end the war sooner. His superiors relented and, after the sub was refitted, Fluckey took *Barb* on his final patrol. He called it a graduation patrol.

On the twelfth patrol, *Barb* again returned to the Sea of Okhotsk. The fifty-six-day patrol, from June 8 to August 2, 1945, was special in that *Barb* was equipped to fire a new weapon at Japan: a rocket launcher and seventy-two 5-inch rockets.[34] The idea to bombard Japanese coastlines had come of age. Additionally, Fluckey promised to sink fifteen vessels of some sort, not necessarily ships. He was committed to total war against the Japanese war machine.

On June 22, *Barb* became the first ballistic missile–firing submarine as it launched twelve rockets against the rail junction town of Shari on Hokkaido. She would make three other rocket attacks against targets on the Japanese portion of Sakhalin Island called Karafuto. Rail junctions, canneries, repair yards, and factories felt the rain of Fluckey's twelve-shot salvos.[35]

He also sank three more ships by torpedo attack, becoming the first sub to sink a ship using a sonar homing torpedo called a Cutie. True to his word, he sank a total of fifteen vessels, expending every bit of ammunition in the process, so that when he attacked the fifteenth vessel, he was forced to ram it to send it to the bottom.

But of all the achievements of this last patrol, the highlight was a saboteur attack conducted by an eight-man patrol landed in rubber boats. The target was to bag a train running along the coastal rail tracks carrying supplies.

Using one of the 55-pound high-explosive scuttling charges designed to be the last resort to prevent the sub's capture, the patrol paddled to the shore, found the track, and set the charge. A sixteen-car train rolled over the makeshift detonating device and set off a massive explosion. Fluckey had seen his dream from when he was "co-commander" fulfilled.

The crew added the symbol of a train to *Barb*'s cluttered battle flag, and the eight-man saboteur patrol became the only American ground forces to ever invade Japan. Four days after the twelfth war patrol of *Barb* ended on August 2, the atom bomb was dropped on Hiroshima, and then on Nagasaki. The war in Japan ended on August 15.

Fluckey's detailed examinations for years after the war, including a 1991 visit to Namkwan Harbor and Japanese records, credits his submarine with 29⅓ ships sunk, a total of 146,808 tons. The Joint Army-Navy Assessment Committee, convened to determine statistics as to who sank what, only credited *Barb* with seventeen vessels, 96,628 tons, but JANAC did not have the benefit of the years when more detailed assessments could be made. But, regardless of the numbers, she was indisputably one of the top three submarines in the war.[36] The U.S. submarines sank virtually the entire Japanese Fleet, sending more than five million tons of shipping to the bottom.[37]

Eugene Fluckey was awarded his fourth Navy Cross after the twelfth patrol, and he and his crew became living legends in the naval history of World War II. Under his command, during five war patrols, crew members were awarded six Navy Crosses, twenty-three Silver Stars, and an equal number of Bronze Stars. The boat was awarded the Presidential Unit Citation, the Navy Unit Commendation, and five battle stars.

But of all the awards amassed by *Barb* and her warriors, the one that Fluckey was most proud of was the one that no one under his command ever received—the Purple Heart.[38] Fluckey completed a career of thirty-seven years' service in 1972 and retired with the rank of rear admiral.

DEATH VALLEY, IWO JIMA

February 25, 1945

PFC Jay Rebstock, USMC (E Co., 2nd Bn., 27th Marines)

On June 19, 1944, as the Japanese unleashed their air offensive against the U.S. Fifth Fleet in the Philippine Sea, 101 land-based Japanese aircraft scrambled off the island of Iwo Jima. They were to lend their weight to the combined air attack to regain Japanese naval strength in the operation known as A-Go. None of the 101 planes ever returned.[1] They became part of the one-sided statistics in the staggering losses suffered by the Japanese in the Marianas Turkey Shoot.

With the loss of the sea battle, the Imperial Japanese Navy was a navy in name only. The losses of planes and pilots, even though most of these pilots were inexperienced, meant that despite the existence of a few surviving carriers they were now useless—there were no aircraft and no men to fly them. Japan could not mount an offensive challenge to the mighty U.S. Fifth Fleet. The great carrier battles that had begun at the Coral Sea were over.

With the elimination of the Japanese Navy, Marines invaded and secured the islands of Saipan, Tinian, and Guam between June 15 and August 10, and then set their sights on the next set of islands leading to the gateway of Japan itself: the Bonin and Volcano Islands, only 660 miles from the Japanese mainland. The most prominent island, with terrain suitable for airfields, was the tiny island of Iwo Jima.

For the Japanese, the defeat of Operation A-Go meant a change in tactics. Their defense would be without the support of naval or air forces, and while they had substantial ground forces—almost thirty untouched divisions—the question was, could they be used effectively in the continuing island campaign of the Pacific?

Imperial Japanese headquarters had little choice. To continue the war—surrender was not an option—they would dig in and fight to the death. They decided to fortify the islands of Iwo Jima and Okinawa and conduct a war of attrition against the invading Americans. The 109th Division was assigned to be the main force to defend Iwo Jima.[2]

The Japanese premier, Gen. Hideki Tōjō, recognized the seriousness of the American advance across the Central Pacific but had little with which to stop them. For the defense of Iwo Jima, he called upon a fifty-three-year-old samurai warrior, Lt.Gen. Tadamichi Kuribayashi, who came from a military family that had served six emperors in the Army. He had commanded Imperial troops in their glory days during the conquests of Manchuria and China. Because of his excellent credentials during his thirty-year military career, Emperor Hirohito personally picked Kuribayashi to be the defender of Iwo Jima. But it was more than defending a small island; Iwo Jima was, in fact, part of Japan proper, and allowing an invasion of Iwo Jima would carry the same disgrace as an invasion of the Japanese mainland.[3]

The general accepted his post without hesitation, but revealed his sober understanding of the consequences of his assignment in a letter to his brother. He was being called upon to defend Iwo Jima; not to save the island from conquest, but to defend it and make the American invading forces pay a staggering price for its possession. "I may not return alive from this assignment," he wrote, "... but I shall fight to the best of my ability, so that no disgrace will be brought upon our family. I will fight as a son of Kuribayashi, the Samurai."[4]

• • •

While Kuribayashi had been leading victorious troops in Manchuria and China in 1940, sixteen-year-old Jay Rebstock was a student at Gulf Coast Military Academy in Gulfport, Mississippi. Rebstock was born on February 2, 1924, and, at the tender age of eleven, had played peewee football while attending school at St. Stanislaus Academy in Bay St. Louis. Playing on the varsity, several years older than he, was a big kid named Doc Blanchard who pounded through the lines of opposing schools and ran roughshod over frustrated tacklers. This big, bruising kid with the pounding running style would become a household name several years later during a glorious football career at the United States Military Academy.

Gulf Coast Military Academy was a long way from West Point, but so was an island named Oahu and a place called Pearl Harbor. Rebstock heard those names for the first time while watching a movie in a Gulfport theater. Suddenly the screen went blank, the house lights came up, and an announcer came on stage and said that the Japanese had bombed the fleet at Pearl Harbor. Most of the youngsters didn't even know where that was, and the audience buzzed with questions. While everyone was puzzled by the announcement, Rebstock's friend, sitting next to him, nudged him. He leaned over and said, "I know where Pearl Harbor is. It's in Hawaii. My brother is serving on a battleship named *Oklahoma*!"

Young Rebstock went back to the campus that night, and began to figure out his next move. He decided that the one way he could get out of school, which he detested, was to join the service. He mustered his courage and went to call his family at the only pay phone for miles around, only to find a line that wrapped around the block. Finally, after three hours of shuffling forward a few feet at a time, it was his turn, and he stepped into the booth and dialed his familiar home number. His father answered and Rebstock cleared his throat and spoke forcefully into the receiver. "Daddy," he said to the elder Rebstock on the other end, "I'm quitting school and joining the Army to fight the Japs!"

At first there was silence on the other end, but then he heard his father's curt voice telling him that if he tried to do that, and if he walked away from the academy, he wouldn't have to wait for the Japs to fight. He would personally give the youngster all the fight that he could ever want. More than a little discouraged, Jay hung up and realized as he trudged back to his room that his short fantasy about the Army was over.

He stayed in Gulf Coast Academy and finished school, graduating in June of 1943, on crutches. In his final football season, he had torn a cartilage in his knee. Corrective surgery was successful, but it left Rebstock 4-F with the selective service, much to his family's delight.

Rebstock found a job in the oil field and served as a roughneck doing backbreaking work for six months. His heart was not in it. All of his friends were in the service, and that's where he wanted to be. Some 4-Fers were delighted to take a pass on serving, but not Jay Rebstock. He'd gone to Keesler Field to try and join the Air Corps, but had been turned down, and then he tried the Merchant Marine at Pass Christian on the Gulf Coast, but the answer was the same. The bad knee was not acceptable. He simply could not pass the physical.

In 1943 there was a mandatory draft to fill the needs of the services. A young man could not just join the service he wanted. He had to be drafted, and then Uncle Sam decided where he was needed. One morning, while working in the oil field, Rebstock decided to give it one more try. He went to his foreman and told him that he was going to Thibodaux to visit the draft board, and then hitchhiked to the small south Louisiana city. He went to the draft board and asked to be drafted, and in two weeks his "greetings" came. Rebstock's father was not thrilled that his young son had persisted in trying to get in the service and even criticized him for not just taking the 4-F classification and sitting it out. But young Jay was of a different mind; he felt left out. He felt that he had to do his duty, as all his friends were doing. He, like the rest of the nation, had been energized by the sneak attack on Pearl Harbor, which was a call to arms. He had also heard the words "chicken" and "draft-dodger," and bristled at the accusation that he had been able to avoid the draft because his father was the head of the ration board. Even the head of the draft board had joked that if he drafted young Jay, he'd have his rations cut. Of course, there was no truth to that, but that didn't stop it from being said.

Finally, Rebstock reported to New Orleans and lined up with a thousand other young men at the draft headquarters. He talked with several of his friends about joining the Marine Corps, especially the Raiders. He'd read about the Raiders in an issue of the *Reader's Digest,* and their bold fighting spirit appealed to him. His friends agreed and, like most young men, they wanted to be in an elite force.

When the time came to line up for selecting the service that they might want, the Army and the Coast Guard recruiters spoke to them using very civil language. It was "Gentlemen" this, and "Gentlemen" that, and "Please fill out this," and "Please line up over there." But the Marine Corps representative was having none of that. He was a small tough-as-nails Marine sergeant who was a veteran of Guadalcanal.

"He only weighed 140 pounds," Rebstock remembered, "but he talked as if he weighed 250 and could whip everyone there."

The Marine veteran sneered and talked down to everyone as he sauntered in front of the men. He used words like "worthless" and "scum" and "maggots," as he paced back and forth. When he flashed a look at anyone, that person could not hold his stare, and usually ended up looking at the ground. Everyone else was wide-eyed.

Finally the sergeant bellowed out for those who thought they could make it in the Corps, and who wanted to be Marines, to take two steps forward. He stood at parade rest, with his arms folded as he waited for the answer to his challenge.

Jay Rebstock straightened his shoulders, took a deep breath, and stepped forward. He looked straight ahead and waited for the next order. When it didn't come, he chanced a look over his shoulder to see where his friends were; they were all back in the ranks, shaking their heads and avoiding his eyes. He was the only person standing two paces in front of the formation, and the feisty sergeant claimed his prize.

The next step was the dreaded physical and, as each phase of it was conducted, Rebstock held his breath. It was a very fast examination, and he passed. He breathed a sigh of relief while a young Navy doctor went over his papers and asked if he had any identifying scars. The "identifying scars" question was a standard on all the physicals, and Rebstock remembered that the tough little Marine sergeant had mockingly told them it was so that someone could identify your dead ass after your face was blown off.

Jay began showing every little nick and cut, and finally showed the big scar on his knee. The doctor raised his eyebrows and wanted to know how he got it. Rebstock explained the football injury and the resulting surgery, and watched as the doctor shook his head. He told the eager young man that there was no way he could get into the service.

Young Jay looked as if he had been struck with a hammer, and then completely broke down and began to cry. He begged the doctor to let him in. He said he had been doing hard manual labor, and it didn't bother him; he swore he could bend his knee all the way—which he couldn't—and that he could do anything that anyone else could. The doctor was so moved by the young man's pleading, with tears running down his face, that he stamped his papers and told him that if he wanted in so badly, he was in.

A delighted Jay Rebstock was off to boot camp. By December 1943 he finished boot camp, and, in February 1944, he was assigned to the newly created 5th Marine Division.

The 5th Division may have been new in name, but it was very old in experience. It boasted of old raider veterans and experienced para-troopers, as well as veterans from the early fights at Guadalcanal and Choiseul and Bougainville. In those elite numbers was the legendary John Basilone, who had won the Medal of Honor on Guadalcanal and opted to go back into combat rather than sit on the sidelines. The presence of all these veterans gave confidence to the newer Marines like Rebstock. For the next seven months, the 5th Division trained in the United States and Rebstock was assigned to Company E, 2nd Battalion, 27th Marines. The three regiments forming the 5th Division were the 26th, 27th, and 28th Marines.

By August, the division was sharp and went to Hawaii for additional training, making numerous amphibious landings in preparation for the next assault. The Marine tactics that had been developed for this island-hopping war were attack and push; attack and keep advancing; don't stop unless it was unavoidable; bypass the enemy and let the following troops mop them up; charge, attack, push; give the enemy no rest. The division practiced until they could all do it in their sleep.

The scuttlebutt all through training was that the division would be used in the next landings, in either Formosa or China. Rebstock had a Marine emblem tattooed on his arm.[5]

While young PFC Jay Rebstock was getting his arm tattooed, Gen. Kuribayashi was busy facing a daunting task on the island of Iwo Jima. He had arrived on June 13, 1944, in a flying boat at the East Boat Basin and had trudged up the sloping terrain to his headquarters at the village of Motoyama, which sat just above Chidori Airfield (Airfield No. 1). Motoyama was at the second dormant volcano on the island. The other was Mount Suribachi.

After his first inspection, he was disheartened at the state of defensive preparations. There had been no unity, no coordination in preparing the defenses, and, in fact, the job of fortifying the island had been hindered by interservice rivalry and distrust between the Army and the Navy.

To make matters worse, one month before he arrived, Gen. Obata and MGen. Tamura, who would command the embattled troops on Saipan, had made an inspection of Iwo Jima. Gen. Tamura concluded the inspection with an order that any guns located in the north on the high ground should be brought down and placed in pillboxes to defend against the enemy if they landed on the beaches. The guns in the northern regions of the island, he claimed, were useless where they were and must be put into a position to conform with the Tamura Doctrine.

The problem was that the American invading forces had never been annihilated on the beach, and the beach line had never successfully been defended. Even the huge German Army had been unable to throw the American forces back into the sea at Normandy. How this would be successfully accomplished now was not a subject that Gen. Tamura addressed.

He simply championed this beach-line tactic, which was, in his mind, plain common sense. He wasn't alone in his thinking. It was a tactic that was recognized and accepted by most tacticians. The idea was that the defending force would keep a big force in reserve and, after observing where the enemy was making his landing, would attack with that reserve and crush the attack at the water's edge, where it was most vulnerable. It was taught in the Japanese Military Academy and the War College. But Gen. Tamura had not heeded a small caveat listed in the operation manual, *Sakusen Yomurei*. There was a warning stating that, against an overwhelmingly armed enemy, a defense in depth must be made with a series of strong fortified positions.[7]

After his proclamation of the beach-line defense at Iwo Jima, Gen. Tamura, along with Gen. Obata, went off to defend Saipan with the Tamura Doctrine. On June 15, two days after Gen. Kuribayashi arrived at Iwo Jima, the thirty-two thousand troops on Saipan were in a position to defend the beach line and hurl the Marines back into the sea once they touched down.

After two days of shore bombardment from the Americans, most Japanese beach defenses were nonexistent, and eight battalions of Marines made their run into the Saipan beaches. Eight thousand Marines reached the beach in the first twenty minutes. By nightfall, twenty thousand had landed and, even though they had sustained two thousand casualties, they had a toehold. Two days later, the overwhelming American force had reached the opposite side and began a pivot to the north to take the rest of the 14-mile-long island.[8]

For two weeks, the Japanese fell back, inflicting many casualties on the Americans while dying by the thousands themselves. At the end, Gen. Tamura's force on Saipan was annihilated, and Gen. Tamura himself was dead, along with the Tamura Doctrine. For Gen. Kuribayashi on Iwo Jima, his doctrine would be a defense in depth.

On June 29, 1944, two weeks after Gen. Kuribayashi arrived at Iwo Jima, one of his staff officers, Maj. Yoshitaka Horie, joined him, landing by aircraft at Motoyama No. 1. As he approached the island, the major could see the remains of aircraft victims of constant American air attack, pushed to the sides of the runway. On the southern tip, Mount Suribachi thrust its ugly 550 feet into the sky. The volcano was attached to the rest of the island by a narrow neck that widened into an ascending plateau on which the airfields were built. From the air, the island resembled a pork chop.

The black sand beaches on the east coast were in several distinct terraces; the sand on the western coast was more golden. The land to

the north was as different as the plateau was from Suribachi. The
northern third of the island was a land best described as a moonscape
of rocky outcroppings. It looked prehistoric, with deep canyons and
jutting rocks, countless caves, and steaming sulfur hissing out of the
ground. Many Marines described it as the worst badlands they had ever
seen. Iwo Jima was an evil, foreboding, waterless, lifeless place.

Maj. Horie thought it would be a wonderful thing if somehow he
could sink this wretched island into the sea. Then it would have no
interest for the Americans, and they would not come here, and Japan
could be spared a great tragedy. He knew that from Iwo Jima, even
the slowest planes were only three hours from Tokyo.[9]

After the fall of the Marianas, it was obvious that the Bonin Islands
and Iwo Jima, because of its airfields, would be the next target. The
Japanese wanted to defend at all costs because of the danger Iwo Jima
would present to the motherland if it fell into enemy hands; the Americans needed Iwo Jima out of the way, since its radar gave the mainland
ample warning of approaching bomber strikes. Early warning meant
fighters scrambled to greet the bombers, which flew with no fighter
escort. But with Iwo Jima in American hands, American bombers
would have only a short flight to drop their devastating loads.

Bombing missions, especially those being flown by the newly arrived B-29s, had a 3,000-mile round-trip flight from Saipan. That distance limited the big airplane to a maximum bomb load of three tons,
not the ten-ton load it was designed to carry. It also meant bomb runs
to Japan with no fighter support, and that required the aircraft to climb
to 28,000 feet, where precision bombing was impossible. There was also
no friendly island on which the big bombers could land if they became
disabled. From the Marianas to Iwo Jima and back, pilots and crews
could expect no help or support. Iwo Jima was the key. In the eyes of
both the Americans and the Japanese, it was a vital piece of land.[10]

The evening he landed on the island, Maj. Horie had dinner with
Gen. Kuribayashi, and the general discussed Iwo Jima and the upcoming operation. He told the young major that when the enemy came,
they could contain them. They would fight a delaying action until the
Combined Fleet could come from the mainland, or from Okinawa, and
smite the American Fleet. "Our role would be a great containing op-

eration," he said while smiling and pouring whiskey for himself and his young guest.[11]

The depth of the official Japanese cover-up of the disasters suffered by the fleet over the years was revealed in Kuribayashi's statement. He knew nothing of the large numbers of Japanese ships at the bottom of the ocean. He did not know of the disaster at Midway, or the more recently crushed Operation A-Go.

But Maj. Horie knew. He had been a staff officer with the Army Shipping Headquarters and had served as a liaison officer between the Army and the Navy, and he had been privy to the vast message traffic that had told the story of the Japanese defeats. Now he looked at Gen. Kuribayashi, who toasted the upcoming glorious battle to defeat the Americans, and swallowed hard.

"General," he began, "we have no more Combined Fleet in Japan. Some tiny naval forces remain, but there is no more striking power."

Kuribayashi showed no expression. He listened.

Maj. Horie continued. He revealed the results of Operation A-Go, and details of all the other naval defeats, and concluded by saying, "The death date of Japan was ten days ago. It was June 19, 1944."

Kuribayashi calmly looked at him and nodded and said, "Then you mean that we must just die at the entrance of Tokyo, don't you?"[12]

The next morning, Kuribayashi and Maj. Horie went to the southern beaches, and the general lay on the black sand just as if he were an invading soldier. He looked up and down the beach, and then up at Mount Suribachi, and then turned and watched the waves breaking on the shore behind him. "This beach is very wide," he said. "The airfield is also very wide. The enemy must come here; there is no alternative."[13]

For the next two hours, the general and the young major drove around the airfield in an old car, making frequent stops. At each stop, Gen. Kuribayashi made Maj. Horie lie down as if he were an enemy soldier. While the major did as the general directed, Kuribayashi observed the lines of fire necessary to stop the enemy. Maj. Horie departed Iwo Jima the next morning and flew back to Chi Chi Jima to begin setting up the shipping and supply operations that would send the men and weapons to Kuribayashi for his Iwo Jima fortress.

Since the Americans bombed the islands in the daytime, Horie's operation was limited to the nighttime. Transports were unloaded, and their cargoes taken by truck into the hills for concealment. The following night, these same trucks would bring the cargo back to the pier, where it would be reloaded onto sailing and fishing boats. Three thousand men were used in the unloading and reloading, along with thirty trucks and twenty landing craft. Fifty sailing and fishing boats made up the supply fleet, and it took four days from the time the cargo arrived at Chi Chi Jima to make its way to Iwo Jima. Everything was done at night.

It was backbreaking work for the three-thousand-man labor force, and officers often beat the men to move them, but in July and August, Horie was able to send Kuribayashi most of the twenty-one thousand men who would comprise his defensive force—a force the Americans estimated as thirteen thousand.

On August 10, Maj. Horie returned to Iwo Jima to visit Gen. Kuribayashi. Despite the fact that the general was now reconciled that Japan was at its end, he was smiling and busy with building his defense.[14] He had also replaced all of his aged battalion commanders with young officers. He would fight with officers who understood his tactics. The disagreement over his defense-in-depth tactics had resounded throughout his command and even as high as Imperial Headquarters itself, but, in the end, he prevailed. He had made a few compromises. A particular compromise was to allow 135 pillboxes to be built on the beach, but that was to get a like number built in his defensive line. In the end, he fired eighteen unyielding senior officers including his chief of staff. If he was to defend the island, his subordinates would do it his way.[15]

But tactics was not the only problem facing Kuribayashi. Iwo Jima had no water. There were no streams on the island, and the only way to accumulate drinking water was to catch it when it rained. Hundreds of cisterns had been built over the years around Motoyama, but Kuribayashi had to provide water for more than twenty thousand men. He built more cisterns and storage tanks, one holding 10,000 gallons, and issued strict orders that no water would be used for anything other than drinking. Baths were taken with seawater.

The trees that existed were cut down for fortifications, and concrete was poured by the thousands of yards, and the Japanese tunneled like moles. Kuribayashi ordered that all strong points be connected by a tunnel, including one from Motoyama to Suribachi. Fifteen miles of tunneling was ordered.[16]

Throughout the months of work preparing Iwo Jima as a fortress, Gen. Kuribayashi had pounded his orders for defense into the head of every man under his command over and over. He made it clear that he expected all personnel to construct his fighting position so that it would be impervious to the heavy shelling that would come prior to the invasion, and that he expected that position to also serve as the man's tomb. There would be no surrender. It would be a fight to the death, and in death, Japan could win in spirit.

His orders were sixfold: to defend the island with an all-out effort; to destroy enemy tanks with explosives; to infiltrate and annihilate; to kill one enemy with every shot; to not die until each man had killed ten enemy; to harass and conduct guerrilla tactics even with only one soldier remaining.[17] Slowly the Japanese defending forces disappeared underground. The defense was hardened.

From December 8, 1944, until D-Day, February 19, 1945, B-24 bombers attacked the fortress every day, dropping 7,000 tons of bombs. Supplementing this enormous bombardment, naval ships hammered the island with twenty-three thousand rounds from 5-inch and 16-inch guns. Deep inside the island, Kuribayashi's men absorbed this pounding little the worse for wear. Inside Suribachi, the Japanese had built a seven-story defensive structure with 35 feet of overhead cover. Steam, electricity, and water had been piped in, and all entrances in the mountain were angled 90 degrees after the first several feet to protect against flamethrowers. The blast revetments were solid concrete.

In the northern regions, where the main line of defense was set up, there were two massive defensive positions near Motoyama and Kitano Point. Kuribayashi's headquarters at Kitano Point had 500 feet of tunnels, some as deep as 75 feet underground. All through the island, thousands of feet of tunnels connected positions, and hundreds of different entrances gave the Japanese excellent mobility and protection.[18]

• • •

Instead of being disheartened, as one might expect of soldiers preparing for a last stand and absorbing a massive daily bombardment, most of the men were in good spirits. They waited for the invasion, and while waiting, like all soldiers, they dreamt of home and wrote letters.

On December 18, Lt.Col. Nishi, who commanded the 26th Tank Regiment, but whose soldiers would fight as infantry because their tanks were at the bottom of the ocean thanks to an American submarine, wrote to his wife: "I sympathize with you," he said, "because it is very cold in Tokyo. . . . This place is like a winter resort. If we stay in our caves we don't feel the cold. . . . We are concentrating our energy in cave digging and expansion of our underground living rooms. Even B-29s can do nothing to these rooms. We are going to dig the land 20 meters deep, and make underground streets."[19]

On the same day, Lt.Col. Nakana, the operations officer, wrote his wife that the enemy air raids were sometimes more than ten a day, but there was no damage. He said that everyone was vigorous and begged her not to worry. He was very upbeat: "Now we have saved enough water," he wrote. "Yesterday we had a bath. Everyone is happy, and we even get some fish, because whenever the enemy makes air-raids, many fish . . . are killed by the bombs."[20] Little did the Americans realize that their bombardment was, in fact, helping to feed the Japanese forces on Iwo Jima.

"The enemy air-raids come almost every day," Lt.Col. Nakana continued, regaling his wife with the resulting feast from the sea. "If they do not come, we miss them." He concluded, "We are gladly waiting for the enemy."[21]

In the first week of January, Jay Rebstock, along with the entire 5th Marine Division, mounted out from the big island of Hawaii while the 4th Division embarked from Maui. It would be the 4th Division's fourth major assault and the first action for the newly formed, but veteran-laden 5th Division.[22]

The 3rd Marine Division would round out the attack force and would be the reserve division. This three-division Marine force was the largest ever committed to a single battle in the history of the Corps. It would bear the title of V Amphibious Corps or VAC.

As Rebstock and his fellow Marines boarded the troop transports, they still thought that their target was either China or Formosa and the scuttlebutt was that those targets would be just a warm-up for the real destination, which was the island of Okinawa. They knew nothing of the plan called Operation Detachment, which had been issued on December 23 and which called for the direct frontal assault on the 3,000 yards of black, sandy beaches on the east coast in the shadow of Mount Suribachi. The 5th Division would assault the left of the beaches and the 4th would assault the right.[23]

The naval force, with which they would rendezvous, was enormous. For the Guadalcanal veterans, the amount of materiel and ships was staggering in comparison to the few ships and supplies available to them in 1942. The force of the U.S. Fifth Fleet consisted of 485 ships including twelve aircraft carriers. The combined strength of VAC was more than seventy thousand men, and the 5th Division alone was going in with over a hundred million cigarettes.[24]

Onboard the APAs, Marines geared up for battle. Weapons were cleaned and recleaned, knives were sharpened and resharpened. Rebstock loaded machine-gun belts and magazines for his Browning automatic rifle. The ammunition was packaged loose in crates, and he spent hours belting it. Down belowdeck, they slept five high in cramped quarters and, during the day, there was nothing to see but the endless ocean.

About one week out of Hawaii, Rebstock's company commander called all his Marines together and informed them that their target was the island of Iwo Jima. The Marines of Company E, 2nd Battalion, 27th Marines, looked at each other with puzzled stares. The captain uncovered a map on the bulkhead, revealing a diagram of the pork chop–shaped island, and pointed to the eastern beaches, which were labeled: Green Beach, Red 1 and 2, Yellow 1 and 2, and Blue 1 and 2.

"We'll be landing on Red Beach 1," the officer said, holding his pointer on the second invasion beach north of Mount Suribachi. "Company E will be in the second wave," he said, but it was, in fact, the first infantry wave, since the first wave would be armored LVT(A)s to provide fire support with their 75mm guns.[25]

When the convoy got to Saipan, Rebstock and Company E loaded onto LSTs. They made a practice run on February 12 and, for the final time, the Marines loaded onto their amtracs, rolled out of the LST tank decks, and circled in the water. Then there was the final run to the beach, with the Higgins boats bobbing in on later waves. When they got close to the Saipan beaches, the craft turned and went back to the ships.[26] It was a practice of coordination to land the landing force. There was no need for the Marines to disembark and hit the beach. They had all done it countless times, and knew what to do: attack. Attack and pin the enemy down. Bypass when possible and let the later waves mop up. Push, push, push. It was the tactics of unrelenting pressure, and from the first attack at Tarawa, the Marines had perfected it.

Back on the LSTs, Rebstock found a place to sleep on the deck rather than being confined in the lower quarters of the ship. It was cooler at night, and the fresh air felt good.

Briefings were held every day. Maps and models of the island were available for each man to see. They examined the terrain models and pointed to the beaches where they would land. Some squatted down to get an idea of the elevation. All eyes eventually focused on Mount Suribachi, and it was Mount Suribachi that had to be taken.

The company and platoon commanders kept the troops up to date, and the word was encouraging. Intelligence had concluded that since Iwo Jima had no water supply, the most that the rainfall could support was thirteen thousand men.[27]

As the Marines circled around and sat on deck for these briefings, they were more convinced that Iwo Jima would be the rehearsal for the big push at Okinawa. These thirteen thousand Japs had to be sick and disoriented by the isolation on the island, and the constant pounding of the last seventy days would make them a less than effective fighting force. It would last maybe five days, and once Suribachi was taken, it would be over.

In the evening, PFC Rebstock and his friends listened to Tokyo Rose tell them that the Imperial Japanese forces were waiting for them on Iwo. The music was good, they thought, even though her propaganda was bad.

The final briefings, as they approached the battle area, included estimates of the length of the battle. No more than three to five days, the young BARMAN heard, and even less if the Nips made their usual banzai charge for the emperor, allowing the Marines to cut them down.

And then they were given the passwords: state capitals and presidents. These were not easy. Had they been baseball and automobiles, the Marines would have had no trouble, but most of the men didn't know the capitals and were stumped past Washington and Roosevelt. They would have to study these passwords. Franklin Roosevelt was the only president these nineteen- and twenty-year-olds had ever known.[28]

As the transports arrived at the assembly areas, the Marines were on deck, transfixed by the spectacular display of the power of the shore bombardment. Even at night, they watched the orange flashes and explosions of what many thought was the greatest Fourth of July fireworks that they could ever see.

That night, February 18, the night before D-Day, sleep was almost impossible. Weapons were checked for the thousandth time, and although there were religious services on board, the attendance was light. Some letters were written, but mostly the Marines spent their time checking everything over.

The landing force was called to chow at 0300. The Marines formed in their interminable lines to be fed. It was steak and eggs in the galley, standing up. Some couldn't eat. Others ate as if there were no tomorrow, scooping up food from the untouched plates of those who couldn't. Rebstock ate in the crowded galley where the only sound was of metal utensils on metal trays. There was little talking.

Small-unit leaders went around and gave final instructions. Each man was given something extra to carry in. Jay Rebstock was handed a 5-gallon can of water to carry in and drop on the beach. Others were given extra ammunition, or explosives, or mines, and it was all tucked away with packs and rifles.

For the Marines of 2nd Platoon, there would be no disembarking over the side and down a cargo net into Higgins boats. They would ride their LVTs out the bow of the LST, and down the ramp into the water.

At 0630, everything was in position, and the thunderous roar of the shore bombardment began. It was a meticulous bombardment plan, with each vessel given exact targets to hit with an exact number of shells at an exact time. What looked to the observing Marines as ships firing at will was the execution of the detailed bombardment plan.

The island was swept yard by yard with a rain of steel. Five battleships pounded Iwo from the east coast while two other battleships steamed to the west coast and smashed it from there. For almost an hour and a half, the battleships poured more than five hundred rounds onto their targets, and the cruisers chipped in with seven hundred.[29]

As the bombardment shrouded Iwo Jima in clouds of dust so that it was often obscured, the landing force debarked. Rebstock and his members of the 2nd Platoon of Easy Company were called to the tank deck of the LST to board their LVTs. He hustled down to the tank deck with his heavy pack and his 5-gallon can of water. Other Marines scrambled over the steel decks, loading their gear and materiel, and the drivers started the vehicles. The noise in the closed hull was deafening, and blue exhaust from the engines filled the compartment.

PFC Rebstock thought he would be asphyxiated before he ever got to the Japs. He held a cloth in front of his face, and then everyone put on their gas masks, but the masks were designed for filtering, not for creating fresh air. For thirty minutes, they sat in their veritable execution chamber, coughing and gagging, eyes blinded by fumes.

Finally, the big steel doors in the bow began to open, and the blue haze and fumes were dissipated by the sudden rush of fresh air, bringing relief to tortured lungs and eyes. The sunlight of a beautiful day streamed into the cavernous hold as the first tractor creaked toward the inclined deck leading to the lapping blue water. Like a great hippo, the ungainly tractor waddled down the ramp and went in nose first. Its steel tracks ground on the steel ramp until it plunged in and bobbed up, righting itself in the light seas. It churned away as the next tractor followed, and then the next, and it was now time for the 2nd Platoon to enter the water.

Rebstock and the other fifteen Marines felt the vehicle dip down the ramp, and suddenly they were floating and crawling off to join the other launched tractors and they circled in a great rendezvous.

The air was crisp, and the sun was clear and bright. Rebstock looked all around and remembered all the small American flags flying from every tractor. The explosions from the great guns of the battleships and cruisers were hardly audible over the noise of the amtracs. The concussions and the great orange flashes as the ships shelled the island brought smiles to the faces of the circling Marines. They watched as the island seemed to literally explode. This would be over soon they thought: When Suribachi falls, it's over.[30]

At a few minutes past 0800, the naval gunfire stopped. The amtracs churned toward the line of departure and, as they passed the navy ships, sailors waved and yelled encouragement to the passing Marines. Nothing could be heard above the roar of the tractor engines, but the Marines gave thumbs-up.

As the 2nd Platoon tractor reached the line, 120 carrier-launched aircraft roared overhead to further bomb the island. The Marines cheered as they saw forty-eight of the aircraft were Marine planes. They watched the squadrons drop their high explosives and napalm on the slopes of Suribachi and on the Motoyama airfields.

The embarked Marines watched the planes hammer the beaches that they would soon invade. Napalm, rockets, and strafing chewed the area until it seemed that no one could be left. The Marines cheered and slapped one another, happy not to be defending the beach against such an awesome display of firepower. For twenty minutes, they watched the grand spectacle, and as the planes flew away, the navy bombardment started again. This time every gun concentrated on the beaches.

Rebstock was at the line of departure, and the first wave of armored support tractors with their 75mm guns started in, as if they were the front rank of a parade, small American flags snapping from antennas.

It was 0830, and five minutes later, the first wave of infantry formed their line and followed the LVT(A)s toward the beaches. Second Platoon Marines could see the sterns of the preceding tractors in front of them and, as they looked over the gunwales of their own craft, could see adjacent units churning forward with them. Their destination was Red 1 and they marched onward under the greatest cannonade of naval gunfire that they could ever imagine. The only thing missing from this colossal parade was the brass band, and for the thirty minutes that it would take for the run to the beach, the American ships salvoed over eight thousand rounds of fire, completely obliterating Kuribayashi's reluctantly built beach defenses.

In the 2nd Platoon tractor, the Marines looked over the sides. Rebstock held on to his 5-gallon water can and watched as some waves broke over the gunwales and splashed onto the deck. Despite the relatively calm seas, some of the men were seasick. The motion and the thirty minutes in the buttoned-up deck of the LST, with those terrible fumes, was taking its toll.

The tractors approached the beach like giant waterbugs; Rebstock observed splashes in the water. He assumed the navy had fired some short rounds. Then there were more splashes and suddenly an exploding LVT. Men were screaming in the water, and heads ducked below the gunwales with the realization that these were not short rounds. The recent smiling and backslapping and the atmosphere of a grand parade was now gone, replaced with the deadly seriousness of men under fire.

It was 200 yards to the beach. Rebstock sneaked a peek over the side, and he could see that the armored tractors were not on the beach; in fact, they had backed down and were firing their guns from the water. Rebstock's LVT churned past the firing LVT(A)s.

What the hell was going on, he thought. He looked out again and, to his amazement, he could see the top of a beach-defending gun firing at the aircraft that were strafing the beach. He could only see the top of the gun and the top of a helmet as the gun slewed around from its position atop the second terrace.

The tracks ground on the sand as his LVT landed and lurched up the slope, but then ground to a halt as the tracks continued to turn and cut a groove in the soft sand. "Over the side," was the order. The Marines scrambled over and jumped to the black sand.

Rebstock moved forward past the grinding vehicle, but his feet moved as if they were in slow motion. He struggled up the first terrace weighed down with his enormous combat load and dragging his 5-gallon water can. He was not even aware that he had not dropped the cumbersome can because his eyes were set on the 5 feet of gun barrel that now was directly in front of him on the second terrace. It was 20 feet away, and again he caught glimpses of the tops of some helmets. The gun continued to fire at the low-flying planes.

The young PFC crouched low and tried to move forward, but his feet sank into the sand up to his knees. He cursed the forty-day ship ride to get here, which seemed to have left him so out of shape and wheezing for air. He felt like a salmon trying to swim upstream. As he alternately struggled up and slid down the terrace, Rebstock chanced a look down and was horrified to see that he was still lugging the water can. His hand opened as if he had grabbed a hot iron, and he half threw, half kicked the offending can away.

He also, now, ditched some of his gear. His load was so heavy he could hardly move. In addition to his heavy weapon, he had 240 rounds of ammo, plus an extra bandoleer slung around his chest, as well as grenades, an entrenching tool, canteens of water, a bipod for the BAR, and a .45 pistol. It didn't take him long to send the bipod and the pistol to join the 5-gallon water can on the beach.

When next he looked up, some of his squad had surmounted the terraces, had jumped into the gun pit with the Japanese gunners, and were clubbing them to death. With his lighter load, Rebstock struggled up the second terrace and ran into his assistant BARMAN, who like him was carrying an extra load and who was equally anxious to lighten his load. When he saw Rebstock, he threw his extra load of ammunition to him and said, "The BAR is your weapon, so you can carry your own ammo!"[31] With that he was off at a half lope across the flatter land.

The 2nd Platoon suddenly found itself up the terraces and free to move forward. "Go, go, go," the NCOs shouted, and they moved forward in a half crouch. Rebstock moved forward with his weapon at the hip. He could hear sporadic firing, and a puff of dust occasionally erupted in front of him, but the going was pretty easy.

They moved across the neck of land joining Mount Suribachi to the rest of the island, constantly casting wary eyes up the forbidding slopes, expecting a hail of fire to rain down on them at any moment. But Suribachi let them pass.

They came across a big blockhouse, which held them up momentarily, but they were able to bypass it and continue on toward the western coast. As they approached a small sugarcane field that had remarkably withstood all the bombardment, Rebstock watched in amazement as a Japanese soldier charged toward him. It was almost unreal, as if in a dream, and it took him a moment before he leveled his weapon at the charging figure to knock him down with a short burst. Lt. Kellogg came up and screamed at the panting BARMAN that he thought he had killed a fellow Marine. Rebstock was horrified, but not for long, as a fellow Marine presented him with the insignia that he had cut off the fallen soldier's shirt: He had been a Japanese Marine.[32]

Again they pushed on, and by early afternoon they reached the opposite side of the island, which was solid rocks and cliffs. They stopped and took up defensive positions and counted their casualties. It was not too bad. Easy Company had lost their company commander and had six other men killed and nine wounded, but they had cut a wide path across the island, isolating Suribachi from the northern reaches.[33] The company took up defensive positions and evacuated their wounded. They were ready for orders to swing to the north, but those orders did not come, and would not come, at least not on this day.

In fact, within an hour of being evacuated, most of the wounded men were back, saying it was safer in the lines than on the beaches. The beaches were catching hell.

As Rebstock's 2nd Platoon scurried across the island between 0905 and 1000, Gen. Kuribayashi's gunners were underground, protected from the shelling. As the fire lifted, they came out, and in the hills to the north, they swung their gun barrels to prepare for action.

The third and fourth waves landed behind the 2nd Platoon, dumping twenty-eight hundred more men on the beach. They too began their ascent up the double and triple terraces to reach the flat land and the airfield. An increase of small arms fire was detected. Marines that had landed to the left of Rebstock and the 2nd Platoon on Green Beach headed for the base of Suribachi.

The invasion was thirty minutes old, and progress was good. But in the hills, hand wheels spun, setting elevating and traversing data on hundreds of guns. The data had been memorized for months, and gunners easily slewed the barrels to the proper attitudes.

A quick pull of a handle by an artilleryman opened the breech, rounds were rammed home, and the blocks slammed shut. One by one, the gun crews signaled "up." The northern defense force waited only for the order to fire. Not one inch of the landing beach would be exempt from the imminent bombardment.

From their positions on the high ground, the Japanese could see small clusters of Marines move forward and then stop while other groups moved. It was like watching a game of leapfrog. The anxious artillery-men watched the tempting targets moving before them and were itching to fire, but the orders were firm. The commanding general would give the order to fire, and until he did, the defense would remain silent.

At a few minutes past 1000, as the landing Marines, now packed on the beaches, struggled to overcome the damnable, sliding terraces, Gen. Kuribayashi gave that order.

The roar was as deafening as it was frightening. Artillery and mor-tars, along with big coastal guns and antiaircraft guns with barrels deflected for direct fire, unleashed a terrifying volley. The beaches were pulverized with every conceivable type of fire, and the waves of raining shells swept back and forth like a giant scythe. Marine bodies were crushed, and landing craft on the beaches exploded. Craft and vehicles close to the beach were instantly destroyed. Men from the first waves, already wounded and awaiting evacuation, were now annihilated, along with the medical personnel attending them.[34]

Kuribayashi's bombardment came from more than one hundred guns with a caliber of at least 6 inches, and more than three hundred guns that were more than 3 inches. Supplementing this formidable bombardment force were another three hundred assorted howitzers, self-propelled guns, tank, and antitank guns.[35] Kuribayashi also had a special weapon with which to punish the invading Marines: the colossal 320mm [13 inches] Spigot mortar, which some Marines would come to call the "screaming Jesus." This monster mortar was the pride of the Japanese 20th Independent Mortar Battalion, and its 675-pound round had a range of more than 1,400 yards.[36]

Kuribayashi's order to fire brought this massive cannonade to bear on the 3,000 yards of landing beaches, and the slaughter was indescrib-able. A veteran Marine correspondent said, "At Tarawa, Saipan, and Tinian, I saw Marines killed and wounded in a shocking manner, but I saw nothing like the ghastliness that hung over the Iwo Jima beach-head."[37]

In the hills, the Japanese fired with the fury and vengeance of men who had been pinned and bombed for more than seventy consecutive days. They fired as fast as they could at the targets of packed Marines and equipment on the beach.

Second Lieutenant Nakamura, who commanded the 12th Independent Anti-Tank Gun Battalion, was everywhere directing fire, and his gunners took a heavy toll. Twenty vehicles and tanks were destroyed under his onslaught, and Gen. Kuribayashi had already telegraphed Tokyo of the lieutenant's feats when naval gunfire finally pinpointed his position and killed him.[38] He had more than fulfilled his ten-for-one pledge to his general, and Kuribayashi posthumously promoted him to the rank of captain. The general cited others, including the entire 145th Infantry Regiment, and then gave orders to collect all the money in the possession of his entire force to send back to the National Treasury. For Kuribayashi and his men, the sacrifice would be total.

On the beaches, the Marines still scrambled ashore, and each wave of men faced the terrace climb. To the right of Red 1, Baker Company landed on Red 2. They did not have the immediate success of scaling the terraces as had Easy Company, and when Gen. Kuribayashi ordered his bombardment, Baker Company was pinned down.

Marines dug into the soft black sand to try to escape the rain of steel. One machine gunner, PFC Tatum, dug furiously as he watched the world erupt around him. He felt every concussion vibrate through the sand and chanced a look at the beach. Everybody was down as the fire swept over them, except one solitary figure who walked among the prone figures shouting and cursing for everyone to get moving off the beach. He was impervious to the falling shells that impacted all around him. As he got closer, Tatum recognized this Marine as the legendary Medal of Honor winner John Basilone. An officer had joined him, and the two men were the only leaders trying to get the pinned-down Marines moving. As Tatum buried his face in the sand, he felt a smack on his helmet and looked up to see Basilone pointing through smoke and erupting sand to a target. He was pointing to a large bunker, and he wanted Tatum to fire on it.

Basilone got the Marines moving. Tatum's gun hammered at the aperture, forcing the enemy away from the opening. His next bursts forced the soldiers in the bunker to close the metal door. Then Basilone directed a demo man to blow the door, and after the explosion, followed with a flamethrower that incinerated the Japanese inside. The screaming survivors, on fire from the napalm, rushed out the back, only to be cut down by the Basilone-led group.

With Basilone as their leader, this group left the beach and pushed up the terraces and toward the edge of the airstrip, which looked more like a junkyard for wrecked aircraft. Up and down the beach, small groups slowly moved forward, pushed into action by leaders such as Basilone, but the Japanese fire did not diminish in ferocity. Marines fell by the hundreds. Manila John Basilone's luck finally ran out, and he too went down in a hail of mortar fire.[39]

As evening approached, the Marines dug in where they were. On the west coast, Easy Company prepared for the inevitable banzai counterattack, which had become a predictable Japanese tactic. Jay Rebstock occupied a fighting hole with four other Marines, and he trained his BAR toward the north, envisioning the coming screaming charge. He wondered if he would be able to fire fast enough to beat back the enemy.

Darkness came at 1845, and the night turned cold. Marines shivered in their holes, straining their eyes forward. The Japanese bombardment continued without letup. Each slackening of fire was followed by an increase in intensity.

At command posts all along the tight perimeter, commanders added up their casualties. The numbers were bigger than the whole Guadalcanal operation. Six hundred Marines were dead and almost two thousand wounded, and it was only the first day.

The reports flashed back to headquarters in Guam, and then to Pearl Harbor, and finally to Washington. President Franklin Roosevelt was seated at his desk when the figures came in. He had just returned from the Yalta Conference with Churchill and Stalin, and the president looked frail and stooped. An aide reported the Iwo Jima casualties to him, and those in the room heard the exhausted president gasp with horror. In all the years of the war and his presidency, no one could ever recall seeing that reaction from Franklin Roosevelt, even during the darkest days after Pearl Harbor.[40]

• • •

The night banzai charge never came, as Gen. Kuribayashi forbade any such meaningless charges, which he concluded only played into American hands. Instead, he pounded the invading force with ceaseless incoming and waited for the invaders to come to him, where he could bleed them white.

War correspondent Robert Sherrod surveyed the scene of the invasion beaches with the first light of the new day of D+1. He wrote in his dispatch back to the United States, "The first night on Iwo Jima can only be described as a nightmare in hell." Speaking of the dead, whose bodies lay strewn on the beach, he said, "They died with the greatest possible violence. . . . Legs and arms lay 50 feet away from the body."[41]

The first night had produced the first difficulties with the passwords for the jittery invasion force, who challenged everything that moved. One anxious guard at the beach challenged a figure in the dark by calling out one president's name, expecting another in return. The answer came back, "Fillmore," not exactly a household name. The guard hated wiseguys, and shouted back, "All right, you son of a bitch. One more like that and you're dead."[42]

On the west coast, Company E prepared to attack to the north on D+1, but as they advanced, their positions were pounded by Japanese artillery and mortars. All Rebstock and the men from 2nd Platoon could do was advance and then burrow in the ground, but the unseen enemy continued to inflict horrific casualties on the Marines. Except for the one enemy soldier that Rebstock had seen and killed on D-Day, and the antiaircraft defenders at the water's edge as they landed, no one had seen any enemy at which to fire. Yet the enemy could see them, and Company E was being drained. In the attack on D+1, as the 26th and 27th Marines advanced, there were six hundred casualties. On February 21, D+2, Company E lost their second company commander.

The attack on the west coast became an attack of prep fires in the morning, followed by the assault, and then a return to previous positions to count casualties. On February 22, D+3, as the entire 5th Division tried to attack forward, ten officers were killed. Ten had been killed the day before, and in four days of combat, thirty-five officers of the division had been lost. The west coast, like the rest of the island, had become one giant killing field.[43]

Rebstock and the members of the 2nd Platoon prepared for yet another attack on February 23. Suddenly wild cheering was heard across the front, and ships' horns and whistles could be heard from the sea. "The flag's up," someone said, and all eyes turned to Suribachi. There it was. The Stars and Stripes beating stiffly in the wind. The men of Company E lent their voices to the cheering and hollering.

Rebstock felt tears well in his eyes, and he was bursting with pride. Best of all, he knew that the battle must be close to being over. He'd remembered the briefing onboard ship where the end of the battle had been predicted in three to five days with the fall of Mount Suribachi. Well, he thought, this is the fifth day and the flag flies atop the mountain. The end is in sight.[44]

But the battle was not over, or even close to being over. In fact, it was only the beginning, and once the euphoria of the flag raising on Suribachi had passed, the battle went back to being a contest of attrition. A few days after the flag raising, the world would be presented with the most famous picture of World War II: Associated Press photographer Joe Rosenthal had snapped the perfectly framed exposure of five Marines and one Navy corpsman raising a second, larger flag on top of Suribachi. Emblematic of the ferocity of the fight for Iwo Jima, three of the six flag-raisers would not make it off the island alive.

Remarkably, a color motion picture film of the historic flag-raising was also made by Marine Sgt. William Genaust. He panned his camera as the flag went up and continued filming as the flag-raisers secured Old Glory into the ground. Genaust would be killed several days later.

The following day, February 24, Company E, with the rest of the 2nd Battalion, moved in an area along the western coast that would be known as Death Valley. The attack began in the morning and was strictly by the book: lay down a base of fire, bring up demolitions and the flamethrower, and destroy the position; move to the next bunker and repeat all the steps.

The attack pushed along along the west coast, which was one series of pillboxes after another. To the left, the Marines could see the peaceful waves breaking on the sandy beaches, and many fantasized about what a marvelous spot it would be to spend a lazy afternoon. To the front was one ridgeline after another, and the never-ending Japanese artillery and mortar fire.

Rebstock fired his BAR at the first strongpoint he could see. The weapon bucked in his shoulder as he poured fire into what looked like an aperture. Other Marines attacked the flanks of the positions, and then the flame man was down before he could reach the pillbox. Another took his place, and he too went down. Rebstock increased the volume of fire at the position, cursing the bastards that he could never see. A third man retrieved the flamethrower and soon there was the familiar *whoosh* and the telltale orange tongue of fire spitting into the rocky seams, and he too went down. Life expectancy of the flamethrower man was short; he was a prime target for every Japanese soldier who could see him.

The squad rushed forward, past the neutralized position, only to be pinned down again from the relentless small-arms fire. Rebstock could see nothing, but fired in the direction that his comrades pointed. They attacked throughout the day, and dug in for the night.

On the twenty-fifth, the officers decided to try a different strategy. Instead of the preparatory fires, which drove the Japs underground but also announced the beginning of a ground attack, they would attack in the afternoon, without prep fires, hoping to catch the Japanese off guard.

Death Valley was a deep indentation like a stadium field, with high ridgelines surrounding the field. The attack would carry down the slope into the valley, and then up to seize the ridgeline that guarded further northern movement. The whole attack down into the valley and up the other side could be seen by the enemy, but there was no other way.

As the jump-off hour approached, Rebstock and his fellow Marines of 2nd Platoon checked their weapons again and again. Each man knew that this attack would expose him to the full force of the firepower of the entrenched defenders who held the high ground.

At 1500 the attacking force stood up and began to advance, but Rebstock's feet were frozen in place, and an unquenchable thirst suddenly overtook him. "I guess that is what's called being scared shitless," he recalled. "I could not move, and I drank almost an entire canteen of water, and only then did my legs move forward."

They moved no more than 50 yards, and the whole world exploded on them. Everyone dived for cover, and Rebstock and his squad leader jumped into a hole with two other men. As one of the men looked up to see who their new companions were, a Japanese bullet hit him directly in the middle of his forehead, and he slumped over dead. The second man had a bullet pierce his helmet, deflect between the helmet and liner, and come out the other side.

Rebstock and his squad leader lay in the fetal position in the hole with the dead and wounded men, and the Japanese incoming thundered all around them. The ground shook, and rocks and stones buried the huddled Marines. Just when they thought nothing could be worse, the first airburst artillery detonated above them, hurling deadly steel fragments down from above.

Rebstock could not move. Like a worm trying to dig deeper, he flattened himself into the hole. He remained pinned there until, finally, he heard the familiar clanking of friendly tanks arriving on the scene. An earsplitting *crack* signaled the fire of the Sherman, just to the side of him. He crawled to the edge of the hole and began laying down fire with his BAR and sent a stream of fire, marked with red tracers, into the terrain to the front. As the smoke cleared, he could see a new bunker and what looked like an aperture. Again the BAR went to his shoulder, and the rounds poured into the slit. Marines inched and crawled forward toward the bunker. Rebstock changed magazines and bore down on the opening.

To his right, a similar scene unfolded. PFC Leonard Nederveld, in the adjacent platoon, moved forward and flipped a white phosphorous grenade into another opening. The soft explosion of the phosphorous was what the Marines expected, and they kept their eyes glued for a Japanese defender who would try to run out, but the explosion was anything but soft. Instead, a gigantic, deafening explosion, sending out an enormous shock wave, obliterated the bunker and clouded the battlefield. Rebstock was thrown to the ground, and his BAR shot from his hands as if it were a toy. The other Marines in the area were flattened to the ground like knocked-out fighters. The explosion seemed to echo over and over, and Rebstock could only hear a ringing in his ears. The pillbox had, in fact, been an ammo dump.

The young PFC staggered to his feet, dazed and disoriented, and looked for his weapon. For the second time in a few seconds, he was thrown down again by a force as mighty as that of the exploding dump. The Sherman tank erupted in a ball of fire and smoke as a Japanese artillery shell found its target.

The tank continued to explode as its munitions cooked off and was joined by more exploding ammo from the pillbox. After long minutes, the roar from the two near-simultaneous detonations ebbed, and the area was engulfed by silence. It was as if the ferocity and savagery of the battle had reached its zenith, and now collapsed under its own weight. What moments before had been the roar and fire from some separate chamber in hell was now eerie silence.

Stunned Marines picked themselves off the ground and made hesitant steps, first in one direction, and then another. Rebstock twisted around looking for his weapon and cradled the damaged piece in his arms. Instinctively, he found another from a fallen comrade, and smashed the first one against a large boulder, swinging it by the barrel.

Other Marines appeared, like figures in a dream, in the settling dust and smoke. Someone passed the word to return to the original lines, and the battered Marines limped back, dragging wounded buddies with them as best they could. The whole attack had not lasted long, and the company added sixteen more casualties to its growing list.

That night, an unforgiving cold rain beat down on the 2nd Platoon. They shivered in their holes and cursed the island of Iwo Jima. The misery of the weather was topped by a renewed Japanese bombardment, making sleep impossible for the exhausted Marines. The next morning, with the rain continuing in a steady beat, the order was passed to stay in the holes. Ammo would be reissued, and replacements would be sent to the platoon.

All day, the platoon traded fire with the enemy. At 1630, the Marine next to Rebstock nudged him and warned that a Jap was crawling in on him. Through squinted eyes, Rebstock picked out a crawling figure, 50 yards in front of him. As he crawled, the man raised his hand, and then continued to crawl. He alternately crawled, and stopped to raise his hand. The Marines in the line watched this agonizing, snail-like movement.

Rebstock sighted in on him. "Don't shoot him. Let him get close before you do," his buddies said, and Rebstock held his fire.

As the crawling man got close, someone recognized that this was not a Jap at all, but a Marine. Two men ran out and dragged the gray, dust-covered figure into a hole. He was all shot up, his leg was hanging on by a thread, and he was unrecognizable. Encrusted dust and sand was caked on his face, pasted there by an undercoat of blood. Rebstock stared at him, and then thought he recognized the man from another company, Watson.

The corpsmen patched him up as best they could, and then made a makeshift stretcher and attempted to evacuate him to the rear, but as they picked the wounded man up, the Japanese opened up on the rescue party. The stretcher crashed to the ground as the carriers dived for cover. The wounded man screamed as he hit the ground, and the shells exploded around him. Finally someone pulled him into a hole, and Jay Rebstock leaned over to comfort him.

"You'll be okay, Watson," he said, and patted the man on the shoulder. Another Marine asked, "Why are you calling him Watson? That's not Watson," he informed Rebstock. "That's Nederveld." Rebstock took a closer look, and, unbelievably, it was the man who had dropped the grenade in the bunker and detonated the massive explosion the day before. He had survived and had spent twenty-four hours in the Japanese lines.

Company E did not attack forward again. With their depleted numbers, they were pulled off the line and, mercifully, sent to the rear for what was to be a form of R&R. The word was that they were through at the front. They would not be put back into the line. The rest area turned out to be anything but R&R. On their first evening back, the Japanese hit the 5th Division ammo dump, which erupted in a spectacular explosion that continued to explode throughout the night.

When daylight came, Rebstock was treated to the sight of a mass burial of his deceased 5th Division comrades. A bulldozer cut out a huge swath of black, volcanic earth. One by one, bodies were laid side-by-side, until the bottom of the trench was filled. Some of the bodies consisted only of an arm or a leg, or some other body parts. Each position was surveyed and recorded in a log, and each body was covered with a thin layer of earth, delicately spread by a fellow comrade. Then the trench was filled by the bulldozer, and markers set up over each body.

After that sobering sight, Company E began its first day in the rest area and took up their new duty. In addition to their regular weapons and gear, each man was issued satchel charges, and they went to the mountain. They were assigned to clean the Japanese out of the caves on Suribachi. For six days, they rooted and burned the remaining force of three thousand Japanese defenders out or sealed them forever in the mountain.

"R&R," Rebstock noted, "was killing more Japs!"[45]

The promise that Company E would not go back into the line was broken on March 4, the fourteenth day of the five-day battle, and the ninth day after the flag-raising on the mountain. When they returned to the line, the line had moved all the way to the northern end of the island, and Rebstock could see the ocean over the northern shore from an elevation of 300 feet.

He was in an area around Kitano Point, and the attack resumed just as it had before R&R at Suribachi: attack, attack, and attack. But Company E was not the same company as it had been when it landed. In numbers, it was the equivalent of a good platoon, and half of the people were new and unfamiliar. The casualty ratio among these new men was horrific; without experience, they fell at an alarming rate.

Jay Rebstock decide to get behind a veteran who was good and knew the ropes during the attacks. It was the only way to survive, and as the battle seemed to be drawing to an end, everyone was thinking about the possibility of being the last man killed. At night, the Marines dug in, and anyone out of his hole was the enemy.

From March 4 to March 11, Company E attacked against the final

Japanese defenses. Rebstock got his first view of a Zippo tank. The fire-breathing armored machines could sustain a long stream of napalm fire for over a minute, and as new holes and bunkers were discovered, the Zippo went into action. The Japanese were immolated in their defensive positions, and the few who charged out were immediately dropped by the waiting Marines. With each step, the Japanese became more frantic. They dropped mortars as if there were an unending supply. At night, the Japanese soldiers infiltrated looking for food and water, and crawled into the lines stabbing many Marines.

On one of the last days of battle, 2nd Platoon had moved to the final ridgeline, and as they stared down into the canyon below, they could see that the rocky precipice on the other side looked down into the water: The end of the island was at hand. A Marine descended into the canyon. As he approached the bottom, a shot rang out, and he slumped in his tracks, dead from a sniper's bullet. One solitary Japanese soldier came out, waving his hands, but the infuriated Marines on the high ground cut him down. Then a second Japanese soldier came out with something in his hands, and some of the Marines said to hold fire and see what this guy was up to. But a nervous shot was fired and that triggered fire from all the jumpy Marines on the ridge.

Still a third soldier appeared in the bottom of the canyon, and again someone shouted, "Hold your fire," but again, after a pause, another shot was fired and the reaction shooting began again.

Rebstock put his weapon down. He could kill no more. Other Marines did the same, and finally it was silent.

On March 27, Rebstock and the remnants of his company were back at their starting point on the west coast in the shadow of Mount Suribachi. Just before first light, there was tremendous shooting in the area of the Motoyama airfield. It lasted over an hour, and as the sun broke into a clear sky, an LST nudged into the shore to take the exhausted Marines off the island.

The word came out the shooting had been the final banzai charge by the last of the Japanese force: Three hundred Japanese attacked, killing almost one hundred men in tents and dying to the man.

As the ship sailed from Iwo, the survivors could not believe they had made it. Everyone prayed. On the ride back toward Hawaii, there were a number of burials at sea, as some of the wounded succumbed.

As the ship finally approached Pearl Harbor, all of Company E had gathered in front of the pilot house. They anxiously awaited to pass through the submarine gates at the entrance. A photographer came to them and told them to line up for a company photograph. The grim Marines sat in three rows and posed for the picture, and just as the photographer snapped the picture, the loudspeaker came on, and a voice announced that President Franklin Roosevelt had just died.

Rebstock and the assembled men broke down and cried. He was the only president they had ever known, and now he was gone, without seeing the end of the war to which they had just sacrificed so much. They entered Pearl Harbor, where the war had started, and where it would end for them.

EPILOGUE

Rebstock and the rest of the Iwo survivors were reequipped and sent to new training in preparation for the invasion of Japan. They were in the field on maneuvers when the word was passed that the United States had dropped an atom bomb on Hiroshima.

Within days, their company was hustled out of Hawaii and loaded on ship, put to sea, headed for Japan. Three days out of Pearl Harbor, in the evening, as the ship sailed under blackout, the lights suddenly came on, and the captain announced that the war was over. Iwo Jima would be the only battle for Jay Rebstock and the 5th Marine Division.

The battle of Iwo Jima could more fittingly have been fought in hell. Had that descent into the underworld been possible, its participants could have seen no greater slaughter or horror. Gen. Kuribayashi's defense inflicted almost thirty thousand casualties on the Marines, with approximately seven thousand killed. Kuribayashi's own force was virtually annihilated, with more than 20,000 killed.[46] Adding to the Marine casualties, and robbing units of leadership, was the slaughter of the officer corps. Fifth Division alone had more than one hundred killed, forty in the first five days. At the end of the long battle, companies fought with PFCs as leaders, and Company E ended the shooting with only one officer from the six that rode in on the LVTs on February 19.

Nor was there a shortage of valor on Iwo Jima. In the four years of war from Pearl Harbor to the Japanese surrender, the Medal of Honor was presented to 353 men in all theaters; twenty-seven were awarded on Iwo Jima, half of them posthumously.[47]

Emblematic of the horrific casualties were the grim statistics offered by 2nd Battalion, 28th Marines, which had stormed and captured Suribachi. On February 19, the battalion had gone into action, reinforced with fourteen hundred men. On March 27, as the unit came down from the mountain to board ships, only 177 originals were left, one-third of whom were wounded.[48]

The official records listed the final strength of Jay Rebstock's company as two officers and fifty-six enlisted men from a starting strength of six officers and 235 enlisted. But as Jay counted the faces in the photo taken as Company E waited to enter Pearl Harbor on the day Franklin Roosevelt died, he could count only thirty-one originals. A thirty-second face belonged to the only replacement out of fifty who escaped Iwo Jima. What happened to all the replacements that were fed in as green troops? "They were green and inexperienced," Rebstock remembered. "They were cannon fodder."[49]

On April 7, 1945, land-based fighters began accompanying the giant B-29 bombers on missions over Japan. The island soon became known as an emergency airfield for crippled bombers, with 186 landing on July 24. By war's end, more than 2,400 B-29s had used the Iwo Jima airfield.[50]

THE SINKING OF USS *INDIANAPOLIS*

JULY 30, 1945

SEAMAN 2/C HAROLD ECK

The second week in August 1945 was hot and humid in the semi-tropical climate of New Orleans. Charles Eck was a second-generation American of German descent, and operated a small grocery store in the uptown section of the city. He had barely made a living during the days of the Depression and, like most Americans in the grocery business, had found himself sometimes selling groceries on credit and, quite often, not being paid by families worse off than himself.

Those dire economic conditions had mostly changed after Pearl Harbor and America's entry into World War II. But the war had also called Charles's two sons into the service of their country, and now, as the war drew to a close, he was anxious to have them return home.

His older boy, Charles, was in the Army Medical Corps and had already been wounded three times in action against the enemy in the European theater. His younger, Harold, was a seaman, 2nd class, and currently serving with the Navy in the Pacific onboard the cruiser USS *Indianapolis*.

Harold was like most other young boys throughout America who had been too young to serve during the early years of the war. He had watched the older boys in his neighborhood leave for the service while he itched to go himself. On several occasions, the youngster had approached first his father and then his mother, Florence, and asked them to sign the waiver so he could join the service before his eighteenth birthday and fight the accursed enemies of the United States. But his parents had always managed to put him off, telling him that he was too young and that he shouldn't rush into anything, but as the boy approached his eighteenth birthday, his father knew he could hold him off no longer.

Harold would become eighteen on August 11, 1944, and two weeks before that magical date, his father relented and went with him to the enlistment office, giving his permission. Nor was it a reluctant permission, since Charles Eck was himself a proud veteran of the Great War, having served honorably in the army of Black Jack Pershing. One of his prized possessions, which he kept in his closet, was his service rifle. He proudly showed it to anyone who was interested.

Harold went through the procedures of enlistment with several of his friends, and when they were finally "in," they celebrated with back-slapping and congratulations.

Within days, they were off to basic training, full of youthful confidence. They quipped among themselves that since the older boys from the neighborhood had not been able to end the war, and defeat Hitler and Tōjō, they would be the new warriors and provide the decisive force to bring down the Axis.

Harold spent three months at boot camp in San Diego, and then came home for a two-week leave before his first assignment. And what a first assignment it was. The young seaman beamed as he announced to his family that he would be aboard the proud Navy ship *Indianapolis*. He already knew much of the ship's long history.

The heavy cruiser was indeed a proud vessel. Its name had been associated with the Commander-in-Chief himself, President Franklin Roosevelt. It was officially FDR's "Ship of State," since the president used her for his personal transportation on Atlantic and South American travel. Over the years, other world leaders and foreign dignitaries had walked her decks on official visits.

Among the favorite stories of the crews of *Indianapolis* was that of President Roosevelt participating in the ritual of initiation during crossings of the equator. The ignominies experienced by first-time crossers were made extraspecial when FDR was aboard. Those sailors who were now initiated into the realm of Davy Jones as "Shellbacks," having previously existed only as lowly "Polliwogs," would forever remember that day when they found their certificates had been signed by the president himself.[1]

But *Indianapolis*'s fame was more than just glitter. She was the state-of-the-art ship of her time. Her keel was laid in March 1930 and she was launched in November 1931 as a treaty cruiser. The Washington Naval Conference of 1921–22 had attempted a form of naval disarmament after World War I, and the ensuing Naval Armaments Treaty of 1922 called for a moratorium on building warships of more than 10,000 tons. *Indianapolis* weighed in at approximately 9,900 tons.

To come in below the 10,000-ton displacement limit, *Indianapolis* had to forfeit something, and that something was the customary armored belt of steel that usually ran near the waterline from bow to stern and protected a ship from mines and torpedoes. While this extra protection had to be abandoned, the unintended benefit was that the ship acquired fantastic speed. Without the bulky armored belt having to plow through the water, the hull was now sleek and smooth, and she was like a racehorse, capable of speeds in excess of 32 knots.

While she forfeited the extra armored protection, *Indianapolis* forfeited nothing in armament. Her decks sported nine 8-inch guns supplemented by four 5-inch guns. Her antiaircraft protection included twenty-four 40mm guns and sixteen 20mm guns. She also had catapults to launch up to four float planes.[2]

So Harold Eck had set off on his great adventure on one of the most storied ships in the U.S. Navy. His family had been left to hope and pray for his safe return, and they followed his whereabouts through news releases and censored letters home.

Eight months had gone by, and now in August 1945, the news was

that Japan was on the verge of collapse. On August 6, the War Department had released the news that a new type of weapon called an
atomic bomb had been dropped on the city of Hiroshima causing great
devastation. Certainly the end was at hand.

Three days went by, and America sat on the edge of its seat hoping
that the war would end. On August 9, a second atomic bomb was
dropped on the city of Nagasaki. Hopefully this was the end. How
could Japan risk its total destruction?

For Charles Eck, the final day could not come soon enough. He
mentally projected the wonderful reunion with his two sons after their
long absences. God had protected them both. Even though his elder
son had been thrice wounded, he would come home, and Harold was
surely safe as the war ticked down its final moments. The dreaded
invasion of Japan now seemed to have been avoided. He was a very
lucky man and gave thanks to God.

In the days following the news of the Nagasaki bombing, Charles
Eck busied himself at his corner grocery. He read the newspaper each
day, always hoping for the headlines that would announce the end, and
tended his store alone. The year before, Harold would have been in
and out of the store, making deliveries, and helping out during the
summer months and after school. It seemed so long ago.

Glancing out the front door, he was distracted from his work by
the unusual appearance of a special telegram carrier walking on the
street. Someone's getting a telegram, he thought, and he hoped it wasn't
bad news.

He watched the carrier come down the sidewalk, waiting to see
him turn up the front walkway of one of the neighboring houses, but
the young man did not turn, and, in fact, crossed the street corner and
entered his small store. Looking around, he spotted the grocer behind
the counter and asked for Mr. Charles Eck.

"I've got a telegram for you," he said, after the older man had
identified himself. He produced the small, distinctive envelope, handed
it over, and waited for a signature. In the next moment, the carrier
was gone, and the store, once more, was empty. Charles Eck stared at
the unopened telegram in his hand.

Finally, he nervously fingered opened the envelope, unfolded the paper, and read the few words that brought his world crashing down around him. It was simple, just two lines, regretting to inform him that the ship, with his son Harold as a crew member, had been sunk and all members were officially classified as "Missing in Action."

He slumped forward and leaned against the counter, his mind trying to comprehend what he had just read. He reread the awful paper and unconsciously stuffed it into his shirt pocket, then tried to go about his business in the store, as if nothing had happened.

For the rest of the day, he served customers, absent-mindedly waiting on them, sometimes getting their orders wrong, and punching random keys on the cash register. There was no way that he could break this terrible news to Florence and the rest of the family. He walked around, the shell of the man he had been before the arrival of the telegram.

In the next few days, Charles Eck became a person that few people knew. His customers, some of whom had their groceries delivered, suddenly found strange, unordered items in their bags, while things they had ordered were missing. That was not like Charles, who had always been very precise. One after another they called, or came by to correct the mistakes, or to return the unordered items, and many observed his strange behavior.

Florence knew something was terribly wrong with her husband and suspected a sudden failure of his health. He had become a man she hardly knew, who had little to say and spent hours alone.

On the third day, shortly after he had come home from the grocery, the family physician suddenly walked in, having been summoned by Mrs. Eck. Charles was puzzled, and looked up and wondered what this was all about. The doctor began to question him about his health, and under the strain of questioning Charles broke down, revealing the message in the black telegram. The family was devastated.

Numerous phone calls were made to military authorities to try and learn more: Were there any survivors? Where did it happen? Was a search being made? But at each turn, they received the same answer: Harold was missing in action. There were no further details.[3]

On August 15, the war ended. The headlines in newspapers around the world simply said "Peace" in huge block letters. At the bottom of the page, some newspapers also carried a story few people read or cared about. On August 14, the Navy had released the following information concerning *Indianapolis:* "Lost with all hands. Washington D.C. The Navy Department announced tonight the loss of heavy cruiser *Indianapolis* with 1196 casualties—every man aboard the ship."[4]

Harold Eck had joined the crew of *Indianapolis* in December 1944, only three months after he had convinced his father to sign the waiver for him to join the service. The ship was at Mare Island, California, being overhauled and refitted with the latest in armament and fire control radar.

Harold's first view of the ship was spectacular. She was more than 600 feet long, and abovedeck she seemed to bristle with guns. She was the home of twelve hundred men and was a seasoned battle veteran, having participated in action against the enemy from the very first day, December 7, 1941, when she searched, in vain, for the Japanese task force that had launched the strikes against Pearl Harbor.[5]

She had participated in action in the Aleutians and had bombarded Tarawa, islands in the Marshalls and the Marianas, and, more recently, Tinian and the Western Caroline. She had earned eight battle stars[6] and was scheduled to depart for further action in the Pacific as soon as her refitting was completed.

Indianapolis, to her crew, was not just another cruiser. She was "the" cruiser, the flagship of the Fifth Fleet and its commander, Adm. Raymond Spruance. On occasion, she also served as flagship for Adm. "Bull" Halsey's Third Fleet.

For young seaman Harold Eck, his boarding of *Indianapolis* was the equivalent of being transported to another planet. All around him was a bustle of activity, and he quickly became part of that bustle. He was everywhere, painting, scraping, hauling, working. He was assigned a battle station at one of the port 20mm antiaircraft gun mounts toward the bow of the ship.

He learned of the new renovations. The ship had received a new fire control radar, and the twin 40mm mounts on the stern had been replaced with quad 40mm gun mounts. In the midship section, he was surprised to see that the cruiser had four float aircraft stowed on a hangar deck. These aircraft could be catapulted and then recovered after landing on the water.

Finally, after a month, the painting, refitting, additions, and testings were finished, and *Indianapolis,* with an impatient Harold Eck aboard, set sail for Hawaii. On January 14, 1945, she raced across the Pacific toward Japanese waters.

By February 10, *Indianapolis* had joined Task Force 58. Harold had never seen so many ships, and could have hardly imagined the number that now sailed toward Japan in a massive armada. There were seventeen fleet and light aircraft carriers, eight battleships, and sixteen cruisers, plus numerous destroyers and submarines. It was the most powerful armada in the history of naval warfare.[7]

By February 16, this massive fleet lay 100 miles off Tokyo and launched the first fighter strike of the war against the Japanese homeland. By the end of the next day, Task Force 58 had accounted for 340 shoot-downs, and 200 planes destroyed on the ground. Simultaneously, B-29 superfortresses had flown strikes from the Marianas Islands and had pounded other Japanese targets. Harold Eck was proud to be part of this American juggernaut.

The following day, Task Force 58 swept to the south, toward the tiny island of Iwo Jima, and by February 19, the battleships and cruisers began a three-day bombardment of the island prior to the Marine amphibious invasion. *Indianapolis* provided security for the invasion fleet, and lent its 8-inch guns to support the Marines on Iwo. From the deck, Harold Eck watched the tiny island disappear under the smoke of the bombardment.

During all this action, Eck stood at his battle station, ready for action. When his gun went into action, he hustled ammo to the loaders for the 20mm guns. Everyone cast watchful eyes to the skies looking for a Japanese air strike, but no Japanese aircraft ventured out.

But with the Iwo Jima invasion barely under way, *Indianapolis* steamed away from the battle. She again headed for Japan with the Carrier Task Force. The Marines on Iwo complained bitterly when they saw their gunfire support sail away, but the fleet moved on, following a tight schedule to hammer Japan into submission. On February 25, the Navy again struck the Japanese homeland. This time the great armada claimed 158 more aircraft, along with five small ships. Carrier aircraft continued to tear up targets on land until they had expended all ammo and bombs.

A week later, on March 1, the armada arrived in Ulithi, and Harold Eck received his first liberty. He was now a combat veteran, and the two-week stay to replenish and refurbish the fleet was a welcome respite.

On March 14, the carrier force was off again, heading north. This time it settled in a mere 100 miles southeast of Kyushu and launched more air strikes. For three days, the aircraft destroyed airfields and ports, and finally shot down forty-eight enemy aircraft that had made a feeble attempt to attack the great fleet.

Some of the Japanese aircraft avoided the Hellcat air cover and bore in on the outer defensive rings of the carrier task force. *Indianapolis,* as part of that outer defensive ring, went into action. Every gun was trained on the sky and fired on the attacking aircraft in a dizzying display of firepower. At the 20mm gun mounts, the action was fast and furious. The guns fired in their staccato rhythm at the swerving, diving aircraft, and Eck humped ammo to the position as fast as he could. Expended brass covered the deck at each gun, and the barrels smoked. At the end of the short ferocious battle, *Indianapolis* gunners claimed six enemy shoot-downs.[8]

For her part in the Iwo Jima operation and for the raids on the Japanese homeland, *Indianapolis* was awarded her ninth battle star, and a jubilant Harold Eck was part of that crew. Every man was proud to be part of the force that carried the war to Japanese soil.

On March 24, the cruiser moved offshore from the island of Okinawa, which would be the next Allied target. Okinawa was not just another target. It would be the last island taken before the invasion of Japan itself.

For seven days, *Indianapolis* bombarded targets on the island with its 8-inch guns. The bombardment continued around the clock, and the crew was on constant alert, particularly the 20mm antiaircraft crews who kept their eyes peeled for the dangerous kamikaze aircraft. D-Day for the invasion was set for April 1, 1945, April Fool's Day, but on the day before, *Indianapolis* had its first and only encounter with the "divine wind," the Japanese offensive using kamikaze pilots.

In the early morning light, the loudspeaker on deck barked the order, "Set condition one in antiaircraft battery."[9] Gun crews turned their eyes skyward to see a tiny speck breaking through the clouds.

Fire from the 20mm guns began immediately. Tracers streaked into the sky at the ever-closing black speck. Harold Eck passed the ammunition to the loaders and watched the gun blaze away at the Japanese kamikaze. Despite the increasing volume of fire, the plane bore in on the cruiser. With each second, more weapons, including the 5-inch guns, joined in to hurl a wall of steel at the attacking plane.

Still it came. The 20mm guns poured fire into the aircraft, and it seemed to falter, and then swerve, but righted itself and dived toward the evading cruiser. From the port side, the 20mm guns followed the dive pattern and sent a fire-hose pattern against the closing enemy.

But the flying bomb came on, undaunted by the fusillade of steel tearing it apart. Harold Eck and the rest of his gun crew watched helplessly as the pilot released the bomb when he was barely 25 feet above the deck. The bomb fell away and preceded the aircraft into the stern deck by a fraction of a second.

The plane crashed into the ship, bounced off the side, and fell harmlessly into the water. But the bomb smashed into the steel deck and plowed down through the crew's mess hall and berthing areas. Still unexploded, the bomb ripped through the ship's bottom and, only then, exploded with a terrific concussion. Nine sailors were killed and another twenty-six wounded.[10]

Indianapolis was badly wounded, but damage control crews contained the flooding. The bomb had destroyed fuel tanks, the water distilling plant, and two prop shafts.

"We got orders to return to the States for repairs, but no one thought that we wouldn't be back. Everyone knew that Japan had to be invaded so there was no thought that it was over for us," said Harold Eck.[11]

Indianapolis buried her dead at sea and limped the long 6,000 miles back to Mare Island in California for major repairs. She sported her tenth battle star for her participation in the Okinawa campaign.[12]

On May 2, one month after the kamikaze struck her, *Indianapolis* sailed under the Golden Gate Bridge. If anyone had thought that the ship was out of the war for good, that thought was dispelled when she underwent repair and refurbishment with the latest in armaments and technology. Even the main 8-inch gun batteries were replaced. The ship would be ready by July 14.

Two days earlier, Capt. Charles McVay III had received top-secret orders to be prepared for a high-speed run across the Pacific to the island of Tinian, in the Marianas, to deliver a top-secret cargo. On the day the "secret" cargo was loaded, no amount of silence could camouflage the special mission. The presence of a dozen admirals and generals on the dock, at seven in the morning, did not go unnoticed. The crew also watched cranes hoist a large crate aboard, and two sailors were seen carrying black cylindrical containers, safari-style, up the gangway. "We always had Marines on board, because we were the flagship," said Harold Eck, "but when I saw them assigned as guards on this big box by the hangar deck, I knew we were carrying something special."[13]

Word quickly spread that the canisters had been placed in the captain's quarters, and two mysterious men, who avoided all questions from a curious crew, were never far from them. Unknown to the crew of *Indianapolis,* the cargo was the firing device and uranium core for the new atomic bomb developed by the top-secret Manhattan Project.

Indianapolis sailed on July 16, an hour after the cargo was brought aboard, and the novelty of the cargo and the mystery men soon gave way to the routine of shipboard life. "We had daily duties to perform," said Eck. "We'd yell at the Marines, and ask them what was in the box, and they'd shrug their shoulders, and we'd get on with our business. A lot of us thought that it might be weapons of germ warfare."

The heavy cruiser streaked across the Pacific, following the path on which it had limped home in April, and covered the 6,000 miles in nine days, including a fuel stop at Pearl Harbor. Its racehorse speed had never been so useful. Its average 26-knot speed was a record-breaker.[14]

Early in the morning of July 26, *Indianapolis* arrived at Tinian and immediately unloaded its secret cargo. The two mystery men disembarked, following two grunting sailors who carried the black canisters as they had when they were loaded. The big box was lowered onto a truck and whisked off under a sizable guard.

Having completed its high-speed mission, *Indianapolis* received new orders from Adm. Chester Nimitz, Commander-in-Chief, Pacific, to proceed to Guam, and then set a course to Leyte in the Philippines. From there, the ship would join the battleship *Idaho* and undergo gunnery training.

All parties concerned with *Indianapolis*'s new orders were radioed copies and, after refueling, the ship was again under way that evening for the 100-mile trip to Guam. She arrived without incident on the following morning, July 27.[15]

Capt. McVay was ordered to proceed as soon as possible to Leyte to begin the scheduled gunnery practice. He was told that he should depart Guam no later than the morning of July 28. His orders were to proceed directly to Leyte, zigzagging at his discretion, at a speed of 15.7 knots, to arrive at 1100 on July 31. He was briefed that the passage was routine, with two "possible" enemy submarine contacts, and one "doubtful" contact reported by merchantmen in the vicinity of his planned route.[16]

What Capt. McVay had not been told was that there had been more than just a couple of "possible" and one "doubtful" sub contacts. He had not been told that the American destroyer *Underhill* had been torpedoed and sunk in the middle of the afternoon just four days earlier, with the loss of 112 men of its 228-man crew. He was also not told that four Japanese submarines were known to be operating in the area of his proposed route to Leyte, and, in fact, was told to proceed at an average pace along the most direct route.[17]

So after his briefing, Capt. McVay sailed *Indianapolis,* with her 1,196-man crew, out of the harbor at Guam, on the morning of July 28, and began the 1,200-mile journey to Leyte.

For most of the crew, the sailing on the next two days was uneventful. The hot days and humid nights made for uncomfortable sleeping, and many men went abovedecks. *Indianapolis* plowed through the seas at a leisurely 16 knots, with only four of her eight boilers lit.[18] It was quite a change from the top-speed trip from Mare Island to Tinian with the mystery cargo.

Harold Eck retired to his rack at ten o'clock on Sunday evening, July 29. Although the berthing quarters were hot in the equatorial climate, they were made a bit more bearable by a modification in the ship's watertight integrity. Since Capt. McVay had no intelligence report indicating the threat of an enemy attack, he routinely allowed some of the watertight doors to remain unsealed to ease the suffocating conditions in the sleeping quarters. That condition would be immediately changed with any threat of attack, and all watertight doors would be sealed.[19]

Even with some of the doors unsealed, many of the crew still escaped the steaming interior of the ship and sought the upper deck for relief under the stars. Sailors, sprawled on blankets and mattresses, could always be found on the open decks. For Harold Eck, used to the heat of New Orleans, the unsealed doors offered enough air circulation for him to sleep below, and he drifted off, knowing that in two days the ship would arrive in the Philippines, and they would engage in gunnery practice. He knew that the war was in its final stages, but there was no thought of returning home soon. Japan had to be invaded, and it would certainly be much worse than the bloodbaths of Iwo Jima and Okinawa. Then home would be a possibility.

There were a lot of new men aboard, and Harold could not help but think back to when he had first boarded *Indianapolis*. Now he was a veteran on the ship that had earned two battle stars with him as a crew member. He wondered what lay ahead. The ship sailed on, now almost 600 miles from Guam and halfway to Leyte.

Eck had been asleep for almost an hour when the surface of the black ocean suddenly turned white with foam, 10,000 yards from the cruising *Indianapolis*. Leaping from the ocean depths, the giant hull of the Japanese submarine *I-58* entered the atmosphere, nose first, and quickly settled her massive hull on the calm waters of the Pacific.

The conning tower hatch clanked open, and Capt. Mochitsura Hashimoto climbed to the bridge, with his binoculars almost immediately fixed to his eyes. He rotated 360 degrees, scanning all quarters.

The 330-foot submarine, larger than any of its American adversaries, was the most modern in the Imperial Japanese Navy. It could travel 17 knots on the surface and could fire six torpedoes at one time. These torpedoes were the submarine version of the deadly Long Lance torpedoes used with such devastation against American ships earlier in the war. It also carried four human-guided torpedoes called kaitens, the submarine equivalent of the aerial kamikaze.[20] The kaiten steered the torpedo into its target and became part of the explosion.

The moon alternately appeared and disappeared in the cloudy sky as Hashimoto peered through his binoculars. His submarine had finally arrived at its patrol station at the busy crossroads of the Okinawa-Palau and Guam-Leyte shipping lanes. It had been two weeks since *I-58* had departed Kure Harbor, several miles southeast of Hiroshima, on a last desperate mission to try to delay the American invasion of Japan. It was one of six subs whose mission was to sink American ships.[21]

Hashimoto was disappointed that he could see no prospective targets and was almost ready to conclude that there were no enemy ships on his small part of the ocean, when his eyes caught a dark speck, barely visible on the horizon. The moon, alternately appearing and disappearing, backlit the approaching vessel, and when he was sure that it could be a target, Hashimoto ordered *I-58* to dive to periscope depth, and continued his observation underwater.

His eyes were pressed hard to the periscope, and the excited crew buzzed around him, anxious for a chance to sink an American ship. The speck had now became a black object and, at certain angles, Hashimoto could see two masts. From its profile, the captain determined it to be a large ship of the line—a battleship of the American *Idaho*-class.

For the better part of an hour, the Japanese commander plotted his course and planned the attack. He issued orders for course and direction and gave the data for torpedo settings, range, and fan.

The ship was now large in his periscope, presenting its starboard side to the Japanese submarine, and he estimated the range to be a mere 1,500 yards, almost point-blank. He gave final angles, deflection, and depth settings, and fired his torpedoes just a little after midnight. The huge 30-foot torpedoes sped toward their target at almost 50 miles an hour. Fifty-one seconds later, Hashimoto saw two large geysers erupt from the forward section of *Indianapolis,* followed by muffled explosions.[22]

Harold Eck was thrown out of his rack to the hard floor at approximately ten minutes past midnight on July 30. He lay on the floor stunned by the fall and unable to grasp what had happened, when a second explosion shuddered the deck where he lay. The entire berthing quarter was pitch-black, and other men started to shout to get topside.

Harold's first thought, after recovering his wits and putting on his life jacket, was to go to his battle station, which was on the port side. Bodies pressed all around him as he staggered and felt his way toward the ladder leading topside.[23] As he struggled among a sea of arms and legs, the ship was already in a three-degree list.

The first torpedo had struck *Indianapolis* just aft of the bow and severed the first 60 feet from the ship, but it was the second one that was the mortal blow. Exploding 180 feet from the bow, the second torpedo ignited a fuel tank and powder storeroom, and severed water main lines and the electric power.[24] The ruptured fuel created a raging fire on the ship and in the ocean.

With no shipboard communications, Capt. McVay had ordered that word be sent to the radio rooms to transmit a distress signal. But his messengers did not make it. Radio 1 was the main radio shack where all the messages were transmitted and received, and Radio 2 housed all of the transmitters. The cables connecting Radio 1 with Radio 2 were all severed, but in Radio 2, seven or eight technicians were assembled with Mr. Woods, the communications officer. Herbert J. Miner, one of the radio technicians, warmed up a transmitter with the waning power from the aft engine room as he put his life preserver on. When it was ready, he watched Chief Warrant Officer Woods tap out an SOS, using an emergency key attached to the transmitter.

"I know the message went out," Miner said, "because I stood right beside him and watched the needle jump in the power meter of the antenna circuit."[25] Technicians Fred Hart and Joseph Moran had also keyed out messages but could not be certain they had gone out.[26] In the few minutes it took to attempt to send the messages, *Indianapolis* was already listing 20 degrees.

On the main deck, Harold Eck finally emerged topside and tried to move toward his battle station, but the severe list made it almost impossible to walk. No sooner had he arrived on deck than he got the word to abandon ship. Already he could see men sliding down the side of the ship, which was now nearly horizontal. He stepped over the rail and slid toward the water, trying to avoid any place where there was fire.

Once in the water, he swam as hard as he could to get away from the ship. He was glad that he had been trained as a lifeguard back home in New Orleans, and his powerful strokes carried him away from the burning hulk.

When he had swum a hundred yards, he turned around, just in time to see the stern of his ship rise into the air with its props slowly turning, pause momentarily, and then sink, bow first, beneath the waves. It was hard to believe that less than fifteen minutes earlier, he had been peacefully sleeping on the ship. The burning oil on the surface illuminated the final moments of the doomed cruiser.

He stared at the foaming surface that marked the spot of *India-napolis*'s dive for several moments, and then thought about his own situation. Many men in the water were screaming in pain from horrible burns, but he seemed to be okay. His first sensation was that he was covered with oil, and his eyes burned. Rubbing only forced more oil into them.

His main worry was that if they had been torpedoed, perhaps the enemy submarine would surface and shoot the survivors. Eck didn't know it, but that was exactly what Hashimoto was trying to do.

Fearing a possible attack from an escorting vessel, *I-58* had dived and remained underwater for almost thirty minutes. When he thought it was safe to surface, Captain Hashimoto surfaced to attempt to capture several survivors to confirm his success. His second-in-command, To-shio Tanaka, wanted revenge and would advise that survivors should be machine-gunned.

But to Hashimoto's disappointment, he could find no survivors. Nor could he find any evidence of the ship he was sure he had sunk. He circled around the battle area once, examining each wave and trough, but he found nothing.

Finally, fearing that another ship might find him, Hashimoto abandoned his search and gave orders to set a northeasterly course. Thirty miles later, he transmitted a message to Tokyo that he had sunk a battleship. By early morning on July 30, the Americans at the combat intelligence office on Guam had intercepted that message and decoded it, and then cast it with the hundreds of other unbelievable messages from Japanese commanders who continually claimed to have sunk the entire American fleet. Besides, there had been no SOS. No one investigated.[27]

Harold Eck spent the remainder of his first night in the water shivering with cold. He hugged his kapok life jacket around him and was thankful it was not winter. The flames in the water quickly died after the ship sank, and he was only aware of men around him, some yelling in the dark. He concentrated on his belief that after dawn, search vessels would be out in force to rescue them.

The night seemed endless, but finally gray skies appeared in the east, and the welcome red ball of the sun was beautiful to behold. Now he could see a small group of men, and others like him floating like bobbing corks in the calm water.

He swam to the larger group and saw that they were holding on to a cargo net, held afloat by corks. They placed the wounded men on top of the net, and all held on to the strands. Eck did not know anyone, and no one was recognizable. Each sailor was coated in the black oil that smeared the water's surface.

Someone made a head count and discovered that there were 124 men. They looked around, but could see no others and thought they were the only survivors of the sinking.[28] They were not. Scattered over miles of the ocean, more than eight hundred men had escaped with their lives, but were floating helplessly, waiting to be rescued.

As the sun climbed in the sky, Harold stopped shivering, and then became very warm. He tore his shirt and made a cap for his head to ward off the burning rays of the sun. The oil that covered his skin and that had been such an irritant now became a soothing salve to protect his skin. The men in the group all ripped shirts to make bandages for the wounded.

As the morning wore on, the men conversed about their possible rescue. The consensus was that they would be rescued today. Certainly an SOS had gone out and that would bring search planes and ships. After all, they were in a well-trafficked sea lane. Others thought that the rescue wouldn't come until tomorrow and prepared themselves for a day in the water. They factored in time for the SOS to be received and search craft to be dispatched and, of course, they had to be found. Everyone agreed that the worst-case scenario would have them reported missing on Tuesday, July 31, the day they were to arrive in the Philippines. That would be tomorrow.

Harold listened to the speculations but was suddenly interrupted when the man next to him slapped him on the shoulder and shouted, "Look!" Eck followed the pointing finger and, at first, could see nothing. But then he saw the fin. It was large, and grayish-brown, and it cut through the water on the periphery of the group. Then there was another, and another. The men were yelling, "Sharks," and pushed themselves into a tighter circle.

There now seemed to be hundreds of fins all around the area. The first attack came on a sailor who had drifted slightly away from the net, and there was a great scream and violent thrashing, then red, foaming water. Other sharks rushed in on the hapless victim. The men witnessing the attack were frozen in horror. They pushed the circle in as tight as they could, but their dangling legs were constantly being bumped by the great fish swimming beneath them.

On and off on that first day, the sharks came and went. Sometimes they would attack, and other times they would just circle. In the group, the sailors debated what tactic they should employ. Some felt that when the sharks came close, everyone should thrash violently and beat the water with their arms in an attempt to frighten them away. Others felt they should remain motionless, hoping the sharks would not attack.

They employed both tactics. Sometimes they worked; other times they didn't. During that first day, a number of the wounded men who had been placed on top of the net died. Their jackets were removed, and they were set free from the group and quickly found by the sharks.

The end of the first day brought relief from the blistering sun and the shark attacks. Harold Eck prayed for tomorrow, the day of rescue.

The harsh sun and fear caused by the shark attacks had hastened the dehydration process, and the small group of men now experienced a terrible thirst.

The cool of the evening was the only time to relax. Harold had found himself floating the whole day with his feet drawn up into a tight ball, held upright by his jacket. His worst nightmare had not equaled the terror of voracious sharks swimming below him and bumping his legs, just to let him know they were there. The monster that lurked under his bed when he was a child was nothing compared to this reality.

During the night, he tried to sleep, but it was impossible. The jacket held his head upright, and on the few occasions that he dozed, his face fell into the water. The only way that sleep was possible was if someone held his body horizontally. After the sun went down, he shivered through the night.

Harold thought of home, his old neighborhood, and his group of friends, nicknamed the Tornadoes. They played ball and were a force with which to be reckoned. He thought of his mother and father and his family and how wonderful it would be to be back at the corner grocery. He could taste a long cool drink of water. Tomorrow he would be rescued.

The sun rose on the second day. Once again, the survivors faced the grisly task of freeing from the net those terribly wounded men who had succumbed during the night. And then the sharks showed up again. The floating dead were taken in a feeding frenzy. Attack after attack claimed more and more. Then it subsided.

Far above the floating circle, an airplane droned. The shout went up, and men waved their jackets and arms, but the plane continued without any sign of a wing wag. Throughout the morning, more planes passed overhead. Their rescuers were just overhead, if only they could see them.

Harold Eck and his circle of survivors did not know that these aircraft were not looking for them, and only happened to be flying overhead. The nonarrival of *Indianapolis* at Leyte had been of no concern to anyone. The fact that she did not show up at her appointed time did not set off any warning lights because of a monumental Navy snafu, originating at the very top of the chain of command.

In 1945, Leyte, and the harbor at Tacloban, was the busiest port in the world. The majority of the traffic was transport traffic to feed the enormous demands of the war effort. Combat ships were treated separately. In an effort to reduce the huge volume of radio traffic, and for security purposes, local port directors were instructed not to report the arrival and departure of ships of the line. Because of these rules, combat ships were generally ignored.[29]

This order, not to report the movements of combat ships, came from none other than the Commander-in-Chief, Pacific, Adm. Chester Nimitz. However, couched in the wording of this order was the question: If a report is not necessary for the arrival or departure of a combat ship, is one necessary for a nonarrival or nondeparture? The answer lies in the reality that *Indianapolis*'s nonarrival raised no eyebrows. Combat ships had, in the past, been diverted from their destinations, and *Indianapolis,* as Adm. Spruance's flagship, was even more likely to be diverted without warning.

At 1100 on July 31, the small fleet of ships that were to participate in the gunnery practice for which *Indianapolis* was scheduled sailed for the training exercise without her.[30] Because of Navy bungling, she was not missed. By the end of that day, 500 miles away, *Indianapolis*'s survivors had been in the water for forty hours.

At the end of the second day, the survivors holding on to the cargo net huddled together encouraging one another. Certainly rescue would come with the dawn. By now the ship would have been missed and search parties would be looking. Those overhead aircraft must be part of the search party.

They pressed together, their common bond being the life-saving cargo net. Again the night brought shivering that wracked their bodies, and thirst had seduced some to drink seawater, worsening dehydration. During the night more men died, but the hours of darkness meant that at least there were no sharks.

At dawn, on the third day, August 1, Harold Eck was shocked to see the condition of his fellow survivors. Many had started to hallucinate and experienced other signs of delirium. Dehydration, exposure, and shock strained each man's mind. Hunger, thirst, and open sores added to their misery and, for the first time, many abandoned all hope of rescue.

For Harold Eck, there was one moment of relief from agony. It came in the form of gallows humor when the man floating next to him suddenly tapped him on the shoulder.

"Hey," he said. "Check that tag on your life jacket."

Eck looked down and read the tag attached to the jacket, just under the water. It said, "Good for forty-eight hours."

Harold turned to his companion and asked, "Where can I go to survey this and get a new one?"

It was one of the few laughs of the day. Later on, some men drifted away from the group, swimming toward imaginary islands, ships, and horizons. Mirages had become reality, and as the doomed sailors swam feebly toward the illusion of rescue, the sharks attacked them. Blood and parts of bodies mixed with the oil slick. Half-eaten corpses, still in their life jackets, bobbed like corks on the still waters.

One man in the center of the group suddenly began to take off his jacket. Harold tried to restrain him, but was pushed away.

"You don't understand, man," he told Harold. "The ship is just below us, and there's water in the scuttlebutt [water fountain]. I'm just going down to get a drink. I'll be right back."[31] The man slipped out of his jacket and sank beneath the surface. Others did the same. By now, the group had shrunk to less than half of the original 124.

Again, aircraft flew across the skies. Those still able to wave did so, but their energy was diminished. Other men died that day from exposure, burns, or simply succumbed to the trauma of their wounds. The ever-present sharks performed their grisly cleanup.

The fourth night passed, and dawn brought the fourth day of their ordeal. By now the remaining survivors had given up all hope. Harold lost track of who was still there. His head and body were now lower in the water as the waterlogged kapok jacket sank deeper. He was still secured to the cargo net, and his mind wandered. He was aware of sharks attacking, concentrating on the bodies of the men who had died and drifted away.

Despite the growing despair of the group on the cork net, a miracle was, at that moment, unfolding several miles away. A Navy aircraft on a routine antisubmarine patrol flew over the oil slick from *Indianapolis.* Lt. Wilbur Gwinn was the pilot of the *Ventura,* but was not at the controls. He was in the aft section of the aircraft, crouched in the tail section and fuming about the second antenna that had failed him that day. The weight that stabilized the antenna had broken off, and the trailing wire whipped uselessly in the wind.

He ordered one of his crew to reel the flailing wire into the plane and just so happened to gaze down to catch a glimpse of a black oil streak. He straightened up and rushed back to the cockpit. An oil slick: the sure sign of a crippled Jap sub.

Gwinn prepared for a bomb run, arming the depth charges and opening the bomb bay. In moments, he was swooping down on the slick ready to release his explosives when he saw what looked like black bumps in the middle of the oil. He secured the run, pulled out of his dive, and circled back for a second pass.

To his shock, the black bumps were people, floating in the vast expanse of water. On a third run, he dropped a raft, life jackets, water, and a sonobuoy, which would allow communications. He also counted thirty heads and sent a message to his squadron headquarters.[32] He had also seen sharks swimming among the floating men.

The survivors in Harold Eck's group knew nothing of their imminent salvation. They were miles away, floating in their own world of endless time and attacking sharks. They could not know that Gwinn's message had been received at Peleliu. After a second and third transmission, the number of survivors counted and reported was up to 150.

Finally the Navy rescue machinery cranked into action. Unbelieving Navy commanders, hearing about the report of a large number of men drifting in the ocean, suddenly checked, and realized that several ships were unaccounted for, including *Indianapolis,* and ordered other ships and aircraft to move to Gwinn's coordinates.

All afternoon several aircraft provided initial assistance. One daring pilot actually landed his PBY on the water, contrary to all Navy rules, and succeeded in using his craft as a rescue float to get men out of the water. Using every available inch of space, including his wings, the pilot managed to pluck fifty-six survivors from the water.[33] A second aircraft also set down, but neither were in the vicinity of the survivors of Harold Eck's group.

Nightfall of the fourth day found Eck more dead than alive. Darkness fell on what Harold believed was the last night of his life. Around him, the group had diminished to a pitiful few. Some hallucinated, others were unconscious, and still others prayed for an end.

A hundred miles from the scene of the disaster, the destroyer *Cecil J. Doyle* raced through the night toward the rescue area. Its captain, W. Graham Claytor, Jr., stared into the cloudy, moonless night. He was in a combat zone and was rigged for blackout, but a second consideration forced him to break all the rules of blackout. Claytor tried to place himself in the position of the men he was racing to rescue. He only knew that floating helplessly in the dark had to be a frightful experience, and he ordered his searchlights turned on and aimed at the clouds. Maybe some poor devil would see the light and know help was coming.[34]

One poor devil who saw it was Harold. He could not believe his eyes. Some of the others saw the reflected beams also.

"They're coming," he said. "Someone's coming."[35]

Others in the group, who were on the point of despair, now took new hope. They braced themselves to hold on a little while longer.

At 0100 the transport *Bassett* arrived. Like *Doyle,* she had her searchlights on and had lowered three LCVPs into the water to conduct a search after spotting a life raft. The boats moved slowly, fearful of running over survivors, their search made more difficult by 6- to 8-foot swells. Crew members held lanterns aloft to light the way. Slowly, suvivors were found and, one by one, the floating men were picked up. The rescuing crews were horrified to see the condition of the survivors.

Ens. L. Peter Wren, in *Bassett's* LCVP #2, recalled coming upon a large group of men. He could not tell their nationality and initially thought they might be Japanese. He held his battle lantern high, shining on some of the group. "I am looking at black face, white teeth, round white-eyed men," he said. "All they can see is a round white light shining on them."[36]

Some of the survivors, who were conscious enough to think, feared that their rescuers were actually the Japanese coming to kill them. Others offered remarks that evidenced their delirium.

Plucking the men from the water was no easy task. In fact, it was backbreaking. A 150-pound man with an equally heavy water-saturated life jacket was a tremendous load.

"I was trying to lift 300 pounds over the gunwale on a moving, bobbing craft," Ens. Wren described. "The man let out a scream of agony. . . . I feel like I am pulling his flesh and muscle away from the bone."[37]

Some of the men who had the luxury of a raft were in fair condition, but most had to be treated with kid gloves. Most had spent the four days completely immersed. Some of the skin and muscle was so ulcerated and waterlogged, it split and came off with the slightest lifting pressure. Others had bones protruding through the ruptured skin. Still others had horrible shark-bite wounds.

In LCVP #1, William VanWilpe dived into the water to try to assist the weakened survivors. He led a group of six or seven to the stern of the landing craft and positioned himself underwater, under each man, and then boosted him up by the rear end to other crew members in the LCVP who would grab him and haul him to safety. When those half-dozen were aboard, VanWilpe swam off to get others.

He had to deal with a new phenomenon—delirium and hallucinations—and he found himself having great difficulty gaining the survivors' confidence. He tried everything, but discovered that telling big lies got the best results. The men did not believe that he was there to help them or rescue them, but they would believe stories they had fantasized about during their days of despair.

"I told them I was going to a ferry boat and some followed me." To others he pointed to the LCVP and told them, "We are going on shore leave."[38] He even formed some up in a conga line as if they were going to do the popular dance.

Those who were still nonbelievers he overpowered and dragged to safety. Slowly the boats were filled and returned to *Bassett* to unload their human cargo, and then back to the rescue area for another load. Crewmen lost count of how many trips they made.

First there were dozens brought to the mothership, then fifty, then the number surpassed one hundred. During the rescue, one of the boats approached the cork net.

Joseph Dronet, a survivor with Eck, and a man who had gone to boot camp with him, saw the lights and fell asleep as his rescuers approached. He awoke when the lantern light shone on his face.

Harold Eck looked up and saw a light over him. He wondered if he had died and was approaching heaven and this was perhaps the entrance? His eyes focused on the sides of the LCVP, and he saw hands. The next thing he felt was his body being hoisted from the water. As he was dragged over the gunwale, he sensed salvation, and his body ceased all resistance and he abandoned himself to unconsciousness. He came to briefly onboard *Bassett* and found himself on deck in a wire basket. He heard himself moaning, but fell unconscious again. Of the original 124 men on the net, 26 survived and were rescued by the *Bassett* crew.

Time had no boundary, and the next time Eck awoke, he found himself cleaned and resting on fresh sheets in clean clothes. He had no recollection of anyone cleaning him, washing away the oil that had become part of his body during the last five days. He had been in the water for more than one hundred hours, and had lost thirty pounds.

Eck asked for water and could only remember that some kind sailor gave him a wonderful gift, a fresh orange. He thanked God he was alive and slept again. When he finally fully regained consciousness, he was in a hospital on the island of Samar at the entrance to Leyte Gulf. It was midday on August 4. *Bassett* had recovered 152 *Indianapolis* survivors and brought them to Samar.

Other ships brought the remaining survivors. Of the eight-hundred-plus men that had initially survived the torpedoing of *Indianapolis* and had slipped into the burning, oil-covered waters during those first few minutes on July 30, only 317 were pulled from the ocean on August 3. Five hundred died after the ship sank.

On their second day of rescue, August 6, 1945, the 317 survivors had no way of knowing that, in the early morning hours, the B-29 superfortress *Enola Gay* had lifted off from Tinian carrying the atom bomb, whose components *Indianapolis* had raced across the ocean the previous week. Several hours later, Hiroshima was destroyed.

The Navy's reaction to the tragedy was shameful. First, it withheld the news for almost two weeks, not even informing the families of the survivors until the day before the newspapers had the story. While the men were recovering in the hospitals, they were told to write home as if nothing had happened. Harold Eck obeyed that order and sent a letter to his parents that conveyed none of his recent ordeal.

That letter, received two weeks after the telegram notifying them that their son was MIA, was the first news that the Eck family had that Harold was okay. The letter, and its nonchalant tone, so shocked and confused his mother and father that they guessed that since he was such a strong swimmer he must have saved himself by swimming to a nearby island.[39]

When the official news was released, the Navy released it to hit the papers on the day Japan surrendered. The euphoric joy of the world at peace buried the story. Other than the grieving families, who would care? The war was over.

An inquiry into the sinking was convened by Adm. Chester Nimitz on August 13 on the island of Guam. All of the survivors were transported there, and Nimitz wanted an inquiry as soon as possible while everything was fresh in everyone's minds. The most obvious question to be answered was the one that Capt. McVay had posed to reporters when he met them on August 5.

"Why didn't this get out sooner?"[40] he asked, referring to the delayed search efforts.

During the week-long proceedings that ended on August 20, forty-three witnesses were questioned. All of the commands that had any responsibility in briefing, dispatching, or receiving messages concerning *Indianapolis* during its fateful voyage paraded their witnesses to testify that they had nothing to do with the ensuing disaster.

There was finger-pointing and dodging, and other self-defense tactics, but the most serious breach of justice occurred when Vadm.

George Murray, who was in charge of the Marianas Command, and whose subordinates were responsible for briefing Capt. McVay about possible Japanese submarines, was made one of the three judges. He would pass judgment on whether he or anyone in his command had been negligent.[41] By any definition, this was a conflict of interest.

In the end, the judge advocate falsely accused Capt. McVay on three charges: First, that he had been warned of the submarine menace and did not zigzag; second, that visibility was good (it was mostly poor), requiring zigzagging; third, that McVay delayed sending an SOS.[42] The surviving radio operators knew that was false. The trumped-up "zigzagging" charges were weak, at best, since orders issued at Guam left zigzagging to the discretion of the captain, especially when the submarine threat was "minimal."

McVay received a Letter of Reprimand and was ordered to stand trial by general court-martial. Capt. McVay would become the first captain to ever be court-martialed for losing his ship.

In September, the *Indianapolis* survivors boarded the aircraft carrier *Hollandia* and sailed home. They had no duties aboard, and it became a holiday cruise. They spent their time between meals playing cards, listening to music, and lounging around. Home was at the end of their cruise.

They arrived in San Diego, where they were given leave and then sent home. Harold arrived in New Orleans in October and finished the last year of his enlistment stationed there. In the fall of 1946, he was released from active duty and joined the fire department, where he spent the rest of his working career.

Fireman Harold Eck was as brave as Seaman 2/c Harold Eck had been during his days on board *Indianapolis*. He was cited by the City of New Orleans for bravery for rescuing a woman from certain death by carrying her down from a burning building to safety. Years later, he would recall his own brush with certain death and that wonderful searchlight in the sky. "That light saved my life," he said. "It helped me muster up enough courage to not give up. I would not have made it . . . as I was more dead than alive."[43]

• • •

The inquiry in August and the upcoming December court-martial of Capt. McVay had allowed the Navy to sidestep some of the damning questions that the brass needed to answer. Some of those were questions about the failure to brief McVay on submarine danger; the failure to investigate the intercepted message from *I-58* concerning a ship sinking; the failure to investigate *Indianapolis*'s overdue status; the failure to divert or escort the doomed cruiser in the face of a known danger; and the ambiguous order not to report the arrival or departure of combat ships.

As the proceedings against the most likely scapegoat were about to commence, there was a brief moment of courage in the face of injustice. Adm. Chester Nimitz, perhaps bothered by his conscience or moved by a sense of fairness, recommended that a court-martial be set aside, since it was unwarranted. His plea was overruled by the Chief of Naval Operations, Adm. Ernest King, who wanted someone to pay. Navy Secretary James Forrestal sided with King, and the trial would go on as scheduled. Curiously, it was later revealed that Adm. King had once been reprimanded as a young officer by none other than Capt. McVay's father, Adm. Charles McVay II. Another troubling conflict of interests.

The court-martial convened on December 3 and ended on December 19, 1945. For most observers, including many of the survivors, it was a "farce" and a "kangaroo court,"[44] complete with all the trappings of railroading. The Navy even called Captain Hashimoto, the skipper of *I-58,* to testify as a witness, adding to its list of inglorious firsts: No enemy commander had ever been a witness for the prosecution against his U.S. adversary.

On December 4, *The Washington Post* tweaked the Navy's nose in an editorial entitled, "Navy Secrecy." It called attention to the top brass's whitewashing of themselves and their actions.

Despite numerous incidents of injustice, and notwithstanding Capt. Hashimoto's own testimony that zigzagging would have made no difference, Capt. Charles McVay was convicted on one count of hazarding his ship by failing to zigzag. He was sentenced to lose seniority, but the sentence was remitted by Navy Secretary Forrestal in February 1946.

McVay thereafter was forever hounded by hate mail and recriminations from some of the families whose loved ones had died in the *Indianapolis* tragedy. Twenty-three years later, Capt. McVay himself became a victim of the sinking. On November 6, 1968, he stepped out onto the front step of his house, took his service revolver, and shot himself.[45]

Of all of the disturbing events surrounding the *Indianapolis* tragedy, none is more disturbing than information that surfaced as the result of two articles appearing in 1955 editions of *The Saturday Evening Post* and *The Los Angeles Times,* on the occasion of the tenth anniversary of the sinking.

After reading the stories in these two publications, Mr. Clair Young, a former seaman 1/c who had been stationed at 3964 Naval Shore Facility, Tacloban, Leyte, Philippine Islands in 1945, refuted the parts of the stories that claimed that though a number of SOS's had been sent from *Indianapolis* before she sank, none had ever been received.

He had been attached to shore patrol security and, on the night of July 30, was on the 10 P.M. to 2 A.M. watch on Nob Hill, which overlooked the anchorage at Leyte. His particular duty was security at a small Quonset hut, which was the quarters of Commodore Jacob Jacobson, the Senior Officer Present at the Naval Shore Facility.

About thirty minutes after midnight, a man approached and Young challenged him. He identified himself as a messenger with an urgent message and said he had been ordered to wait for a reply. Young told him to wait, took the message, and went to the light by the side door to read it.

The message was garbled, but had been repeated. It identified a ship, its position, and its condition, and looked like an SOS. Young had no idea what the ship's identification was since it was only listed as CA-35, meaning it was some type of cruiser.

He brought the message to the commodore, awakening him in the dark and shining his flashlight on the message. The commodore propped himself on one elbow, read it, and told Young that he had no reply at that time, but if any further messages were to come in, he was to be notified immediately. Young gave this answer to the messenger, who left and went down the hill.

On August 6, 1955, Clair Young wrote a letter to the Chief of Naval Operations in Washington detailing this information. He sent copies to Sen. William Knowland and the editors of the two publications. No one has ever refuted his story.[46]

NOTES

Chapter 1

1. Henry H. Arnold, *Global Mission* (New York: Harper & Brothers, 1949), 274.
2. Ibid., 289.
3. "Chronology 1933–1944," *History of the Second World War* (BPC Publishing Ltd., 1966), 3540–41.
4. Carroll V. Glines, *Doolittle's Tokyo Raiders* (D. Van Nostrand Co. Inc., 1964), 12–19.
5. Ibid., 36.
6. Ibid., 44; Ronald Drez interview with Robert Bourgeois, December 1998.
7. Ibid., 48.
8. Ibid., 66–68.
9. Pacific War Conference, University of New Orleans, April 12–13, 1991.
10. Ibid.
11. Glines, *Raiders,* 249.
12. Ibid., 251.
13. Ibid., 392–93.
14. Haruko Taya Cook and Theodore Cook, *Japan at War* (New York: The New Press, 1992), 187–92.
15. Glines, *Raiders,* 312.

Chapter 2

1. George Gay, *Sole Survivor* (Midway Publishers, 1979), 82–83.
2. Ibid., 24.
3. Pacific War Conference, University of New Orleans, April 12–13, 1991.
4. Gay, *Survivor,* 46.
5. Samuel J. Rosenman, *The Public Papers and Addresses of Franklin D. Roosevelt,* 1942 volume (New York: Harper & Row, 1950), 216.
6. Mitsuo Fuchida and Masatake Okumiya, *Midway: The Battle That Doomed Japan* (Annapolis: Naval Institute Press, 1955), 70–73.
7. "Symposium '98: The Battle of Midway," Naval Aviation Museum and Foundation, May 7, 1998, Pensacola, Florida.
8. Gay, *Survivor,* 98 and 101.
9. Ibid., 17–20, 103.
10. "Symposium '98."
11. Richard Hough, *The Longest Battle: The War at Sea, 1939–45* (New York: William Morrow and Company, Inc., 1986), 214.
12. Gay, *Survivor,* 105.
13. E. B. Potter and Chester W. Nimitz, *The Great Sea War: The Story of Naval Action in World War II* (New York: Bramhall House, 1960) 221–23.
14. Fuchida and Okumiya, *Midway,* 95.
15. Gay, *Survivor,* 106.
16. "Symposium '98."
17. Gay, *Survivor,* 111.
18. Potter and Nimitz, *Sea War,* 230.
19. "Symposium '98."
20. Pat Frank and Joseph Harrington, *Rendezvous at Midway* (New York: The John Day Co., Inc., 1968), 115.
21. Gay, *Survivor,* 111–15.
22. "Symposium '98."
23. Gay, *Survivor,* 117–23.
24. "Symposium '98."
25. Fuchida and Okumiya, *Midway,* 174–75.
26. Frank and Harrington, *Rendezvous,* 126.
27. Clark G. Reynolds, *The Carrier War,* from *The Epic of Flight* series (Alexandria, Va.: Time-Life Books, 1982), 93.
28. Fuchida and Okumiya, *Midway,* 177–78.
29. Frank and Harrington, *Rendezvous,* 130–31.
30. Gay, *Survivor,* 133.
31. Ibid., 139.
32. Ibid., 140.

33. "Symposium '98."

34. Reynolds, *The Carrier War,* 99.

35. Potter and Nimitz, *Sea War,* 247.

Chapter 3

1. Jack Bolt oral history, Naval Aviation Museum Foundation, Pensacola, Florida.

2. Martin Caidin, *Golden Wings* (New York, 1960), 140.

3. E. B. Potter and Chester W. Nimitz, *The Great Sea War* (New York: Bramhall House, 1960), 255–65.

4. John Foster, *Hell in the Heavens* (New York: G. P. Putnam's Sons, 1961), 161.

5. Jack Bolt oral history.

6. Gregory Boyington, *Baa Baa Black Sheep* (New York: Dell, 1959), 120–21.

7. Bolt oral history.

8. Boyington, *Sheep,* 135–38.

9. Ronald Drez interview with Jack Bolt, copy at Eisenhower Center (EC), University of New Orleans.

10. Boyington, *Sheep,* 127.

11. Bolt oral history.

12. Boyington, *Sheep,* 153.

13. Bolt interview.

14. Frank E. Walton, *Once They Were Eagles* (Lexington, Ky.: University Press of Kentucky), 21.

15. Bolt oral history.

16. Richard Abrams, *F4U Corsairs at War* (New York: Charles Scribner's Sons), 16.

17. Bolt oral history.

18. Boyington, *Sheep,* 155.

19. Walton, *Eagles,* 36.

20. Boyington, *Sheep,* 160.

21. Walton, *Eagles,* 110.

22. Ibid., 41.

23. Ibid., 48–49.

24. Ibid., 51.

25. Mark Styling, *Corsair Aces of World War 2* (London: Osprey Aerospace, 1995), 54.

26. Bolt oral history; Bolt interview.

27. Walton, *Eagles,* 52.

28. Ibid., 53.

29. Bolt interview.

30. Boyington, *Sheep,* 283.

31. Ibid., 357.

32. Ibid., 184.

33. Ibid., 194.

34. Bolt oral history.

35. Bolt interview.

Chapter 4

1. E. B. Potter and Chester W. Nimitz, *The Great Sea War* (New York: Bramhall House, 1960), 405.

2. Ibid., 316–18.

3. Henry I. Shaw, Jr., *Tarawa: A Legend Is Born* (New York: Ballantine, 1969), 32.

4. Potter and Nimitz, *Sea War,* 311.

5. Shaw, *Tarawa,* 12.

6. Ibid., 32.

7. Earl J. Wilson et al., *Betio Beachhead* (New York: G. P. Putnam's Sons, 1945), 9.

8. Ronald Drez interview with James Russell, April 21, 1999.

9. Shaw, *Tarawa,* 19.

10. Ibid., 20.

11. Russell interview.

12. Shaw, *Tarawa,* 26.

13. Russell interview.

14. Shaw, *Tarawa,* 26.

15. Russell interview.

16. Ibid.

17. Lieutenant General Julian Smith oral history, 1973, Marine Corps Historical Center (Washington, D.C.), 285.

18. Shaw, *Tarawa,* 30.

19. Russell interview.

20. Quoted in Rafael Steinberg, *Island Fighting* (Alexandria, Va.: Time-Life Books, 1978), 106.

21. Ronald H. Spector, *Eagle Against the Sun* (New York: Vintage Books, 1985), 262.

22. Quoted in "Our Century—Death Tide at Tarawa," A&E telecast, 1993, Lou Reda Production.

23. Wilson, *Betio Beachhead,* 25.

24. Russell interview.

25. "Death Tide at Tarawa."

26. Shaw, *Tarawa,* 42–45.

27. Russell interview.
28. Shaw, *Tarawa,* 45.
29. Quoted in Wilson, *Betio Beachhead,* 38.
30. "Death Tide at Tarawa."
31. Joseph H. Alexander, *Utmost Savagery: The Three Days of Tarawa* (New York: U.S. Naval Institute, 1995), 129–30.
32. Russell interview.
33. Alexander, *Utmost Savagery,* 182–83.
34. Ibid., 183.
35. Shaw, *Tarawa,* 98.
36. Ibid., 110–12.
37. Ibid., 118.
38. Russell's citation reads that the action took place on November 22. This is clearly a clerical error, made months after the battle was over. Russell received his award in 1945 while in a hospital. The action occurred on November 21.
39. Quoted in "Our Century—Death Tide at Tarawa."
40. Ibid.

Chapter 5

1. Quoted in Gordon A. Harrison, *Cross-Channel Attack* (Washington, D.C.: Office of the Chief of Military History, Dept. of the Army, 1951), 467.
2. Erwin Rommel, *The Rommel Papers,* ed. B. H. Liddell Hart (New York: B. H. Liddell Hart, 1953), 466.
3. Omar N. Bradley, *A Soldier's Story* (New York: Rand McNally & Co., 1951), 235.
4. Ken Russell interview by Ronald Drez, September 23, 1988.
5. Napier Crookenden, *Dropzone Normandy* (New York: Charles Scribner's Sons, 1976), 31.
6. This was true in all wars following World War II. The author's own experience in Vietnam found him hard-pressed to gather 10 pounds for an attack against a bunker, from a company that started with 30 pounds of plastic explosive.
7. Stephen E. Ambrose, *D-Day, June 6, 1944: The Climactic Battle of World War II* (New York: Simon & Schuster, 1994), 154–55.
8. Crookenden, *Dropzone,* 111.
9. Ibid.
10. Ken Russell interview.
11. Ibid.
12. Ronald L. Lane, *Rudder's Rangers: The True Story of the 2nd Ranger Battalion D-Day Combat Action* (Almonte Springs, Fl.: Ranger Associates, Inc., 1979), 1–2.

13. Ibid., 67.

14. Ibid., 71–72.

15. Ronald J. Drez, *Voices of D-Day: The Story of the Allied Invasion Told by Those Who Were There* (Baton Rouge, La.: Louisiana State University Press, 1994), 258.

16. Quoted in Lane, *Rudder's Rangers,* 68.

17. Bradley, *Soldier's Story,* 269.

18. Lane, *Rudder's Rangers,* 73.

19. Drez, *Voices,* 258.

20. Ronald Drez interview with Leonard Lomell, March 16, 1993. Copy at Eisenhower Center, University of New Orleans.

21. Lane, *Rudder's Rangers,* 76.

22. Ibid., 77.

23. *Small Unit Actions* (Washington, D.C.: Historical Division, War Department, 1946), 11–17.

24. Lomell interview.

25. Lane, *Rudder's Rangers,* 130.

26. Bradley, *Soldier's Story,* 270.

27. Lomell interview.

Chapter 6

1. Ronald Drez interview with Arthur Abramson, January 19, 1999. Copy at Eisenhower Center, University of New Orleans.

2. Ibid.

3. E. B. Potter and Chester W. Nimitz, *The Great Sea War* (New York: Bramhall House, 1960), 348–54.

4. Clark G. Reynolds, *The Carrier War* (Alexandria, Va.: Time-Life Books, 1982), 140.

5. Ibid.

6. Ibid.

7. Arthur Abramson presentation onboard *Mississippi Queen,* July 23, 1997. Copy at Eisenhower Center, University of New Orleans.

8. Reynolds, *Carrier War,* 142.

9. Abramson presentation, Eisenhower Center, University of New Orleans.

10. Potter and Nimitz, *Sea War,* 357.

11. Ibid., 358.

12. Barrett Tillman, *Hellcat: The F6F in World War II* (Washington, D.C.: U.S. Naval Institute, 1979), 87.

13. Potter and Nimitz, *Sea War,* 358; Abramson interview.

14. Tillman, *Hellcat,* 87.

15. Ibid.

16. Potter and Nimitz, *Sea War,* 359.
17. Tillman, *Hellcat,* 89.
18. Abramson interview.
19. Potter and Nimitz, *Sea War,* 359.

Chapter 7

1. This was different from United States Army and denoted reserve status.
2. Ronald Drez interview with Lyle Bouck, October 13, 1999.
3. ASTP had been jokingly called "All Safe Till Peace" because of the seemingly remote possibility of being called to duty.
4. Hugh Cole, *The Ardennes* (Washington, D.C.: Dept. of the Army, 1965), 64–68.
5. Quoted in John Eisenhower, *The Bitter Woods* (New York: DaCapo Press, 1969), 117.
6. Eisenhower, *Bitter Woods,* 120–22.
7. William I. Goolrick and Ogden Tanner, *The Battle of the Bulge* (Alexandria, Va.: Time-Life Books, 1979), 51–52; Cole, *Ardennes,* 263.
8. Quoted in Goolrick and Tanner, *Bulge,* 53.
9. Bouck interview.
10. William Slape memoir, September 7, 1966. Copy at Eisenhower Center, University of New Orleans.
11. Bouck interview.
12. Richard H. Byers, *Battle of the Bulge* (Mentor, Ohio: Richard H. Byers, 1996), 25.
13. William C. Cavanagh, *Dauntless: A History of the 99th Infantry Division* (Dallas, Tex.: Taylor Publishing Co., n.d.), 106.
14. Eisenhower, *Bitter Woods,* 182–83.
15. Bouck interview.
16. Eisenhower, *Bitter Woods,* 184.
17. Quoted in Byers, *Bulge,* 25.
18. Adolph Schur interview. Copy at Eisenhower Center, University of New Orleans.
19. Slape memoir.
20. Schur interview.
21. Jack Anderson, "Why Private Tsakanikas Should Get the Medal of Honor," *Parade Magazine* (March 25, 1979), 6.
22. Bouck interview.
23. Slape memoir.
24. Bouck interview.
25. Slape memoir. Later Slape discovered he had a cracked rib and a broken sternum.

26. McGehee, Robinson, and Silvola were cut off and tried to escape toward Losheimergraben, and possible help from the 1st Battalion, but they were captured by Germans in white suits who already controlled the roads.

27. Schur interview.

28. Tsakanikas letter to Maj. Kriz, March 30, 1945.

29. Bouck interview.

30. Al Hemingway interview with Lyle Bouck, *Military History* (August 1992), 55.

31. Slape memoir.

32. Cavanagh, *Dauntless,* 107.

33. Bouck interview.

34. Message sheet from National Archives, printed in Cavanagh, *Dauntless,* 107.

35. General Order No. 26, Department of the Army, 29 October 1981, Distinguished Service Cross-Awards, 4.

36. Jenkins and Preston never found any friendly forces. They hid out for three days before being captured near their old regimental headquarters in Hunningen.

37. Hemingway, *History,* 56.

38. Schur interview.

39. William James [Tsakanikas] memoir, December 17, 1949. Copy at Eisenhower Center, University of New Orleans. In 1947, he dropped his last name and was known as William James.

40. Ibid.

41. Slape memoir.

42. Bouck interview.

43. James memoir.

44. Ibid.

45. Ibid.; Bouck interview.

46. Schur interview.

47. Bouck interview.

48. Eisenhower, *Bitter Woods,* 218.

49. Major Kenneth Hechler interview with Jochen Peiper, September 7, 1945, Freising, Germany. Document entitled, "Ethint 10, Oberst (W-SS) Jochen Peiper, '1 SS PZ Regt.'" (December 16–19, 1944), 15. Copy at Eisenhower Center, University of New Orleans.

50. Bouck interview.

51. Stephen M. Rusiecki, *The Key to the Bulge* (Westport, Conn.: Greenwood Publishing Group, Incorporated, 1996), xii.

52. Bouck interview.

53. Ibid.

54. Ibid.

55. Ibid.

56. Ironically, Col. Waters was not with the column, having been wounded in the groin in the attack of the compound. He was left behind.
57. Peiper interview, 21 and 9.

Chapter 8

1. Jacques Legrand, *Chronicle of the 20th Century* (New York: Chronicle Publications Inc., 1987), 177.
2. Ronald Drez interview with Eugene Fluckey, February 9, 2000.
3. Eugene B. Fluckey, *Thunder Below* (Chicago: University of Illinois Press, 1992), 4.
4. Charles A. Lockwood, *Sink 'Em All* (New York: Bantam, 1984), 33.
5. Lockwood, *Sink 'Em,* 99.
6. Keith Wheeler, *War Under the Pacific* (Alexandria, Va.: Time-Life Books, 1980), 42–47.
7. Lockwood, *Sink 'Em,* 117, 127.
8. Fluckey interview, August 8, 1995, and February 9, 2000.
9. Fluckey, *Thunder,* 4; Fluckey interview.
10. Fluckey interview.
11. Fluckey, *Thunder,* 5, 298.
12. Ibid., 430.
13. Ibid., 239.
14. Ibid., 241.
15. Ibid.
16. Wheeler, *War Under the Pacific,* 89.
17. Fluckey, *Thunder,* 242.
18. Wheeler, *War Under the Pacific,* 90.
19. Fluckey, *Thunder,* 242.
20. Ibid., 245.
21. Ibid., 247.
22. Theodore Roscoe, *United States Submarine Operations in World War II* (Annapolis, Md.: U.S. Naval Institute, 1949), 442.
23. Fluckey, *Thunder,* 258.
24. Ibid., 259.
25. Ibid., 263.
26. Ibid., 263–66.
27. Ibid.
28. Ibid., 268.
29. Ibid.
30. Roscoe, *Submarine Operations,* 443.
31. Ibid., 271.
32. Ibid., 6, 360.

33. E. B. Potter and Chester W. Nimitz, *The Great Sea War* (New York: Bramhall House, 1960), 419.

34. Lockwood, *Sink,* 357.

35. Fluckey, *Thunder,* 352.

36. Ibid., 462; Roscoe, *Submarine Operations,* 528.

37. Ibid., 491.

38. Fluckey interview.

Chapter 9

1. Yoshitaka Horie, "Fighting Spirit—Iwo Jima," 34. Copy at Eisenhower Center, University of New Orleans.

2. Ibid., 28.

3. Bill D. Ross, *Iwo Jima: Legacy of Valor* (New York: Random House, 1986), 19.

4. Quoted in Richard F. Newcomb, *Iwo Jima* (New York: Holt, Rinehart, and Winston, 1965), 19.

5. Ronald Drez interview with Jay Rebstock, March 20, 1999.

6. Horie, "Fighting Spirit," 39.

7. Ibid., 40.

8. E. B. Potter and Chester W. Nimitz, *The Great Sea War* (New York: Bramhall House, 1960), 348–49.

9. Horie, "Fighting Spirit," 44.

10. Potter and Nimitz, *Sea War,* 441.

11. Horie, "Fighting Spirit," 44.

12. Ibid.

13. Ibid., 45.

14. Ibid., 56–57.

15. Joseph H. Alexander, *Closing In: Marines in the Seizure of Iwo Jima* (Washington, D.C.: Government Printing Office, 1994), 6.

16. Newcomb, *Iwo Jima,* 25, 29.

17. Horie, "Fighting Spirit," 76.

18. Newcomb, *Iwo Jima,* 41–44.

19. Quoted in Horie, "Fighting Spirit," 83. Lt.Col. Nishi was a famous equestrian, having won the gold medal in the 1932 Olympics in Los Angeles in the individual jump. Newcomb, *Iwo Jima,* 27.

20. Ibid., 83.

21. Ibid.

22. Alexander, *Closing In,* 6.

23. Ibid., 5.

24. Newcomb, *Iwo Jima,* 33, 39.

25. Ronald Drez interview with Jay Rebstock, March 20, 1999.

26. Ross, *Iwo Jima*, 40.

27. Alexander, *Closing In*, 5.

28. Rebstock interview.

29. Newcomb, *Iwo Jima*, 76.

30. Rebstock interview.

31. Newcomb, *Iwo Jima*, 76–77.

32. Rebstock interview.

33. Henry Gininger and Tony Smith, "27 Marines in Combat." Copy at Eisenhower Center, University of New Orleans.

34. Alexander, *Closing In*, 14–15.

35. Horie, "Fighting Spirit," 73.

36. Alexander, *Closing In*, 29.

37. Quoted in Alexander, *Closing In*, 19.

38. Horie, "Fighting Spirit," 92.

39. Charles W. Tatum, *Iwo Jima: 19 February 1945, Red Blood, Black Sand* (Stockton, Ca.: Charles W. Tatum, 1995), 157–68.

40. Jim Bishop, *FDR's Last Year: April 1944–April 1945* (New York: Morrow, 1974), 479.

41. Quoted in Newcomb, *Iwo Jima*, 103–4.

42. Ibid., 103.

43. Newcomb, *Iwo Jima*, 119.

44. Rebstock interview.

45. Ibid.

46. Newcomb, *Iwo Jima*, 210.

47. Ross, *Iwo Jima*, xiii.

48. Newcomb, *Iwo Jima*, 203.

49. Rebstock interview.

50. Newcomb, *Iwo Jima*, 204.

Chapter 10

1. G. Donald Steel and Patrick Finneran, "USS *Indianapolis* National Memorial," *Naval Reserve Association News* (August 1995), 8.

2. Philip A. St. John, *USS Indianapolis (CA-35)* (Paducah, Ky.: Turner Publishing), 46.

3. Ronald Drez interview with Harold Eck, November 29, 1999.

4. Harold Eck collection. Release 229386, New York Bureau, 8-14-45. BurSpc #1; #70 MCS CAN.

5. Steel and Finneran, "USS *Indianapolis* National Memorial," 8.

6. St. John, *USS Indianapolis*, 46.

7. Ibid., 27.

8. Ibid., 28.

9. Quoted in Dan Kurzman, *Fatal Voyage: The Sinking of the USS Indianapolis* (New York: Atheneum Press, 1990), 34.

10. St. John, *USS Indianapolis,* 28.

11. Harold Eck interview.

12. St. John, *USS Indianapolis,* 28.

13. Harold Eck interview.

14. St. John, *USS Indianapolis,* 31.

15. St. John, *USS Indianapolis,* 32.

16. Ibid.

17. Kurzman, *Fatal Voyage,* 45–47.

18. St. John, *USS Indianapolis,* 32.

19. Kurzman, *Fatal Voyage,* 59.

20. Ibid., 28.

21. Ibid., 23.

22. Ibid., 62–63.

23. Harold Eck interview.

24. St. John, *USS Indianapolis,* 34.

25. Quoted in L. Peter Wren, *Those in Peril on the Sea* (Richmond, Va.: L. Peter Wren, 1999), 137.

26. St. John, *USS Indianapolis,* 34.

27. Kurzman, *Fatal Voyage,* 91–95.

28. Harold Eck interview.

29. St. John, *USS Indianapolis,* 37.

30. Kurzman, *Fatal Voyage,* 124.

31. Harold Eck interview.

32. Kurzman, *Fatal Voyage,* 150–53.

33. St. John, *USS Indianapolis,* 40.

34. Ibid., 39.

35. Harold Eck interview.

36. Quoted in Wren, *Peril on the Sea,* 84.

37. Ibid., 85.

38. Ibid., 82.

39. Harold Eck interview.

40. Quoted in Kurzman, *Fatal Voyage,* 188.

41. St. John, *USS Indianapolis,* 47; Kurzman, *Fatal Voyage,* 188.

42. Kurzman, *Fatal Voyage,* 205.

43. Quoted in Wren, *Peril on the Sea,* 112.

44. Bill van Daalen, Viewfinder Video, *Indianapolis: Ship of Doom,* 1992.

45. Ibid.

46. Clair Young to Chief of Naval Operations, 8-6-1955, original of letter posted on Internet at http://members.tripod.com/IndyMaru.

INDEX